Ɗiscovering S

C
D
St

Verenae

'beati qui audiunt verbum Dei et custodiunt'
Luke 11:28

Discovering Saint Patrick

THOMAS O'LOUGHLIN

DARTON·LONGMAN + TODD

First published in 2005 by
Darton, Longman and Todd Ltd
1 Spencer Court
140–142 Wandsworth High Street
London SW18 4JJ

ISBN 0–232–52498–X

A catalogue record for this book is available from the British Library.

Set in 11/13pt Minion
Designed and produced by Sandie Boccacci
using QuarkXPress on an Apple PowerMac
Printed and bound in Great Britain by
Page Bros, Norwich, Norfolk

CONTENTS

❧❧

ACKNOWLEDGEMENTS

I would like to thank Brendan Walsh of Darton, Longman and Todd for first suggesting this book to me and for keeping up a gentle pressure to get it written; my colleagues in the Department of Theology and Religious Studies, and especially Dr Jonathan Wooding, for many helpful discussions; many friends in other universities whose works appear in the bibliography for answering queries over the years; and the library staff here in Lampeter for much help in locating books and articles for me. Most especially, I would like to thank the students here who have participated in my seminars on insular Latin writings for all their questions and prompts to tease out other aspects of these dense and fecund texts.

❦

Patrick, the British bishop who worked in Ireland in the fifth century, the principal patron of Ireland, continues to fascinate people at the beginning of the third Christian millennium. It is this interest that has inspired this book. Over the past fifty years, there has been a steady stream of new books, articles and television documentaries about him. These productions range from very popular works, often merely retellings of the classic legends, to the most detailed of scholarship on the original medieval sources. It is the aim of the present work to take this scholarly research and make it accessible to a wider and more general readership. Writing for that most elusive reader, 'the interested lay reader', is to walk a tightrope: too much simplification can collapse into a collage of bits and pieces and unwarranted generalisations; too many deviations into the debates of scholars can turn the book into a string of footnotes. If I have fallen from the tightrope in places, I beg the reader's pardon.

This is a book in two parts. The first is an attempt to write a narrative outlining the problems of coming to know Patrick and to outline the earliest evidence for Christianity in Ireland. The second part is made up of fresh translations of the basic sources for Patrick and his cult, with notes that should provide many of the helps to understanding these texts that are available in scholarly editions. Reading Part 1 without Part 2 is to miss the richness of the tradition of Patrick, while I hope that anyone reading Part 2 will find that Part 1 provides a context and a guide to understanding the texts. Each year for the past eight years I have read all these texts with a fresh class of postgraduate students here in Lampeter, and I am continually reminded how interacting with these texts provokes new questions each year (I hope the fruit of

these questions appears in both my text and the translations) and
can help us not only to get a 'feel' for the earliest Christianity in
these islands, but to appreciate further aspects of that 'religion of
historians', to use Marc Bloch's famous phrase, which is
Christianity. Christians since the very earliest times have discovered their identity by looking back to the texts of the past and
comparing and measuring themselves against them: for the first
generation this was the Old Testament confronting the message of
Jesus; then it was the writings of the New Testament compared
with their own experience; and for later generations it was all
those writings together with the writings of earlier Christians
('the fathers' or 'the tradition') that formed the mirror and
measure through which they discovered themselves. Since, at least,
the seventh century Irish Christians sought in the memory of
Patrick a key to their own belief, and this process continues in
many ways even today. I hope that your reading of these ancient
documents – from a world very foreign to our own – whether you
read them as a Christian believer or not, can give you a deeper
appreciation of that great historical mosaic that is Christianity.

THOMAS O'LOUGHLIN
August 2004

Part 1

CHAPTER 1

ℰ.ℰ

Man, Myth and History

Where to start?

Starting at 'the very beginning' is, according to the song, 'a very good place to start'. The problem for the historian is that it is much harder to know what and when is 'the very beginning' of something. For more than a millennium the very beginning of the story of Patrick – and the story of the coming of Christianity to Ireland – was held to have occurred between AD 431 and 461. Patrick was believed to have arrived in 432, to have converted, with his few trusty companions, more or less the whole island, and to have died in 461. So the place to start was the fifth century and then work forwards from that point until whatever date was chosen as the end of the particular story. For those who started with Patrick's 'arrival' in 432, a popular ending point was 795 when the first Viking raid occurred; between those dates was the 'Golden Age' of 'the Island of Saints and Scholars'. This approach started to disappear from historical textbooks from the early 1960s, but it is still used in many popular accounts of 'the Celtic Saints', and in a number that claim to be more than 'popular'.

Another possible starting point is the seventh century, when the documents that provide most of the legends about Patrick were written, including the 'life' of the saint by Muirchú and other writings in which Patrick is central, such as the *Book of the Angel* or the *Collection* made by Tirechán.[1] It might seem strange to start with the seventh century rather than with the man from the closing period of Roman rule in Britain, but there is much to

---

1. The complete text, in translation, of Muirchú can be found in Part 2 of this volume.

recommend this. First of all, most of the information that is associated with Patrick is not about a bishop working on the periphery of the Roman Empire, but about a saint who is seen as an 'intercessor', a 'patron', and an 'apostle'. These are not just inter-changeable titles that can be used for Patrick, but very distinct roles that Christians bestowed on those who were dead yet revered in their memory, liturgy and private devotion as 'saints': while every saint is assumed to be an intercessor, only some are approached as patrons, and very few indeed are venerated as 'apostles'. Thus, most of what we say about Patrick – and, more importantly, the framework within which any facts relating to him are viewed – belongs to the cult of the saint. Such a cult of a saint always involves far more than what most people in the early twenty-first century would associate with the term 'history' or 'biography'. The materials of a saint's cult (by which I mean ancient documents, tombs, relics, customs, traditions about where he visited, and when her/his feast day falls) relate to *the memory of the saint as perceived by a community of religious faith*, who see not just the person someone in the fifth century might have met, but the significance of the person within a story of salvation of which they themselves are part. So the miracles of a saint, both while the saint was alive and after death, are far more important for some-one writing documents relating to the cult than questions of accurate dates, the places visited, and who the saint met and why. In short, there is little in common between a writer of saints' lives (a hagiographer) and a modern historian. However, the two pro-fessions are easily confused in that both write accounts of the life of someone in the past. In very broad terms the difference can be put like this: the historian is interested in what happened *then*, and from her modern vantage point seeing what were the most significant aspects of that past time; the hagiographer is looking at the saint's importance right *now* – at the time the hagiographer is writing – and is only interested in the past in so far as it explains why the holy person is so significant to his community. Alas, ignoring the difference in perspectives between a medieval hagiographer and modern historian has bedevilled much that has been written about Patrick.[2] The interesting thing is that between

2. Until 1962, when D. A. Binchy (see Binchy 1962) wrote a book-length article about the confusion, hardly any historian had drawn attention to this

Patrick's time (whenever that was, but it was most probably in the fifth century) and the seventh century there is almost no mention of Patrick! Therefore, one could say that the story of *Saint* Patrick begins in the seventh century, and everything before that is just the historical prologue.

A third possible starting point is to attempt to draw a clear line between material that can be placed in close proximity to Patrick the bishop and material that belongs to his cult as a saint, which is mainly the seventh-century writings just mentioned. This too, at first sight, seems a good strategy. Patrick did leave us two writings, one is a letter to the soldiers of a Christian brigand named Coroticus, the other is an apology for his own ministry in Ireland and is now known as his 'Confession'.[3] Because these are the very words of the man, they seem to get behind the wall of miraculous stories and the accretions of cult. In addition, we can add a few details relating to fifth-century Ireland that come from elsewhere (a couple of snippets from Prosper of Aquitaine (*c.* 390–*c.* 463) and Pope Leo the Great (d. 461)), and use whatever help the archaeologists can offer, and try to construct a plausible scenario for the missionary from Roman Britain while avoiding statements not 'well based' in 'sources', hyperbole, the fanciful, and the downright daft. This approach would seem to offer the possibility of bringing us to 'the man behind the legends', 'the true Patrick', or to 'the real Patrick'.

This starting point seems both attractive and simple and, at present, it is by far the favourite approach among both academic and popular writers. Among popular presentations, for example, there have been at least half a dozen television documentaries about Patrick in recent years, and the 'real Patrick' offers a new slant on the man who lies behind the festivities of 'St Patrick's Day'. One can use the 'shock angle' in such a programme that the

problem. We can roughly divide modern writing about Patrick into two camps: (1) writings prior to 1962 or written later but outside the influence of Binchy's article; and (2) those who have truly appreciated the nature of hagiographical evidence – in the case of Patrick this is almost entirely post 1962. Binchy himself acknowledged that he was doing no more than applying to Patrick what was the standard practice with regard to saints' lives of the Bollandists (of whom more will be said later in this chapter).

3. The complete texts, in translation, of both of Patrick's works can be found in Part 2.

archetypal 'Irishman' came from Britain (true, but only as a geographical fact) or even England (wrong, and anachronous) and that he never used a shamrock or threatened a snake. For academics it is attractive as it accords with a basic rule of historical evidence: 'use contemporary sources for each period, and do not use later interpretations as a basis for earlier times.' Moreover, for both academics and popular writers, given that it is part of our culture that we are suspicious of the miraculous and make a fundamental distinction between 'an historical event' and 'a miracle', it suggests that we can get to a set of 'facts' (over which there would be little dispute), which could then be subtracted from the overall story/memory/cult. We would then have 'the man' (somehow equivalent to 'the truth') and 'the myth' (somehow equivalent to propaganda, 'the fanciful', and falsehood) in watertight compartments, and would be free to choose between them. We would have the reality as found in the fifth-century documents – and from which a 'real man of faith' might 'emerge' – and everything else would just belong to the background to a big party on March 17; after all, we have great fun with 'Santa Claus' without worrying about St Nicholas of Myra.

Unfortunately, this approach presents as many difficulties as attractions. First, the fifth-century evidence is not only sparse, but comes bristling with historical problems: where do we place Patrick's writings in time, relative to our few sure dates; how do we interpret his references to people and places; do we assess what he tells us narrowly (information on one bishop working in Ireland) or as broadly in line with the seventh-century accounts (that he was the key player in converting the Irish); and what value can we lay on autobiographical material?

Second, 'the past is a foreign country, they do things differently there': historical 'facts' are always a perception and an abstraction, and the historian brings not only her/his prejudices to a topic, but a whole world of understandings and assumptions which give significance to the remnants that have survived over time. Each culture and each generation writes history anew, and while there is progress in the unearthing of discrete nuggets of information (for example, one might discover a new manuscript that allows one to provide a better text of what Patrick wrote, or an archaeologist might find a hoard of coins that can throw light on commerce at the time between islands of Britain and Ireland), since each generation comes with different questions and assumptions, each generation starts afresh and produces their 'real Patrick'.

Third, while we might be very clear on the distinction between facts (alias 'historical events') and religious interpretations (alias 'miracles'), that was not a distinction shared by many prior to the eighteenth century. Patrick's writings contain numerous miracles: the miracle of finding a place on the boat to escape from slavery in Ireland, miraculous food in a desert, and an angelic voice calling him to Ireland as a preacher, to mention but a few. So is the angel calling Patrick back to Ireland a 'fact' – it is contained in a contemporary source: his own *Confessio* – or is it something we can discount? We might get around this by saying that it is a fact that Patrick thought it was a fact; consequently, it is a fact about his mentality and how he saw the world. But that response merely reinforces the assertion that the past is foreign, and reminds us that to study Patrick we have to be prepared to enter a world where religious questions and a religious perception of the universe were central. Not to take account of that religious dimension as a fundamental aspect of every source (whether fifth-century or later) connected with Patrick, is to denature the material, and reduce the study to what we have predetermined as 'the real'.

Lastly, the assumption that we can draw a line dividing the fifth-century material from all else supposes that people (apart from historians working on fifth-century Irish history) would still be interested in Patrick quite apart from the later legend which has ensured his fame and generated our interest.

So if there is no obvious starting point, where do we start? I suspect the place to start is with a study of how memory works within communities as they hand on their traditions from generation to generation: if we can appreciate that process we might have a perspective on both the legends and the significance that has been given to Patrick. This requires that we begin by looking at what we expect from history, and the very different expectations of those who made Patrick famous, gave value to his writings so that they were preserved, and produced the interest that is still with us. Only when we can distinguish between the problems and perspectives of the hagiographer, on the one hand, and the historian, on the other, can we begin to approach Patrick.

Hagiography and history

The notion of 'hagiography', meaning writing intended to praise a saint or demonstrate her/his sanctity (from Greek *hagios*: a holy man/saint; *grapho*: I write), does not sit well with us. In a review of a book about a dead religious leader I recently saw the claim that 'it is not written as hagiography' being used as a term of praise for the book and its author; hagiography is a genre we neither respect nor value. Our experience of heroes and 'saints' is too bitter for us not to be suspicious of any work that praises someone and holds them up for our imitation. Any work that dishes out praise, and sets out deliberately to extol someone and make us admire her/him is seen by us as a 'whitewash', propaganda or simply an attempt to con us. Heroes have failed us and the following of heroes has led whole countries astray. We want to know our people 'warts and all'. Moreover, hero-creators and personality-myth-makers are those who have promoted some of the greatest monsters of modern times. To suggest that Muirchú was to Patrick what Goebbels was to Hitler is to put Muirchú, and all like him, into the category of liars. Indeed, one of the tasks that fall to historians is to expose myths that the propagandists may have spread abroad. In the immediate aftermath of an event or person there are the praises or the denunciations of the media and then, in the longer term, the historians present a balanced view showing the good points and the bad points and, hopefully, presenting an assessment of the impact of a person or a movement, showing both surpluses and deficits. The historian with the benefit of hindsight is to be the final arbiter and we do not expect anyone to be wholly good or beyond criticism.

The hagiographer works in a very different milieu; for him (I cannot think of a single woman hagiographer from the Middle Ages) the question of his subject's perfection is already beyond doubt – the person is a saint in heaven, enjoying the fullness of the vision of God, right now. So dwelling on imperfections is simply silly: the saint is at that exact point of perfection/happiness that every human desires. There may be a dark legacy in the saint's life on earth – indeed the murkier the better – but that is now past for the saint has repented, possibly done penance, and converted to a new way of life. So the saint is a model in his/her present state of what Christians want to become, and in turning from a former sinful life, the saint is a model of what Christians should be doing. The new, reformed, penitent life sets the earlier/former life at nought. We have a splendid example of this standard pattern in hagiography in Muirchú's *Vita Patricii*, in the story of Macc Cuill – who changes from being a murderer to being a monastic bishop and saint: the audience are intended to marvel at the new saintly bishop rather than ask whether ex-murderers should be given positions of responsibility in the Church.[4]

To appreciate this difference in viewing saints we must note a fundamental difference between how people today (including most Christians) view religion (even when they take part in it as active believers), and how Christians in the early Middle Ages viewed religion. In the early Middle Ages to be a Christian was not seen primarily in terms of personal conviction regarding a set of beliefs, but about being part of a society, a group, and a tradition – this was expressed by saying that one 'belonged' to the Church. This was a body, in effect Christ's body, scattered over every part of the earth and over every generation, and it would only become wholly visible and complete at a moment beyond history when 'Christ' would be 'all and in all' (Col. 3:11). Salvation consisted in being fully part of this interconnected network, which, through its union with Christ its head, was able to stand in the presence of the Father. Salvation was being part of the group, and being on one's own was tantamount to being lost. It was with that notion in people's heads that the phrase 'there is no salvation outside the church' (*extra ecclesia nulla salus*) was coined. Put another way, a man or woman was not saved as an individual in a series of private contracts between God and individuals, but rather it was the body of Christ that was saved, and the individual had to seek to belong within that group. Sin cut one off from the group, penance restored one to being fully within the group, and conversion was the decision to join the group, which was seen as literally joining Christ or being 'grafted into Christ'. It was in this way that they read the verse: 'Apart from me you can do nothing' (John 15:5). Christ was the whole tree and individuals were branches or limbs. The language of Christianity was corporate – talking of bodies – at every turn: the Church was the body of Christ; Jesus the Lord was the head; head and body made up the whole Christ (*Christus*

4. Muirchú, *Vita Patricii* 1, 26.

totus); individuals were limbs, branches, members of the body; the Eucharist was the body of Christ – and so in it they participated and shared in the body, they prayed for the whole body's health and the body prayed for the individuals which made it up.

To convert an individual was to make sure that she or he was no longer a loner outside the body or poorly connected to the body; to convert a group was to graft a new interconnected group (a family or a tribe) into the final body that would exist at the Last Judgement when all else would have passed away. In short, to become a Christian was not spoken of in terms of a lifestyle decision, but in terms of joining fully in the whole sweep of history, for at the 'eschaton' (the 'final shakedown' of the whole of creation) only those who were within Christ would survive and have that happiness they desired. It was as part of this view of history that Augustine wrote the opening lines of his *Confessiones*: 'You have made us, O Lord, for yourself, and our heart is unsettled until it rests in you.' And, it was within this view of history that Patrick worked in Ireland, and Muirchú later created the story of the island's conversion.

This community of Christians believed its full identity would not be known until the end of time, but it was bonded together *now* in a whole variety of ways which gave it its self-image, its beliefs, and its agenda for activity. The group began to exist long before Christ, but was given its perfect form when Jesus gathered his disciples and set it on its path through his death and resurrection. Since that time it had gained new members in each generation, preserved its memory through its books,[5] and interacted not only with God but with all its deceased members through the liturgy. The liturgy brought the assembled group not only into the presence of Christ, but through him into the presence of the whole court of heaven: the saints of the time before Christ brought into heaven on the first Holy Saturday; the

---

5. By the fifth century, the notion that Christians had their sacred scriptures was well advanced (they had the 'scriptures' that the earliest Christians had venerated which are more or less equivalent to what post-Reformation Christians refer to as 'the Old Testament', and they had a group of early Christian writings which were also accorded authority. Again, the contents of that group of writings is more or less equivalent to what post-Reformation Christians refer to as 'the New Testament'); however, the notion of 'the Bible' as many modern Christians use the term was still several centuries off.

saints of the time of Jesus (the Virgin Mary, John the Baptist, the apostles); all the saints since then; and all the choirs of angels, for it was with this group that they sang out 'Holy, holy, holy Lord' at their Eucharists. This whole transhistorical community acted as one: the Christians on earth asked for help and offered praise; those in heaven (the saints) interceded, protected, and intervened with their acts of power; those en route from earth to heaven sought to hasten along with help from both sides; while the Lord looked on his people as parts of his own body. Recalling the saints, expressing their identity, all their worship, and their final destiny as a Church were intertwined realities. The hagiographer, through fostering the links between the visible church community around him and the larger Christian community of the saints and angels, was supplying an important service to his own community. He helped it appreciate 'the rock from which they were hewn' (Isa. 51:1), recalled those in whom they could glory, and reminded them where their destiny lay by showing them proven examples of how to get to that destination. From this perspective, a saint's life that did not show how the saint-members of the Church inter-vened right now in the lives of the not-yet-saint-members would be of little worth to those people. Put another way, a saint's life must record the saint's miracles in relation to those who look to him or her as a saint. This is what we see well exemplified in the lives of Patrick: he is the one in heaven who has been given a special care of those members of the whole Church who are Irish: he is their intercessor, their patron, and will look after them now and at the end – hence it behoves the Irish not to forget him!

Lastly, most Christians today look to saints as examples of moral behaviour and right living. This is a view of sanctity that first came to prominence at the Reformation, when many Christians rejected the notion of a cult of the saints or the notion that they had intercessory power. However, the saints were held to be models of how to lead a good Christian life and, as such, a saint's memory was godliness: teaching through example. So a holy Christian might be worth recalling as a model of what discipleship means or costs, but without any hint that you might ask them to help you. So today many Christians look back, rightly in my opinion, to Dietrich Bonhoeffer (1906–1945) as a teacher, an example of discipleship and a reminder in his own death of the demands that a decision to follow Christ might make. And, following from that theme, I have heard people call him 'a modern saint'. That is fine in terms of contemporary Christianity, where even the Catholic Church has modified its manner of presenting the value of saints: 'Father ... you give the Church this feast in honour of Saint X; you inspire us by his holy life, instruct us by his preaching, and give us your protection in answer to his prayers.'[6] However, we must not project this image of a saint as model Christian backwards to the early Middle Ages. One way to note the difference is to ask whether someone who has praised Bonhoeffer or Martin Luther King (1929–1968) has ever thought of adding 'pray for us' after their names in what is the simplest of prayers to a saint – usually the answer is a look of bafflement. Equally, many Christians still pray to St Anthony of Padua (1195–1231) to help find lost keys, but would they promise to build a roadside statue to him or offer 20 kilograms of wax candles at his tomb – typical medieval promises of one member of the Church to another? Or would someone who held up Martin Luther King – who after all has a secular feast day in the United States[7] – as an example of peaceful protest want to present him as someone looking after him or her from heaven? In reality, these are two very different notions of what 'saint' means, and we must recall this when we read earlier material relating to saints. Muirchú rejoices that Patrick can destroy the army of the High King and can bring death upon those who oppose his work in Ireland, but this is a statement about Patrick's power and it is irrelevant that the stories are blood-curdling. Today, if we heard that a nineteenth-century missionary to a group with an organised military force, for example the Zulus, had begun his missionary work by slaughtering their army, we would stand aghast that such an act could be carried out in the name of religion, the missionary's memory would be pilloried, and the notion that he might become the hero of that people would be viewed as a sick joke. Yet, this is exactly the sort of tale that is central to the whole Patrick cult.

However, before we dismiss all those who fostered the memory of Patrick in the early Middle Ages (and without their interest we

---

6. The Preface of Pastors in the 1970 Missal.
7. Martin Luther King Day is held every third Monday of January; the custom began in 1986.

would know nothing about Patrick) as bigots, zealots, primitives, or religious tyrants, we should not forget that their examples came from the fate of Pharaoh's chariot army in Exodus 14 and 15; the fate of the prophets of Baal at the hands of Elijah in 1 Kings 18; and the fate of Ananias and Sapphira before Peter in Acts 5; and indeed many Christians still sing the Song of Moses (Exod. 15), which thanks God for drowning the Egyptians, as part of their celebration of Christ's resurrection at the Easter Vigil.

In writing about Patrick, Muirchú saw himself in continuity with these biblical writers and sought to cast Patrick as a contemporary version of those biblical characters. Indeed, ultimately the hagiographers saw themselves doing for their subjects, who were members of Christ, what the evangelists did for Jesus to show he was the Christ. The evangelist John concluded his gospel by saying that he had 'written' the book 'that you may believe that Jesus is the Christ, the Son of God, and that believing you may have life in his name' (20:31), and so we make a distinction between the genre of gospel writing and the genre of biography. The hagiographer echoes John's words: he wrote that people might believe that someone was a saint and so might be moved to link their own life with that of the saint through entering into that saint's cult. Hagiographers lived in a different world from ours, and even for contemporary Christians, to enter that world requires a leap of imagination and sympathy with religious difference. This stress on the gulf of understanding that separates us from the past is itself part of our very modernity: for most of Christian history it was the continuity with the past that was stressed. Each culture and period imagined their society as having the same understanding as that of earlier Christians: hence the message of the Gospel related directly to their situation, the events of the gospels were pictured as occurring in their landscape and fashions, and they attributed to the earlier period their own beliefs and hang-ups. So, for example, Muirchú imagined that the situation and events of the Book of Daniel and the situation at the court of the Irish High King at Tara were virtually the same apart from the obvious difference in date, location and language. Alternatively, some modern Christians live in a situation where miracles are viewed as childish superstitions and so, to preserve continuity with the desired past, the milieu of Jesus, Jesus is reconstructed without any hint of the miraculous. One myth of continuity makes a seventh-century Irishman into an ancient Babylonian,[8] while the other makes a first-century Jew from Palestine into a twenty-first-century social reformer.[9] In short, continuity is the lifeblood of a community, and so it is a central plank in the worldview of a hagiographer, but it is dangerous for the historian, and problematic in a culture that notes its differences from the past.

Saints, heroes, relics

While we must not try to disguise the differences between our worlds and those of the past, we should also note that there are continuities, and while the cult of saints may mean less within the Christian churches, the human dynamics that are at play in saints' cults seem to be as active as ever. These human dynamics do seem to form a real continuity with the past and serve to remind us that with some imaginative sympathy we can enter into a foreign world, and at the very least experience it through a cultural translation.

Many of the same cultural phenomena that in the past were linked to the cult of saints can be found today in the interest we take in 'celebrities' – 'people', as someone remarked, 'who are famous for being famous.' The devotion given to some pop singers – often referred to using religious terms such as 'pop idol' or 'pop icon' – or internationally famous football players is a modern secular form of saint's cult. The simplest proof of this is that marketers know that these cult images are financially valuable and so place images of these idols where they can influence our behaviour in terms of our use of money, not with reference to either making music or playing sport. A famous footballer can 'sponsor' any product and many of us are moved to buy it: it is as if he becomes the product's patron saint and each advert hoarding showing him with the product is another wayside shrine to his excellence, goodness or prowess in the eyes of his devotees.

---

8. The question of how Muirchú presents identities is even more complicated: in the seventh century AD he wants to imagine Irish pagans from the fifth century, and in order to do this he depicts his subjects as he read about those at the court of Nebuchadnezzar in Babylon in Dan. 1—4.

9. For a stimulating account of how miracle-laden material has been approached since the Enlightenment, see Meier 1994.

Equally, the cult of relics is alive and well, as witness the desire for 'celebrity memorabilia'. The seriousness of this cult, and its organisation, can be gauged by the amounts of money people are prepared to spend on these relics (or as Jesus is reported as saying in Matt. 6:21: 'For where your treasure is, there will your heart be also'), the involvement of famous auction houses in the trade, and the coverage such sales attract in the media. The musical instrument of a pop icon, the dress of a celebrity worn on a particular occasion, or some other personal item will fetch the highest price (equivalent to the older Roman Catholic category of first-class relic: that which belongs properly to the saint), while signed pictures or autographs are next in order of value (a second-class relic: that which was associated with the saint), while programmes from a famous concert or event have least monetary value (third-class relics: material objects which have touched higher relics). Material objects bring us close to our heroes! Other human instincts also seem to be still at work when fans gather to hear or see their hero 'live' when they could more comfortably (and more economically) see an event on TV or listen to a recording: there is just no substitute for 'being there'. The sentiment that one must go to the place and be there with the group and be in the very presence of the hero is something that any medieval pilgrim to a saint's shrine would have understood. The modern pop concert or great sports tournament functions in a very similar way to the feast-day gatherings at the special cult centres of medieval saints. Moreover, this pilgrimage instinct even survives the live experience of the heroes' presence: the houses where the Beatles grew up in Liverpool and the home of Elvis Presley are still attracting devotees.

Devotion to the saints was a group phenomenon and so attaching oneself to the group was a primary task: to become part of the group was seen as attaching one's self to the saint and thus sharing in his/her glory. The same instinct can be seen today in the followers of football clubs, where the club and its fortunes on the field become part of a person's identity: they wear the colours, gather the memorabilia, travel together to the sacred moments of the cult, and seek to move ever closer to the club through their demonstrations of loyalty. In the early Middle Ages the highest form of such loyalty was the desire to be with that saint at the final Day of Resurrection – literally to rest with him in his place so as to rise with him.[10] It is for this reason that sites connected with saints in Ireland are still cluttered up as graveyards: to be buried in a monastery is a definitive statement of attachment to that place made holy by the saint. For that reason Adomnán can tell a story of St Columba telling a monk he must move to another monastery because he foresees that he should be buried elsewhere.[11] However, even this has a modern parallel: several football clubs have scattered the ashes of famous deceased players or a manager on the pitch, while some supporters express the opinion that this would be their preferred 'resting place' if only they too could persuade the club to scatter their ashes at the sacred centre of their cult. I know that only a tiny proportion of supporters go that far in their desire for proximity to their heroes but, equally, only a tiny proportion of early medieval Christians engaged in subterfuge to get their grave that bit closer to the bones of the saint. The instincts of both groups of followers seem to be the same.

As we read a medieval hagiographer we must keep in mind that his religious landscape is as different from ours as his physical landscape is. But we should also note the opposite phenomenon. A medieval writer will tell of massive outpourings of grief at the moment the saint dies – now recall the crowds and the flowers at Princess Diana's funeral in 1997 and the shrine erected as her tomb. When we read of wayside shrines and markers to those who died alongside the road – note the flowers that are left, often renewed for years after the event, where there has been a fatal road accident – and when we read of the desire for relics and to touch the 'very spot' of some wonder – then let's not forget that ful- filling people's desires to get to specific famous spots is a key aspect of the tourist industry and most of those who go there will carry a special relic-collector to link them to that spot: a camera.

The 'dossier' of a saint

So in looking back at someone whom Christians have venerated as a 'saint' we do not encounter historical artefacts together with the interpretations of earlier historians (as we might if we were to pursue the life and times of an early Irish king), but something far

10. See O'Loughlin 2001a.
11. Adomnán, *Vita Columbae* 2, 39.

more complex. We find the strands of historical fact intermingled with the cult as it evolved over time, all set within the larger parameters of how that society and period perceived its universe religiously and adapted the Christian traditions about saints. This whole complex of surviving bits and pieces has been given a label by the Bollandists – a group of Jesuits in Belgium who have become the specialists in matters relating to hagiography[12] – and they call it the 'dossier of a saint'.[13] The starting point in any cult is precisely that: a cult. This means that in the immediate surroundings of a Christian there is a belief that the person is saintly and that, almost from the moment of death, the person is now a saint. In times before modern communications, and leaving aside spectacular exceptions where people (usually bishops) already had a widespread reputation while alive (for example, Ambrose of Milan (*c.* 339–397) or Augustine of Hippo (354–430)), such cults were usually very local affairs indeed. Indeed, if one went through the many thousands of people whom the churches have venerated over the centuries, the vast majority are only known in a particular locality, perhaps one church building dedicated to them and, probably now long forgotten, a tradition that her/his feast falls on a certain day. Today, even that building has often been re-dedicated to a more famous or more recent saint and all that survives is a place name that indicates that once there may have been a cult there.

One can drive through Ireland and find places whose name is in the form 'Kil + a personal name', where there is no other record of such a saint. Likewise in Wales one can find place names beginning with 'Llan', or in France with 'St', where no other trace of a cult survives. In many cases this is the last scrap of evidence of a local cult but one that did not grow to establish itself deeply in the larger memory of Christians. Historians of saints frequently quote the line from Sirach 44:7–8 that the saints 'were' those 'honoured in their generations, and were the pride of their times ... [who] have left behind a name, so that others declare their praise'; and in fact that is often all we have: a name. A cult may begin with just a few people who notice a 'sweet smell of

12. See Knowles 1963 for the origins of the Bollandists; their website contains a great deal of information on the history and work, www.kbr.be/~socboll.
13. Delehaye 1998 [1905] is essential reading for any critical engagement with hagiographical evidence.

flowers' in the room immediately after someone's death and interpret this as 'the odour of sanctity'[14] – and in that local community a cult is born. It may be strengthened if soon after that a child recovers from illness and their recovery is attributed to the new saint's care and to their intercession for the community they belonged to while on earth, and so their gravesite becomes a place of local devotion. And, as anniversaries of death are always recalled within families, so that annual moment is now recalled as a feast of that saint and it becomes the focus point of the cult in time as the tomb/grave is in physical location. These three items – a name, a burial site, a feast day – form the bedrock of every dossier. Moreover, when one thumbs through any martyrology[15] one finds that for many, if not most, saints from the time before AD 1000 that is all we know.

A small local cult may gradually develop and spread, it may disappear altogether, or it may remain local but by chance obtain a mention in a martyrology and so be recalled elsewhere but without becoming a great centre of attraction.[16] However, when we look at the cults that really did take off and become widely known, we notice that one factor is pre-eminent: the saint is adopted by an organised ecclesiastical community that can record and promote the saint, serve the cult centre with all its liturgical needs, and invest energy in the cult as part of their own identity. A layman or laywoman may die with a reputation for holiness and be venerated in their community or parish for generations without anyone outside that area learning of the cult, but things would be very different if that person had been the founder of a monastery of monks or nuns or the first bishop in a region. In the latter situations there is a group who look back to the saint as their origin or 'father' or 'mother in faith' and they have within the structures of the monastery or of the clergy all that it takes not only to preserve the memory *in detail*, but also to elaborate that memory and spread it abroad. Wherever those monks or clergy

14. The origins of this belief lie in interpretations of 2 Cor. 2:16.
15. A martyrology is a liturgical book designed to be read each day in a monastery where are recorded all the named saints, not just martyrs, who are recalled on that day – this list is far greater for every day than just the one or two saints who can claim the day as a 'feast'; see Le Brun 2003.
16. The lists of local saints added to the *Martyrology of Tallaght* is an outstanding example of this process.

go they will take the cult with them and will see it as their own badge of identity. Someone may ask who they are, and their reply is that they are the monks, the spiritual children, of that saint, and so it is important to them that that saint is as widely known as possible. In this process, the formally written life of the saint – what is usually referred to in scholarship as 'the *vita*' – is a key element, and hence it is (or they are – because a successful cult will generate a succession of *vitae*) a key part of the dossier. The written story fixes the memory of the saint so, while bits will be added to that memory, it becomes more difficult for stories relating to the saint or his/her miracles to fall out of memory. Once a saint has a *vita*, he/she has tacitly moved into a higher category of saint – saints that can be read about – and therefore there is an implicit understanding that these saints have more power than lesser-known saints. Any cult that has generated a *vita* can now spread more easily, for the memory can be transferred from place to place in book form. On the feast day there is now material to be read – hence our word 'legend' from *legendum*, that which is there to be read about the power, that is the miracles, of a saint. And there is a way of generating new stories about the saint, for the material in *vitae* seems to have had general popular attraction. Today we find this last point hard to credit, but keep in mind that a *vita* provided exciting stories within their world in a manner similar to the way science fiction tales fit within our worldview. In the late 1960s, *Star Trek* provided as comprehensive a view about its creators' ideal society as a *vita* did in the early Middle Ages – and in both times these projecting-texts had those who simply enjoyed them.

From the insular world we have no better example of this process than with St Columba (*c.* 521–9 June 597) who founded the monastery of Iona. He left a community of monks behind him who drew their identity as a group from him and spread his fame with every new monastery they founded. His memory was preserved formally in the tales they told about him, and by the mid-seventh century they had compiled a *vita* for him. Although this *vita* does not survive, it was one of the sources that Adomnán drew upon when he wrote his *Vita Columbae* towards the end of the eighth century, and in that *vita* we are told how his fame had spread. Many areas of what is now Scotland are presented by Adomnán as being under Columba's protection – so that even in distant Rome his name and cult were known.[17] This example of the spread of a cult also draws attention to other aspects of a saint's dossier. First, a successful cult is always growing by a process of gradual accretion – a moving saint's cult *does* gather moss. Second, once a cult is set in motion it becomes more complex, in that the basic story of the saint is elaborated by standard elements from the larger Christian memory of what a saint should be. So Columba is presented using many features of sanctity that are the common possession of many cults: the figure of the saint is elaborated by seeing in his life imitations of Christ, as well as imitations of the great figures of the Old Testament, the apostles, and the already famous saints of the tradition such as Antony of Egypt (251?–356), Martin of Tours (d. 397), or Gregory the Great (*c.* 540–604). Thirdly, the saint has a definable territory, his lands, where his memory is known, where there are churches or monasteries dedicated to him and the people in those areas see themselves under his special care, or as having placed themselves under his protection.

Once we see the cult of a saint in this way, we realise that it is not something static, but a dynamic process in the life of a particular community interacting over time with new members of that community and with the larger community of Christians elsewhere. Moreover, it allows us to appreciate that the most fundamental rule of evidence in the study of any saint's dossier is this: what a dossier contains tells us *primarily* about how that saint was perceived at the time that element entered the dossier, and it may have little to tell us about the actual life of the man or woman who after death became a saint. Thus Adomnán's *Vita Columbae* is primarily about how Adomnán and his community saw Columba and their own life and work as Christians, but *we cannot* – in the absence of earlier independent evidence – *assume that it tells us anything about the man* who died on 9 June 597. So in a great many cases where we have only a name, a cult-site or tomb, a feast day, and a later *vita*, all we can say about the historical person is that they were a Christian who died in a certain place on a certain day – we may not know the year – and that at a later time (i.e. when the *vita* was written) they were sufficiently significant to merit a written *vita*: not one item in that *vita* can be taken on its

17. See O'Loughlin 1997.

own as providing information about the life and times of its subject. This limitation flies in the face of the human desire for details
about those in whom we are interested and is a lesson that few
were prepared to take on board with regard to Patrick until the
1960s.[18] However, it is with this fundamental rule before our eyes
that we can now set out to find Patrick: *we will seek to use the
various strands of evidence separated by time, allowing to each
moment only that which can be dated to that time and assuming
that we cannot use later fame as a basis for earlier understandings.*
So, for example, if it is only in the later seventh century that we
find Patrick being presented as the patron of the whole island of
Ireland – and so someone significant for the whole island – we
cannot assume that at any time before that picture of Patrick was
presented by Muirchú, Patrick had such a significance for the
whole island.

Signs and wonders

Before turning to Patrick, there are two other topics to reflect
upon: first, how do we approach the issue of the miraculous,
which is found scattered in all the evidence we shall be examining;
and second, if the world of the Christians in early Ireland is so
different from our own, why bother to look at it?

Faced with an account of a miracle most modern western-
educated people are all too likely to dismiss the whole event as
evidence of the hold of superstition/stupidity on previous
generations, the woeful lack of a proper understanding of either
how nature works or how to analyse statistically unlikely
outcomes, or simple frauds practised on an intellectually en-
cumbered population by a literate self-organised elite as part of
their process of domination. The prevalence of such attitudes goes
some way towards explaining why so little study has been devoted
to date on the world-view contained in early medieval miracles.[19]
The temptation is to question the evidence as if our structures for
understanding the universe are absolute, and every other way of
assembling a meaningful universe is inferior. This has been the
western approach to the past and to other cultures since the

18. Binchy 1962.
19. For an examination of the place of miracles see Ward 1976, Stancliffe 1983,
    McCready 1994, and Borsje 1994 and 1996.

eighteenth century, yet even a brief encounter with contemporary non-western cultures will show that human beings can, and do, organise the world very differently. So when we read of a miracle our question should not be 'Did it happen?' – let us assume that if a modern western academic were transported back to that moment in the past, they would not see anything that they would explain in terms of a miracle – but 'What does that story tell us about how those people imagined the world?' As such, the miracle stories are among the most important evidence we have if our aim is to understand the mentality of those who lived in a culture very different from ours.

So how were miracles seen in the early Middle Ages? First, let us dispose of the most common mistake found in works on the period, where Roman Catholic writers take over their modern canonical definition of a miracle as used by officers of their church in 'declaring' a miracle for a saint's canonisation or identifying a location as a pilgrimage shrine, namely that a miracle is a departure from the expected course of events which cannot be explained by scientists according to their knowledge and so can be attributed to the intervention of a supernatural power. The problem with such an approach is that it assumes a far more rigid understanding of the 'laws of nature' than anyone had prior to the rise of modern science. It also seeks to preserve a separation between two orders of existence (the 'natural' and the 'supernatural': where the higher can intervene in the lower but not vice versa) that was unknown in the early Middle Ages, which only began to appear in formal theology in the thirteenth century, and which has still not established itself in popular Catholic culture in many parts of the world.

The early Christian world was one in which God was both beginning and end, expressed in the scriptural shorthand Alpha and Omega,[20] and presided over the whole creation in an act of sustaining it in being, governing it and caring for it. But crucially, between the Alpha and the Omega, the Lord of the creation took a step into the background and allowed a whole series of forces to be at work. In this act of 'stepping back' God has established the domain of the creation's freedom, and while he is not constantly

---

20. See Rev. 1:8; 21:6 and 22:13 for an early use of this image, which was known through its use in liturgy.

fiddling with the creation to bring about his will, he is aware of all
that is happening in it and can 'hear' its cries. Note the image they
used of hearing, where they imagined someone hearing a cry in
the distance, while the image of seeing was too active because it
meant the decision to look at the creation. Within the created
realm all the various capabilities that God has given to creatures
are at work and encountering one another. So stones fall to earth,
water flows and plants grow, while the stars run in their circular
courses and the moon and sun keep regular station to do their
appointed tasks as lanterns and clocks.[21] Spiritual beings both
faithful and fallen set about good and bad tasks: a wicked angel
was at work in the Garden of Eden[22] and a good angel was at work
in the Garden of Gethsemane.[23] When you set out to travel a road
you might meet a good man, by chance, or fall among robbers.[24]
You or anyone you meet might be tempted by a demon or helped
by your guarding angel, and you had to be aware of your needs
constantly. It seemed easier to acquiesce in evil than to do good,[25]
you needed protection from disease and illness, and you knew that
famine, mishap and other dangers stalked your steps: in all these
situations you needed special strength, assistance and care, which
could only come from above. In this universe prayer was a
definitely positive act on the part of humans and a necessary turning towards the good. Prayer was a calling out to God that he
would listen to human requests and turn his face towards his
needy creatures, and so dispose and govern the creation that those
needs were answered. And, as a part of this process of asking God
to step into the foreground and act within his creation, the
Christians forming the Church on Earth could also call on the
saints and the angels to lend their voices, their intercession, to the
cry of need – it is the willingness and ability of saints to assist in
this cry for help that constitutes their miraculous power, their
special skill, their *virtus*, and this power to intercede was seen as

---

21. These are images drawn from the Christian scriptures.
22. The serpent in Gen. 3:1 was interpreted as the devil or as a creature
    possessed by the devil.
23. Luke 22:43–4: these verses have been omitted in some modern translations
    (e.g. the RSV), but they were part of the Vulgate text.
24. See Luke 10:30–7.
25. This was seen as a consequence of the sin of Adam, which was already being
    interpreted as 'Original Sin'.

related to their position within the court of heaven, and their special relationship with the community making the appeal.

One can still see this view of the creation in the language of Christian prayer, especially in the liturgies of those Christians, e.g. the Roman Catholic Church, which still use prayers today that come from the period before the sixteenth century. Thus, Catholics today still use the phrases 'Lord hear us, Lord graciously hear us' (*Domine audi nos, Domine exaudi nos*), and 'beseech' God to visit, heal and protect them. One of the final prayers of the present Night Office is still the ancient collect *Visita quaesumus*, which captures in a few lines that whole concept: 'Visit this house, we pray you, Lord: drive far away from it all the snares of the enemy. May your holy angels stay here and guard us in peace, and let your blessing be always upon us.'[26]

To read of the miraculous in a medieval text is to encounter a different paradigm of science from that which we tend to use, and to enter a different spiritual world from that in which most modern Europeans live, be they Christian believers or not.

Before leaving the topic of the miraculous we should note one other point: theologians of the period devoted quite a lot of attention to the different ways in which God acted within his creation (a good example from the insular region would be Adomnán who adapted many ideas from Gregory the Great).[27] Hence, where we have just one category of 'miracle', they had many well-differentiated categories of actions/divine aid/care/intervention. However, for now, it is sufficient to mention just the two broadest categories: one can be labelled a *miraculum*, and the other a *signum* – although, unfortunately, not every early medieval writer was consistent in this usage. *Miracula* were those special acts of divine care, for which every Christian prayed, that occurred in the course of everyday life and came either directly from God, or through the action or intercession of the angels and saints. We can view them as unexpected help in the normal crises of life and they

26. This prayer is, today, the alternative conclusion of Compline for 'the Easter Triduum and Solemnities which do not fall on Sundays'. Prior to 1971 it was in daily use. The Latin text is even more expressive than the modern official translation: *Visita, quaesumus, Domine, habitationem istam, et omnes inisidias inimici ab ea longe repelle; angeli tui sancti habitant in ea, qui nos in pace custodiant, et benedictio tua sit super nos semper.*

27. See Cusack 1993.

relate to the sort of happening that we would put down to 'good luck'. So, for instance, a child falls in the river – and the prior expectation is that sometimes this leads to the child being rescued and sometimes to drowning – but on this occasion, just when all seemed lost, the child fetched up onto a rock and was rescued. The onlookers noted that they had called out 'O Mother of God' when they saw this, and then the unexpected solution is seen as one more Marian miracle.[28] Events usually take their course for better or worse, but the help of God may, unexpectedly, come to a situation and resolve it in a way that those involved find both good and wonderful.

Signa are far more spectacular, far more rare, and have a very different purpose within the whole divine plan than *miracula*. These are occasions when God, on his own initiative, intervenes with mighty gracious acts (*magnalia Dei*), not to help in a normal problem of life but to advance the whole of the kingdom. The interventions in the life of Israel were seen as the perfect examples of this: dividing the Red Sea and rescuing his people, establishing the truth of his prophet before the priests of Baal,[29] and speaking through his prophets. The coming of the Christ and his wonders also fell into this category; and the form of those wonders, for instance the 'first sign' at Cana or the feedings,[30] were seen to reveal the inner dynamic of Christ's care for the Church. The structure of these *signa* were part and parcel of the way that the Father acted in the life of the Church, so any great movement within the life of the Church on Earth was capable of being expressed within these terms – and that expression was not an act of falsification of the evidence, but a case of understanding the whole inner dynamic of what was going on. We will see a splendid example of this in Muirchú's *Vita Patricii*, where Muirchú knows that a new people have been added to the Church and brought within the whole sweep of salvation history, and so he expresses the event of conversion within the framework of the miracle of the first Easter Vigil on Irish soil – for conversion is, for him, the work of God. Just as on the first Pascha the work of God led the Israelites out of darkened idolatrous Egypt into freedom under

28. See Bull 1999 for a collection of similar incidents.
29. For the biblical references see p. 13.
30. See John 2:1–11.

Moses, so God on another Pascha led the Irish out of a darkened idolatrous Ireland into freedom under Patrick. *Signa* were the stories within which theologians explained, in shorthand, the inner structures of God's relationship with his Church, and these structures were 'great mysteries'.[31]

Looking backwards

This chapter has tried to point out some of the problems and pitfalls in trying to find a fifth-century Roman from Britain called Patrick, who is venerated by Christians as a saint. It has stressed some of the difficulties in that process and how foreign that world is from that in which we live. So before looking any further it is worth asking why we should bother to search through this material. The answer can be sought on three different levels, depending on one's starting point in the quest.

First, for anyone working on the history of Ireland or of the Latin west in late antiquity, there is no choice but to study Patrick for his writings, which constitute our earliest historical evidence produced on the island of Ireland. And, given that Ireland begins to have written materials for its history with the coming of Christianity, the materials relating to Patrick must be studied as the earliest stratum of documentary evidence. Equally, the later writings dedicated to Saint Patrick are important sources for the time of their composition and, given that they have played a crucial role in constructing Irish identity, no historian of Irish culture can afford to ignore them.

The reasons why it is worthwhile for Christians to look back on this material are more complex. Clearly, many branches of Christianity consider it part of their agenda to look backwards to their tradition and it is claimed that this process provides alignment and inspiration for them. However, if we leave aside doctrine-based claims for the value of studying the past, there are still two very good reasons for examining earlier generations of Christian believers. Firstly, looking to the past provides us with a genetic understanding of our present: this is where we have come from, this is how we have changed, and these are the factors that have changed us or influenced us. In a historical/traditional

31. See Eph. 5:32.

religion – and this is what Christianity is, whether it is acknowledged to be so or not, a fact illustrated every time a Christian begins to read the ancient text handed down to them as a 'Bible' – not to reflect on that past, that process of transmission of the ideas believed today, is to make absolute the present as the one and only valid form of the religion and to see what is taken as the present position as perfection. Plato said that 'the unexamined life is not worth living', the Christian could say that 'the unexamined tradition is not worth inheriting.'

Secondly, a study of how Christianity in the past was different and how its beliefs have evolved and adapted to cultures can give contemporary Christians a perspective on their believing, and show that the Christian message is far broader, indeed richer, in its dimensions than any one of its expressions within a particular period or culture. The past will have insights worth taking up afresh and warnings of dead-ends to be avoided. Within a traditional religion, innovation usually occurs through prophetic critique, and the variety of Christian experience – much of which is in the distant past – is one of the great resources for such critique. Christianity is, as Karl Rahner (1904–1984) once remarked, always remembering and always forgetting. Indeed, it is in the tension between the present situation and the experience of the churches back to the time of Jesus, that it moves forward with confidence into new situations. If 'variety is the spice of life', then the variety of ways in which Christians have imagined their world in the past is one of the great sources of renewing life within the churches.

Lastly, encountering cultures – whether contemporary or in the past – very different from our own, with the consequent demands of making the effort to learn a new cultural language and idiom, expands our minds and humbles our certainties. In a time when we hear of the 'clash of cultures' on the one hand, while seeing the effect of globalisation on the other, it is a valuable insight to see just how recent, in the history we see as 'our own', many of our cherished assumptions are. The worlds in which we live are human constructions, and it is a form of blind imperialism to think that our world is the only one in which purpose, meaning or happiness can be found.

CHAPTER 2

❦

The Earliest Christians in Ireland

Empire and boundaries

'Ireland was always outside the Roman Empire' and 'St Patrick brought Christianity to Ireland' are two statements that are taken for granted by millions of people who have heard of St Patrick, but who otherwise do not claim great knowledge of late antique or early medieval Europe. Before we can think of who the earliest Irish Christians were, we need to unpack both of these truisms. Because one can draw a clear and firm line on a map showing the edges of that Empire, one can easily imagine that the actual border was equally clear, firm and hard. There was the Empire, where there was law and order, Latin was spoken, and there were cities and roads and literature and commerce and what not, and by the fifth century an ever-growing Christian Church. Outside that world was the exact opposite! The two worlds were so far apart that it was only a brave explorer that ventured from one world to the other. For much of the twentieth century, writers imagined – often unconsciously – the distance between pre-Christian Ireland and the Roman Empire as being like Europe and the Americas in 1492. Later in the century, writers imagined that boundary as the fifth-century equivalent of the Iron Curtain. It depended on the individual's perspective as to which side of that boundary was full of fun and joy and which was dull and boorish. In recent years the most popular form of this image is that the pre-Christian Celts (outside that boundary) were free, creative and fun-loving, while the Romans were rather a depressing lot, pretty dry and bureaucratic, with little love of beauty or creativity, writing down lots of stuff in Latin. Then Patrick landed as a missionary – more than once this has been compared to Neil Armstrong landing on the moon – and in this wholly alien environment began preaching. Because Ireland now begins to have written records and can generate the material for its own history – and the oldest documents from Ireland are Patrick's – Patrick's arrival can be viewed as marking the arrival of the Church, and this fact alone testifies to Patrick's marvellous success. Little wonder, then, that Patrick became the religious hero and patron of later times. I have drawn this caricature because unless we are aware of its influence on our thinking, we are apt to fit what little evidence we do possess from the earliest period into that caricature and simply repeat the old stories.

Ireland was known to the classical world, that is the world of the Greeks and Romans, for centuries before Patrick's time.[1] It had been described by geographical writers, by soldiers and by travellers. At some time in the second century AD the great Alexandrian geographer Claudius Ptolemaeus (c. 90–168) gave its location with latitudes and longitudes, noted the position of fifteen river mouths right around its shores, and listed some seven inland towns along with some tribal names.[2] Ptolemy intended that his work would enable its readers to construct an outline map of the places he described with the correct location of each place relative to other places, and give each place's correct location on the sphere of the earth. Unfortunately, we have no example of any attempt to convert Ptolemy's text into a drawn map from earlier than the later Middle Ages, but several modern scholars have produced maps that show us just how much information Ptolemy had available to him.[3] What it shows us is that, at least three hundred years before Patrick, there was not only knowledge that Ireland existed 'out there' on the periphery of the continent of Europe, but there was intercourse with its inhabitants and, while not part of the world governed by Romans, it was thought of as a

1. The most comprehensive account is Freeman 2001.
2. *Geographia* 2, 1; cf. Orpen 1913.
3. The best reconstruction is in Freeman 2001, p. 69; for commentary on this map, see Baumgarten 1984, and Andrews 1997, pp. 26–9; on the problems of using Ptolemy for a knowledge of the British Isles in the second century AD, see Jones and Keillar 1996, and Strang 1997.

Christian Europe in AD 450

place with towns and so was imagined as being far less alien from the world of Rome than we often imagine it being. The other significant feature about Ptolemy's knowledge is the number of river mouths he lists: silent evidence that there are plenty of trading links between Ireland, Britain and the continent.

More direct evidence of trade comes from archaeological finds of Roman materials in Ireland. Many Roman coins, and even some Roman silver ingots, have been found in Ireland – and coinage is a very good indicator of trading links. Trade can also be seen in remains of Roman storage vessels, imported wares and occasional Roman burials.[4] And, indeed, Patrick himself supplies our earliest written evidence of this trade when he describes how

4. See Wooding 1996a and 1996b.

he sought and found a ship that was leaving Ireland for either Britain or the Continent. We can discern from his description that the ship was crewed by Irishmen who were not Christian.[5] So when we think of the boundary between Ireland and the Roman Empire we should think of a soft boundary that was frequently crossed and where people either side of that boundary had a fair understanding of the other group, and had the ability to communicate with one another. This is an ability that Roman and Romano-British traders in Britain must have taken for granted (Roman traders in Britain must have already been able to communicate in the local language of Britain – the ancestor of the language we know as Welsh, but which would be better described as 'British' at this period). It is also very likely that some of the inhabitants of Ireland were able to communicate with people from elsewhere, knowing either British or Latin or both.

Along with this trade in goods came exchanges in ideas. The Ogam alphabet (chiselled marks usually along the long upright edge of a stone) was adapted from Latin to record names in Irish in the fourth or fifth century. This adaptation was probably not a direct consequence of the adoption of Christianity by a large proportion of the population, but proceeded as a general result of contact with the Roman world:

> Where, when and by whom the Ogam alphabet was invented is not known. What can be said with certainty, however, is that Ogam existed already in the fifth century as a monumental script. The distribution of inscriptions in the Ogam character suggests that it was at home in the south of Ireland, and as it can be shown beyond reasonable doubt that the alphabet was designed for the Irish language it is likely that its framers were Irish and probable that they resided in the south of the country, possibly in the fourth century. That they were familiar with the Latin alphabet and had at least a rudimentary training in Latin grammar is evident ...[6]

5. *Confessio* 18 and 19.
6. McManus 1991, p. 1. This work, which has mainly attracted interest from linguists, is of great value for understanding the intellectual culture of the earliest generations of Christians in Ireland. Incidentally, despite the work of many skilled linguistic scholars, such as McManus, many popular writings on 'Celtic spirituality' continue to claim that Ogam is some 'secret' priestly language belonging to 'the druids'.

So anyone with a Roman background arriving in Ireland in the fifth century would find a very different culture to that which was familiar, but equally one which was in communication with Latin culture, willing to learn from it, and welcoming contact and trade. He would not find himself in a 'hermit country'. Moreover, if that person already knew Britain, he would be familiar with the co-existence of Latin with a local language, so the notion of a bilingual environment would be nothing new. This visitor would have considered British wholly unrelated to Latin, and when he encountered Irish he would have considered it to be wholly un-related to both British and Latin.[7] Furthermore, while Latin was the empire-wide language in *writing*, from the experience of African visitors to north Italy in the later fourth century we know that there was such a wide variety of accents that it was often difficult for people from one region of the Empire to understand the *spoken* Latin from elsewhere. So the idea of regional variations and difficulties in communication would be nothing new.

This trade between Ireland and elsewhere certainly brought some knowledge of Christianity along with it. In the National Museum of Ireland there are four silver ingots, found in 1940 in a gravel pit at Balline, County Limerick, dating from the late fourth/early fifth century. Three have Latin inscriptions, and one of these has the Christian chi-rho monogram clearly stamped on it. The Irish were trading with Christians, and in all likelihood some of those traders had set up bases in Ireland and were possibly the first Christians living in Ireland. These 'ex-pat' groups of Christians would have organised themselves for worship – the key form this would have taken was gathering for the Eucharist on Sundays – and this would have required clergy probably brought from the ports they traded with. Whether or not these groups would have engaged in 'missionary' work with the surrounding society is a matter of guesswork, but it is more than likely that they did engage in this way – but this is a topic that we shall examine in detail later.

7. The realisation that British and Irish are closely related as 'Celtic languages' did not appear until the work of Edward Llwyd (1660–1709), while the real-isation that Latin and the Celtic languages all came from a common Indo-European stock came even later.

Slaves and Christians

The earliest large groups of Christians in Ireland for which we have certain evidence are slaves, who were either bought in, or stolen, from Britain. Patrick provides us with the evidence when he tells us that when he was about sixteen he was captured from his father's country estate near the village of Bannavem Taburniae along with 'many thousand others' (*cum tot milia hominum*) and brought to Ireland as a slave.[8] Allowing for the exaggeration in numbers that is always part of remembered 'bad luck' (we might doubt if on any one slaving raid someone could take away 'thousands'), the basic fact remains: slaving was a big business. These men and women were obtained by force, traded as a commodity, and formed a key element in the labour force, probably mainly working, as did Patrick, in agriculture. These slaves would have included many – just like Patrick – who were Christians, and these British-born slaves would probably have been the first numerically large groups of Christians in Ireland. How many people were just snatched by slavers is impossible to estimate, as is any attempt to assess how widespread was the practice, because slaves disappear from history. Indeed, it is quite remarkable that of all the slaves in the world of antiquity we have only a handful of names – for example Onesimus who accompanied St Paul for a time[9] – and we can hear the voice of only one of them: Patrick. While presumably some did escape to freedom, none, except Patrick, have left us an account of their captivity and escape.

This slaving activity has appeared to many historians as a pretty straightforward affair. The Roman Empire was 'crumbling', the legions had been withdrawn from Britain in 410 leaving its west coast undefended, and the pagan Irish spotted in this power vacuum their chance to grow rich through raiding. Amphibious operations by these cruel barbarians were the scourge of these now defenceless Christian farmers who were being taken off to the misty depths of Ireland as slaves to pagans. While indeed it must have been easier to engage in slaving raids when there were fewer soldiers around, and while it must have been an awful fate to have been seized – we have but to think of the suffering endured by

8. *Confessio* 1; see Chapter 3 for details.
9. See his letter to Philemon, and see Thompson 1980.

slaves being brought from Africa to America in the late eighteenth and early nineteenth centuries – this slaving activity needs to be set in context. Since people are unlikely ever to volunteer to become slaves, slavery is always a matter of violence. There is always a need for additional slaves: by procreation, by purchase, through criminals and those taken captive in war being enslaved, and, of course, through seeking out new sources of people who can be captured and sold on as slaves. Most of the economies of the ancient world depended on slaves, and it was an important trade in its own right. Although procreation by slaves was seen by some owners as an added bonus, it alone never ensured a sufficient supply: slaves were there to work rather than care for their own families. This meant that the work of the slaver was always hovering in the background of society, and since one could not gather up new slaves within one's own society – that would be theft if the people were already slaves, and unlawful if they were not – the slavers had to operate on the edges of societies, gathering slaves from other peoples' lands and then selling them at home. Hence, around the edges of the Roman Empire there were slaving operations in both directions. We have to imagine slavers working in the lands beyond the Empire and seeking people to be sold into slavery within it – and they might then be sold on to anywhere in the Roman world, and vice versa. We have records of this sort of activity from every Roman frontier, and the situation would change very little for centuries, in that in the eleventh century Icelanders were seeking slaves in Ireland and vice versa. Moreover, we know that this caused Christians little moral anxiety – except that no one wanted to be the object of a slaver's raid.

Christianity arose in a society where slavery was taken for granted, and part of its message was that before God a slave and a free person were equal, and within the Christian community there was to be no distinction between master and slave. It is in this light that we should read the two famous statements of Paul: 'For by one Spirit we were all baptized into one body – Jews or Greeks, slaves or free – and all were made to drink of one Spirit' (1 Cor. 12:13), and 'There is neither Jew nor Greek, there is neither slave nor free, there is neither male nor female; for you are all one in Christ Jesus' (Gal. 3:28). However, if within the ideal society envisaged by Christians there were to be no distinctions between slave and free, this was not an item on their agenda for social change.[10] The Christians lived with slavery and – provided that a master did not mistreat his slaves – they did not raise their voices against it. By the fourth century, church law forbade slaves receiving ordination or entering monasteries to avoid their secular obligations, which can be seen as indirect support for the institution of slavery, and many individual clerics owned slaves. St Augustine viewed slavery as one of the effects of the sin of Adam manifesting itself in human society, but – in a way curiously similar to what we read in Patrick – he was outspoken in condemning slavers who were kidnapping children and other people for the slave market, and he was prepared to use church resources to ransom them.[11] The institution of slavery only gradually disappeared and was replaced by various forms of serfdom, but from our perspective it suffices to note that it was an everyday part of life throughout the period covered by this book. Thus, Bede recalls Gregory the Great seeing English slaves in Rome at the end of the sixth century and the Pope's concern is not with their status but with their religious adherence. Bede takes this as a sign of his loving pastoral care – he does not expect a pope to be critical of slavery.[12] Likewise, Muirchú takes slavery for granted in his society. In his efforts to present Saint Patrick as a model just man who pays his debts, he has the saint make his first journey after arriving back in Ireland to Miliucc – whose slave he had been – to redeem himself. In Muirchú's eyes being holy and running away as a slave were incompatible.[13]

In recent years there has been a tendency to romanticise the world of 'the pagan Celts' as a sensitive spiritual people in tune with the world, placing a high value on women, and without the nasty traits linked to Romans and/or Christians. There has also been a movement within Christianity to see 'Celtic Christianity' as a kind of 'golden age', when Christians had a spiritual 'insight into the depths of their religion' and had not yet been corrupted with the later base metal of law and sophisticated theology – for these Christian romantics this early period was also a time when women

10. See Bartchy 1992 for a summary of the Roman slave trade and system along with a survey of the earliest Christian attitudes.
11. See his *Epistola* 10* (Divjak); and cf. Corcoran 1985.
12. Bede, *Historia ecclesiastica gentis anglorum* 2, 1.
13. Muirchú, *Vita Patricii* 1, 11.

were valued, when freedom was valued, and when poets could sing with clear voices of the lovely creation around them. One can reply to these romantic visions, whether 'pro pagan' or 'pro Christian', in many ways.[14] However, the simplest reply is to note that slavers preferred to capture women who could serve their masters in field, household and bed; next, they preferred boys who could work hard but not be too truculent; and lastly, adult males caught on a slaving expedition would probably be put to the sword. As to the value of women, well the female slave, the *cumal*, was a basic unit of value in early Ireland for centuries after the arrival of Christianity.[15] Christian legislation merely condemned the worst excesses of the trade. We may sympathise with Patrick being captured as a slave, but he grew up on a farm where slaves carried out all the basic labour.[16] Lastly, a soft-focus picture may conjure up a 'mystical' 'Celtic' landscape of the first millennium, but I prefer the shocking image of the ancient slave chain found at Llyn Cerrig Bach in Wales, of the sort that might have been used to bring British slaves to Ireland or Irish slaves to Britain.[17] That is an image a great number of Christians would have recognised, at once recalling either their journey to Ireland, their present status, how they obtained their labour force, or even their trade!

In Patrick's letter to the soldiers of Coroticus we see this world of kidnapping and slavery in miniature. It is not certain whether or not Coroticus – a name in Latinised form – was British or Irish, but we do know that he and his soldiers were Christians. This fact probably indicates that he was a Pict, because Patrick tells us that the Christian Picts and the pagan Irish were allies in the work of taking slaves. Moreover, this alliance of pagan and Christian, and of Irish and non-Irish, was operating in Ireland and its latest target was a group of newly baptised Christians. It is this act, Christian taking Christians as slaves, that Patrick finds objectionable and hence he calls them 'apostates'. Moreover, this band of slavers is prepared to sell their fellow countrymen and women and/or their fellow Christians to whoever wants them. Patrick objects that they are selling them to pagans and reminds his readers of the practice among Gaulish Christians of ransoming

14. See O'Loughlin 2002.
15. See Kelly 1988, pp. 95–7 and 112–3.
16. *Epistola* 10; see Chapter 3 for details.
17. Now in the National Museum of Wales, Cardiff.

the Christians sold as slaves to Franks or other pagans – which we know was practised in southern Gaul by St Caesarius of Arles (*c.* 470–542). The implication is clear: he is concerned about Christians being mistreated by slavers and then being sold to pagans. He would have had no difficulty with Christians owning other Christians as slaves.[18] From the letter to Coroticus we can see that the boundaries between Irish and British, Irish and Roman, Christian and pagan, were all far more fluid than we tend to imagine. Moreover, it is certain that there were sizeable communities of Christians on the island of Ireland – large enough to warrant a bishop being sent to them. These communities were probably made up of slaves for the most part, but there were also non-slaves, such as traders – including traders in slaves – and, almost certainly, Irish converts.

Pastoral care for Christians in Ireland

That there were Christians beyond the Roman Empire was taken for granted in Rome by the early fifth century for at that time Pope Leo the Great noted that the extent of the regions that submit to the apostles of Rome, Saints Peter and Paul, is now greater in extent than the territories that submitted to the Roman emperors.[19] That many of those Christians beyond the bounds of the Empire were slaves was also something that was taken for granted. Prosper of Aquitaine (*c.* 390–*c.* 455) in his book, *On the calling of all the nations* (*De uocatione omnium gentium*) remarks on how providence is at work when Christians are taken as slaves beyond the boundaries of the Empire for 'they hand their captors into the possession of Christ's gospel.'[20] Moreover, these Christian slaves were not only known about, they were the pastoral object of concern for Christians 'back home'. We know from other border regions of the Roman Empire that Christians were concerned about the pastoral welfare of their brethren who had been taken as slaves beyond where the Church had an organisation of clergy to minister to them.[21] Christians needed ministers for several tasks that were seen as central to their religious lives. At a very simple

18. See sections 2, 5 and 14 of Patrick's letter for the basis of this paragraph.
19. *Sermo* 82,1; and see Charles-Edwards 1993.
20. *De uocatione omnium gentium* 2, 33; and see Charles-Edwards 1993.
21. See Thompson 1980.

level, they needed lectors who could read the scriptures to them. The ability to turn written marks on papyrus or parchment into sounds was not such a simple task that anyone with basic literacy could perform it; only someone with training and experience could take a literary text such as one of the gospels and enable it to be heard, and as Paul said: 'Faith comes from hearing' (Rom. 10:17). For the Eucharist they needed both presbyters and deacons – the notion of a single priest celebrating the Eucharist was still centuries in the future. And, so that their teaching could be co-ordinated, these communities needed bishops. This would have been no small number of men. Again we must remember that the notion that a priest and a deacon could serve a group of Christians of more than about one hundred people belongs to a much later image and practice of the Eucharist and of the eucharistic ministry. In several regions we see such ministers being appointed so that they could emigrate and take care of communities of slaves beyond the imperial borders: one such group was in Ireland.

Prosper of Aquitaine records in his *Chronicon* – a history of events in the church written year by year in chronicle fashion – under the year 431, this action by Pope Celestine I: 'To those Irish who are believers in Christ, Palladius, having been ordained by Pope Celestine, was sent as their first bishop' (*Ad Scottos in Christo credentes ordinatus a papa Caelestino Palladius primus episcopus mittitur*). This short statement assumes that not only were there Christians who had been brought to Ireland as slaves, but that there were at least some *Scotti*, that is the natives of the island, who were Christians. We can place great weight on this statement and its date because Prosper was in Rome at that very time, and for the period of his own lifetime his chronicle is very trustworthy. And, from another reference by Prosper we know that not only did Celestine know that there were Christians in Ireland at the time, but he was aware that the island was both barbarian and pagan. Palladius, apart from looking after those who were believers in Ireland, was to work 'to make the barbarian island Christian'.[22] What we can draw from this action in far-off Rome is that by 431 there were not only Christians in Ireland, but Irish Christians. They already had all the personnel structures so that they could be

22. See Charles-Edwards 1993.

recognised as a church. Certainly they would have had lectors, deacons and priests serving them. However, the country was still seen as a pagan region, and there was a definite task given to the Church in Ireland, through its first bishop, that it should convert the nation in which it found itself. With regard to other structures we have no definite evidence, but there is no reason why there might not have been monks and nuns among these groups of Christians in Ireland. We know that there were monks in Britain at that time, and the links which have just been alluded to, for example the alliance we know about between some Irish and Pictish slavers, could have led to the introduction of monasticism to Ireland by the early fifth century. We know on the evidence of Patrick's writings that monasticism was present in Ireland in the later fifth century.

Palladius, 'first bishop of the Irish'[23]

There has been much speculation over the centuries about Bishop Palladius. The traditional picture is that produced by Muirchú, where Palladius lacks zeal and is a failure, and is contrasted with the zealous and successful Patrick. Muirchú's story runs like this. The Bishop of Rome, Celestine, sent his archdeacon, Palladius (Prosper mentions that Palladius was a deacon, Muirchú promotes him to being a specific senior officer of the diocese of Rome) to Ireland. However, this was not something that was within the plan of Providence and so the scheme was doomed from the start. Palladius arrived in Ireland with his assistants. (Muirchú gives the names 'Augustine' and 'Benedict' to the two main assistants and says there were others – giving such famous names shows a certain lack of originality on Muirchú's part.) However, the wild men of Ireland were not prepared to accept Palladius's teaching, while Palladius did not like spending time in a foreign land. So after less than a year – a detail implied in the *vita* since they were not in Ireland long enough to celebrate an Easter vigil – Palladius decided to go home to the continent. But after landing in Britain – Muirchú takes it for granted that he would have gone from Ireland to Britain and then on to Gaul – Palladius died. His

---

23. A bibliography of recent writing on Palladius would include: Ó Cróinín 1986; Charles-Edwards 1993; Dumville 1993, pp. 65–88; and Ó Cróinín 2000.

companions continued on to Gaul and told of the death of 'Saint Palladius' at a place he calls 'Ebmoria' – no such place is known, but many older writers, assuming that Muirchú had a reliable source, made 'scholarly conjectures' about its location. This is the information that leads to the start of the mission of Patrick – a mission that is sanctioned by Providence.[24]

The source of Muirchú's information is clearly Prosper's chronicle and the rationale for the story of his failed mission in Ireland is an attempt to get around an embarrassing fact. Prosper names Palladius as first bishop – by papal appointment – but if Patrick, his hero, is to be the source of apostolic succession, then Patrick must be the first Irish bishop. So how does one retain the latter without ignoring the former? Allow Palladius to be the first bishop appointed, but let everyone know that Patrick was the first who actually worked as a bishop in Ireland. We shall return to this topic in detail when we examine Muirchú's theology, but for now it is enough to note that while we may see him as a 'spin doctor', he was faced with a real problem: he had only one source that told him of the earliest days of Christianity in Ireland (Patrick's writings) and yet he had this chronicle which he also had to accept as recorded fact. His task was to reconcile the two as best he could – in this he acted in a manner little different from most other ancient writers, for example the gospel writers, who had to combine contradictory scraps of information into a consistent narrative.

There is no reason to think that Palladius's mission was short-lived or a failure. In all likelihood he spent the rest of his life working in one of the most difficult pastorates of the time, helping to organise his scattered flock, training and ordaining clergy, and preaching the gospel – but like so many workers, before him and since, he left little that an historian can find. However, there may be a few scraps that indicate that he laboured in Ireland with some success. For instance, among textbooks for working out the date of Easter, which were in use in Ireland in the seventh century, there is one that preserves the method used in Milan and which was different from the method used by the Church in fifth-century Britain. Since one would expect the first communities of Christians in Ireland to follow the British practice, the presence of this very early Milanese text may be due to its being brought to

24. Muirchú, *Vita Patricii* 1, 8–9 (and see 1, 14).

Ireland by Palladius. Another possible reference to Palladius is the statement by Columbanus in a letter of 613 to Pope Boniface IV, when he says that the Irish have kept the faith which 'was first handed on to them from you who are the successors of the holy apostles.'[25] This statement coheres with what Prosper tells us, but from it we cannot tell whether Columbanus had ever heard the name of Palladius or not. However, it would be unusual if he knew that the first bishop in Ireland – Columbanus viewed a bishop primarily as a teacher of apostolic doctrine – came from Rome but did not know his name.

But these 'scraps' on Palladius are just faint or possible echoes. The simple fact is that the first bishop to have ministered in Ireland and whose name we know is Palladius. He is virtually forgotten within the traditional memory of Christians in Ireland and has been so forgotten since at least the seventh century. He is one of those Jesus ben Sira had in mind when he wrote:

> Let us now sing the praises of famous men, our ancestors in their generations ...
> Some of them have left behind a name, so that others declare their praise.
> But of others there is no memory; they have perished as though they had never existed; they have become as though they had never been born, they and their children after them. But these also were godly men, whose righteous deeds have not been forgotten ... (Sir. 44:1, 8–10).

Faced with this silence we want to stretch the evidence to add detail – but that does not add to the sum of our knowledge!

Conclusion

The origins of Christianity in Ireland are obscure. The reason for the obscurity is due, probably, in part to the unsystematic way that Christianity entered the island through captured slaves and random trading contacts, and in part to the fact that the fifth century saw the arrival of the Saxons in Britain and the destruction of many of the structures of Roman administration and

25. Columbanus, *Epistula* 5, 3.

record keeping. From the standpoint of surviving historical evidence we can view the insular region in the fifth and for much of the sixth centuries as being in a 'dark age'. However, we do know that there were sufficient Christians in Ireland by the 430s for there to be concern about their spiritual welfare in Rome, hence Palladius was ordained bishop specifically for their needs. But of the life of that church we know virtually nothing, with one spectacular exception: the two documents by a Roman citizen from Britain who was also a bishop: Patrick.

CHAPTER 3

Patrick the Man

What do we know?

To narrate in detail either the whole story of my labours or even parts of it would take a long time. So, lest I injure my readers, I shall tell you briefly how God, the all-holy one, often freed me from slavery and from twelve dangers which threatened my life, as well as from many snares and from things which I am unable to express in words.[1]

Patrick's desire not to burden his readers with details about his life and work in Ireland may reflect an admirable trait in his character – few forms of narrative can be as boring as those of religious people recounting their experience moment by moment – but it has been a source of frustration for everyone interested in him for at least thirteen hundred years. This absence of detail has been filled using a variety of strategies from carefully constructed saintly portraits to sheer romantic invention. The most usual form has been that of the religious portrait – the saint's life by a hagiographer – that proceeds on the rationale that this is what he *should* have been like, therefore this is what he *must* have been like. More recently, by applying a model of 'the ancient holy man' – a very valuable category for understanding the places of saints in society at that time but about whom we do not have much detailed information – to Patrick, or by treating

1. *Confessio* 35.

every tradition about him as fact, or by creatively locating him in a generic landscape of the period, writers have sought to supply details, but these methods still fail to supply concrete information on him as an individual. So at the outset it is worth recalling that *Patrick's own two short works are our only sources* about him that are contemporary with him. Everything that is said about Patrick that can lay claim to be historically factual about his life, beliefs and mission must be derived from them by textual exegesis. Neither work is dated, and neither contains any reference that would tie down his dates with certainty. Neither survives in more than a handful of manuscripts, although they do survive in sufficient numbers that we can determine the text to the same degree of satisfaction that we have with any other early Christian text – including those writings that are included in the New Testament.[2] Nor can we be sure which of the two texts was written first – but since Patrick says at the end of the *Confessio* that he writes as 'an old man before he dies', most scholars have worked on the assumption that the letter to the soldiers of Coroticus was written first – but the sequence is of little value in adding to our store of knowledge. This and the subsequent chapters are an attempt to draw out a religious description of the man in so far as that can be done on the basis of what he has left us.

Dates[3]

There have been three dates suggested for Patrick's mission. The first is a date some time in the fourth century and perhaps reaching into the early fifth century.[4] While this has received enthusiastic support from a few scholars it is hard to reconcile it with the long family tradition of Roman officials as well as Christian clergy that Patrick proudly announces to his readers. Moreover, that would further increase the gap between the generation of Christians with whom Patrick worked and the time

---

2. There are excellent descriptions of the surviving manuscripts in White 1905 and Bieler 1952; for a fuller bibliography relating to the Latin text of Patrick, see Lapidge and Sharpe 1985, pp. 10–11.

3. The best summary of the issues regarding dates is Dumville 1993, pp. 13–8.

4. The most recent writer to use this date is Freeman 2004.

when Christian remains become plentiful in Ireland. That Christianity begins to be a force in Irish society in the fifth century – around the time of Palladius – make much better sense of the evidence.

The second date is the 'traditional' one: Patrick arrived in 432 or thereabouts. This date is suspiciously close to the date of Palladius's mission.[5] All the sources where 432 is given are from the seventh century or later and were written with an awareness of Prosper's *Chronicon*. Muirchú opts for this date by implication since he needs Patrick to succeed closely on the heels of Palladius, while the various Irish annals are not contemporary records for that period and can be seen as written within an established cult-memory of Patrick as 'the apostle of Ireland' so they too must harmonise their cult-memory with the details founds in Prosper.[6] Moreover, the annals contain contradictory details, especially regarding the date of Patrick's death, which may indicate that there was a variety of traditions surviving about him, and this may indicate developments in the status of Patrick and the size of his cult during the time when annals were being kept. Earlier scholars, faced with these discrepancies but unwilling to doubt the actual assertions of the annals, were even willing to suggest that there were two Patricks![7] However, it is far simpler to say that the annals become a secure basis for dates only when they are contemporary with the events they record – for earlier events they simply record the presence of traditions at their time of writing and should not be used as 'raw' factual evidence. The date 432 is, in my view, most unlikely and simply a reflex to keep both Palladius and Patrick in the memory from a time – the seventh century – when Patrick was emerging as the central figure in the Christian story of the Irish 'nation'.[8]

5. See Dumville 1993, pp. 39–43.
6. The study of insular annalistic materials is a specialist sub-discipline within Celtic studies and this is not a suitable place to discuss the matter in detail. For a survey of their contents with reference to Patrick, see Dumville 1993, pp. 29–33, 45–57; and Maund 1993.
7. See Dumville 1993, pp. 59–64.
8. What 'nation' means in this context will become clear when we examine Muirchú's theology; for now it is sufficient to note that I use 'nation' to translate *gens* as that word is used in the Vulgate of Matt. 28:19: 'Go therefore and make disciples of all nations (*gentes*).'

The third possibility is that Patrick worked in Ireland in the later fifth or early sixth century. There is but one slip of evidence that sets the upper limit to this time. In his letter to Coroticus's soldiers, n. 14, he says that the Christians in Gaul send ransoms for captives taken by 'the Franks and other peoples'. Now this could mean that at the time the Franks and the others were still pagan. Clovis was baptised sometime around 500 and died in 511–512, which would put Patrick's writing in the late fifth century.[9] However, there are a number of possibilities. First, Patrick does not state that the Franks are either pagan or Christian, just that they are slavers and 'the Roman Christian Gauls' send them money – note he does not say simply that the 'Christians' send them money. While it would be nice to think that the baptism of Clovis would have had such an impact on his people that they gave up slaving that very day, the evidence is against it; certainly, as Patrick's own letter testified, baptism did not have that effect on the Picts. Moreover, we know for certain that the ransoming of captives continued as a work of charity in Gaul until long after the Franks had been assimilated within the ranks of the Christian nations.[10] Also, if the Franks did abandon taking Christians as slaves at the time of Clovis's baptism, then it would still take some time for that news to reach Ireland and Patrick. However, if we assume that Patrick is referring to what was happening in the later fifth century, then that would accord with one of the dates, 493, found for his death in Irish annals – but we must still note what we said about annalistic evidence in relation to 432. So, taking these various factors into account, a date for his mission in the latter half of the fifth century seems to fit most closely with the evidence we have. There is nothing impossible about 493 as the year of his death, but then there is nothing to prevent us locating his mission in the early years of the sixth century. *The working assumption in this book is that Patrick was working in Ireland in the latter half of the fifth century.* He probably died in 493, almost certainly on 17 March – his traditional feast day – as the date, but not the year, of a holy person's death is one of the basic elements in any cult. Moreover, we know that this date was being kept on the continent as his feast by the later seventh century because in

9. The traditional date of 496 for the baptism of Clovis is not certain – a date for his baptism as late as 508 is possible.
10. See Bieler 1953, p. 93, n. 38.

the *Calendar* of St Willibrord (658–739) we have this entry next to 17 March: '[The feast of] St Patrick, Bishop in Ireland'. However, we should be careful not to see this as a witness wholly independent of Irish works from that period promoting Patrick's cult, as Willibrord spent time in Ireland prior to going to Fresia.

Family background

Patrick tells us that he was born in Britain, and that his home was at Bannavem Taburniae, and that near that town his family had an estate. So the first thing we can say is that his background was that of belonging to the 'gentleman farmer' class, and this is confirmed by his description of his father as a 'decurion' – a local minor Roman official – and that he was born a freeman.[11] What exactly the duties and role of a decurion were in Britain at this time must remain a matter of doubt, but clearly it was, at least, a badge of social status and one of which Patrick was proud: he is telling his audience that he was 'not a nobody'. This little snippet is crucial for understanding Patrick's sense of cultural identity. He saw himself as a freeman of the Roman Empire, a Roman born in Britain,[12] a fellow with the Romans in Gaul, and culturally distinct from barbarians whether they are the Franks, other invaders on the continent, or the people he was working with in Ireland. In *Epistola* 10 there is a curious echoing of St Paul: both are freemen 'according to the flesh' within the Roman Empire, one comes from Tarsus, the other from somewhere in Britain, but a place a little more unknown than Tarsus. So where was this place? As early as the seventh century no one really knew the location of Bannavem Taburniae, or is it 'Bannaventa Berniae'?[13] And numerous modern attempts have been no more successful.[14]

We know three other details about Patrick's family. Firstly, they were of middle rank economically. Not only because they had an estate or were of decurion status – these might be remnants of

11. *Epistola* 10.
12. Patrick tells us that his parents' home was in Britain in *Confessio* 23.
13. Muirchú did not know its location; cf. *Vita Patricii* I, 1; on the different ways of giving the name of Patrick's home, see Howlett 1994, p. 52.
14. Suggesting locations for this place has been a specific sub-section of interest in Patrick. Places ranging from Cornwall, through Anglesey, to Carlisle, and some places even further away, have had their supporters.

earlier wealth – but because at the time that Patrick was captured they were slave owners. Patrick complains that apart from taking him captive, the slavers killed the male and female slaves of his father. This indicates that the family estate was a 'going concern', that it was relatively prosperous, and indeed it might have been that very wealth that attracted the slavers. The question arises as to why they killed the slaves belonging to the estate, yet took Patrick captive: it could be that those killed were caught up in the fighting during the raid or that the raiders took those whom they thought they could ransom, such as the son of the estate – but we shall never know.

Secondly, we know that Patrick's family had been Christian for at least three generations: his father, Calpornius, was a deacon, and his grandfather, Potitus, a '*presbyterus*' (the rank in the Christian hierarchy now usually referred to as 'priest'). By the fourth century the Christian churches in the Latin parts of the Empire had already evolved quite an elaborate structure of ministries as well as quite a distinct clerical culture. This structure of ministries is far more complex than anything found in any hierarchically organised church today – except that many titles have survived with little practical meaning. In Patrick's time we have to imagine an area with a bishop at its head presiding over several actual communities, but close enough to them geographically that he could really oversee their liturgy and preaching. The density of bishops in other parts of the Empire at the time would equally have applied in Britain and that density meant that every town – what we would refer to as a 'market town' – would have had a bishop. For all we know there may have been a bishop of Bannavem Taburniae – since Patrick thinks of it as a well-known place, it is not impossible. In every place where the Eucharist was celebrated – and we must think of gatherings of a few dozen people rather than the hundreds that can fit in late-medieval or modern church buildings – there would have been at least one priest and one deacon. There would also have been at least one lector and one acolyte: one was the reader at the liturgy and the other a general assistant, while in the community there would have been those with recognisable positions within the group as 'subdeacons' and 'widows'. For all we know, the 'parish' of Patrick's family may have been Bannavem Taburniae, or it could have been just their own estate, or maybe their estate along with those of some of their neighbours.

It is not an accident that Patrick's father is both a cleric and a decurion. By the early fourth century in Spain – even before the Peace of Constantine – the Christian clergy were taking over some of the social roles that had been held by the cult-officials, the *flamines*, within the Empire. The clergy were rapidly becoming the administrative middle class of the provinces.[15] It is more than likely that all those clergy were freemen because to give a slave ordination would have been to give him a place in society that would have been incompatible with his economic status. The Christian ministers already formed an *ordo* (literally: 'an order') within the society. Within late Roman society an *ordo* was a clearly demarcated social group, distinct from the mass of the *plebs* (literally: 'the people').[16] We have to imagine a family that was well connected socially within the area, held a central role economically and ecclesially, and would have had certain well-defined ambitions for one of their sons.

The sort of Christian household from which Patrick came may well have lived in a villa not unlike those Christian houses that have been excavated at Lullingstone in Kent (fourth century) or Hinton St Mary in Dorset (fourth-fifth century). Both houses had rooms set aside for liturgy: the first has a painted portico with the monogram of the word 'Christ' (the chi-rho) set between Alpha and Omega, the second had a mosaic pavement with a picture of Jesus in the form of a chi-rho.[17] The villa, its owners, and the Christian community in those places all seem closely intertwined.

Thirdly, the family had a strong sense of identity and cohesion. Patrick speaks about his family with pride and affection. He remarks how they welcomed him on his return from slavery and how they did not want him to return to Ireland (*Confessio* 23). This might appear to us to be no more than the obvious, but very few ancient writers give us even that amount of detail about their family's opinions. Moreover, Patrick describes his homesickness while in Ireland as a bishop, his desire to be with his people, and how he is without a home for the sake of the gospel (*Confessio* 43).

15. There are few works that study the social context of the Christian clergy at this time, but Laeuchli 1972 is indispensable.
16. See Joncas 1999 for how this clerical *ordo* functioned in fifth-century Roman Africa.
17. Di Berardino 1992, figures 65 and 66.

This raises another question that cannot be answered with any certainty: was Patrick married with a family of his own? For many writers brought up within cultures where being a saintly bishop and being celibate were seen as inseparable notions, this has not even surfaced as a question. But in the fifth century most bishops were married – and in a family like Patrick's, where there was pride in the family's past, there may have been quiet rejoicing that Patrick had reached a grade in the clergy unattained by either father or grandfather. However, while the majority of clergy, including bishops, were married, from the later fourth century a major shift in Christian attitudes to sexuality was slowly taking place, which meant that increasingly marriage and saintliness were being seen as incompatible. Writers such as Jerome saw marriage as tied to the 'Earth', while those who dealt with 'heavenly' things should be celibate; Augustine had set an example for bishops adopting a quasi-monastic lifestyle in Hippo; and monasticism was gradually being take as setting the 'gold standard' for Christian holiness. These and many other factors contributed to a climate in which bishops could be married, but any bishop who was married was seen as of 'inferior quality' compared with those who were celibate. Patrick makes no statement that can be taken as evidence that he was married or that he was not married. However, the fact that Patrick mentions 'monks and virgins' (*Confessio* 41; *Epistola* 12), that he praises women who have remained virgins (*Confessio* 42), and his use of the phrase 'the religious chastity which I have chosen for Christ' (*Confessio* 44), all incline me to think that Patrick was one of those fifth-century clerics who believed that a perfect minister of grace would be celibate.

A moderately wealthy clerical family would have placed a high value on such skills as reading, writing and speaking – all essential to those in the clerical *ordo* – and so have provided a good education for their male children, expecting them to carry on the family traditions. Over the years many have suggested that Patrick was poorly educated, partly because of the opening remarks which he makes in the *Confessio* and partly because his Latin prose seems awkward to anyone whose expectation of what elegant educated Latin looks like is derived from reading the Latin writers of a period much earlier than Patrick. It is worth remembering that we are as far away in time from Shakespeare as Patrick was from Virgil. However, that negative view of his Latinity fails for several reasons. First, Patrick's claim that he is 'the most rustic' of people is based on his desire to claim the extent of his humility and relate himself as the simple Christian in opposition to those who are criticising him and his mission. Second, he writes with real skill when he wants to convey his own message to his audience and the jerkiness of some of his sentences stems entirely from his desire to cite the Christian scriptures or use their figures of speech – themselves clumsy attempts to render Greek and Hebrew into Latin idioms – at every turn in his prose. Thirdly, as David Howlett has demonstrated,[18] he shows both familiarity and fluency in using many complex rhetorical forms within his two writings. The exact extent of his schooling and its content must remain open questions. He would have spoken both Latin and the local British language – probably an earlier form of Welsh – but would have learned to read and write in Latin. Moreover, he would have been given some training in elegantly and persuasively speaking in Latin, that is some basic skill in rhetoric, for that would have been needed for preaching, and the traces of that training are visible in the way he writes.

Education

So what sort of religious culture would he have encountered at home? At first sight the *Confessio* gives the impression that Patrick had almost no contact with Christianity in his youth: 'When I was about sixteen and taken captive to Ireland with many thousand others I was ignorant of the true God', and he proceeds to see his capture and that of the others as being a punishment for his people having 'departed from God, having abandoned his commandments, and having ignored his priests who kept on warning us about our salvation' (*Confessio* 1). However, this statement needs to be set in context. First, autobiography is a strange kind of writing for it is written not only with hindsight, but employing the various explanations that humans use to make sense of their life-story up to the time of writing. And, there is a very particular need for those who believe in God to explain how the 'bad things that happen to good people' can be seen within the plan of a loving God. Patrick – and indeed the whole Church in Britain at

18. Howlett 1994.

that time, which was suffering attacks from east and west – had to explain to themselves why God was letting this happen to them: after all, were they not God's people, was he not a caring God who sought to defend his people – and if so why were they having their lives torn apart and being sold into slavery? One method of making sense of this conundrum – God loves his people, but the people suffer – is to assume that the suffering is a medicinal correction: God is punishing his people to purify them and push them towards a new life of faith. In other words, if we have suffered or are suffering, then we must deserve it, so we must have been bad people, unfaithful to the covenant, living lives that were astray. The sufferings are there to highlight this infidelity of which we were unaware and are a loving corrective if they forestall a greater punishment in the next life. It is from within that urgent question and that perspective on the nature of divine activity that Patrick writes: if he needed the medicinal correction of being taken captive then he must not have been a good Christian, he must not have had a real knowledge of God, nor obeyed his commandments, nor paid sufficient attention to what was being preached by the church's ministers.

Patrick consciously adopts this perspective through his use of quotations from the Old Testament, for it was a strategy of explanation used time and again by the prophets: Israel's woes at the hands of foreign enemies was God's punishment for the people's infidelity. Nevertheless, within it lies the evidence that Patrick was well aware of the Christian life from his youth. When in Ireland Patrick fasted, and prayed sometimes 'as often as a hundred times in the day and almost as often at night' (*Confessio* 16). And, during that time he began to view his whole life within a religious frame. He says that:

> And there [in Ireland] the Lord 'opened my understanding to my unbelief', so that however late, I might become conscious of my failings. Then remembering my need, I might 'turn with all my heart to the Lord my God'. For it was he who 'looked on my lowliness' and had mercy on the ignorance of my youth, and who looked after me before I knew him and before I had gained wisdom or could distinguish between good and evil. Indeed, as a father consoles his son, so he protected me. (*Confessio* 2)

So much so that it was probably his frequent prayers that gained him the nickname 'Holy boy' ('*Sanctus puer*'), which is found in the address given him in a dream by the messenger from Ireland (*Confessio* 23). So we can assume that Patrick grew up in a family where he learned to be a Christian, to pray, to fast, to give to the poor, to take part in the liturgy, and to acknowledge his relationship with God. But from the need to make sense of his searing experience he began to think of having only established that relationship with God after he realised how wicked he must have been! Being taken into slavery was not only the great break in Patrick's young life, it was the defining event for his whole religious outlook. Many today may find Patrick's strategy to explain 'why bad things happen to good people' very strange, but it was a favourite explanation in the prophetic books of the Old Testament and has been an explanation that has been employed time and again by Christians who found it easier to assume they were sinners than that God was not in charge of every detail. Gildas – roughly contemporary with Patrick and the other theological writer from the late British church whose works have survived – also used this strategy to explain the depredations of the Angles and Saxons. Hundreds of years later, preachers in the mid-fourteenth century used it to explain the Black Death, and today there are strands of Christianity who still use it to explain such phenomena as the AIDS epidemic. It is attractive as 'an explanation' as it is simple to communicate and seems to speak to people in their pain. However, it is ultimately destructive of a true appreciation of the Christian view of God as infinite love, for it presents God's interaction with the creation as if God was one more finite actor in the creation exerting his power as 'justice'. 'God' appears close to those who use the strategy, but it is as a juggernaut that can destroy the creation at will as a direct response to human actions, and, what is more, actions done in good faith. Such a God rules by terror, and is not the vision of the infinite beyond the creation who sustains all and can bring all good to completion. Every generation of theists has to face the problem of theodicy ('why bad things happen if God is caring and good'), but it always requires a more sophisticated response than Patrick gave.

Slavery and escape

Of all those taken captive in the ancient world, only one slave who escaped has left us his story: Patrick. He does not dwell on the privations he endured as a slave, instead he tells us of how his religious life developed and how he used his time as a slave to discover the power and mercy of God. From the *Confessio* we can see that at the time he was a slave – from roughly sixteen to twenty-two – he understood his enslavement as a punishment on him and his people. But by the time of writing, another strand of thought had entered his thinking: the time in Ireland was part of the divine providence to prepare him for his later mission. These two strands are intermingled in what Patrick writes and he may not even have been aware of his differing perspectives on his slavery. Patrick, no more than most human beings reflecting on life's turns and changes, never disentangled these themes he saw in his life; for Patrick as for most of us, self-perceptions were not subjected to logical analysis! Incidentally, within this narrative of what God was doing in his life, he mentions that he was looking after flocks (*Confessio* 16), and later when back in Britain he had a vision in which 'I thought I heard the voice of those around the wood of Foclut which is close to the western sea' (*Confessio* 23). These two references have, quite naturally, been put together by those writing on Patrick to assert that he lived as a slave in Ireland near the wood of Foclut, and that the wood was near the west coast of Ireland.

Patrick tells us of his escape as a miraculous intervention of providence: a vision told him to leave where he was and go to a ship 'prepared for him far away, perhaps some 200 miles away' (*Confessio* 17). This distance, combined with the reference to Foclut, has produced some of the most bizarre scholarship on Patrick. This is usually done with a modern map of Ireland and dividers set to inscribe arcs 200 miles distant from a series of ports on the east and southeast coasts of Ireland. Then, according to this theory, we can find the likely locations for the wood of Foclut, and it usually turns out to be somewhere in County Mayo in the northwest of Ireland. It is worth noting just how wrong-headed such calculations are as it illustrates a basic difficulty modern people have in reading ancient, especially religious, texts. First, we all have an image of the shape of Ireland to work with, derived from modern maps, but this image was first known through the work of sixteenth-century surveyors.[19] Patrick would not have been able to imagine his journey in any similar way; in fact, he could have wandered for miles in zigzags up and down valleys despite the fact that his starting-point and finishing-point were only a few miles distant as 'the crow flies' or as we see it on a modern map. Second, how long is a mile? While all are agreed that a mile is 1000 paces, how long that is on the ground has varied over the centuries, and while the Roman road makers were amazingly accurate in giving distances in their miles, that does not mean that they had measured Ireland or that Patrick had that sort of skill. One must not imagine Irish routes marked out with milestones or that at some point on the road there was a sign giving distances to various ports. Third, even if there were milestones, we cannot assume that he was that careful to note the distances down – even today that is not a common skill. Many people may travel a road frequently but can be quite surprised when they are told the exact mileage – Patrick is just as vague: 'perhaps 200 miles away'. Fourth, even if we were sure of all the distances, we still do not know the location of the starting-point – if that was the wood of Foclut – nor of the port. The basic lesson is this: we must avoid imposing our view of the world on to authors who lived long before our world came into being; and we must be aware that we have a love for mathematical precision, but that we cannot impose that level of precision on cultures where it did not exist. Patrick was quite indifferent to these issues of where he was, exactly what he was doing, how long he spent in various places during his life – if he were not so indifferent he would not have generated so much speculation – and this should show us that his interest in his life's story and his notion of precision are quite alien to ours. Patrick's care is to explain the details of his life as the work of God and his care is in the details of his visions, dreams and revelations, topics that we would hardly note as they seem too imprecise, if not wholly irrelevant.

So, if Patrick did pick a figure out of the air to express the notion that he had to travel a great distance to the place where his ship lay – and we are left to imagine the difficulties that such a journey would entail for a foreigner who was on the run – why did

19. See Andrews 1997.

he pick on 200 miles? Why he picked on this precise number may, it seems to me, be related to the expression for a gigantic distance that is found in Revelation 14:20, where one of the angels at the end of the world is seen to reap the final vintage of the earth for the great winepress of the wrath of God. What flowed from that press was a lake of blood as high as a horse's bridle for a distance of 1600 *stadia*. Patrick was deeply interested in the coming end-times and this figure – anyone from a decurion's family would know that 1600 *stadia* was equivalent to 200 miles – may have lodged in his memory as indicative of a great distance, and was then applied with hindsight to his own journey as he thought back to it and its length and difficulties.

Patrick's adventures in getting on the ship, while on it, and then with the crew after the ship had come to land, have all produced an amount of speculation over the years. Where did they wander? How could they have run out of food in agricultural areas of the Roman Empire? How could one wander for so long without meeting a settlement? There have been many ingenious solutions but all depend in one way or another on taking an assumption as a fact and solving the rest of the riddle from that base. The most famous of these solutions was that of J. B. Bury who explained this 'wandering in the desert' as due to the Vandals having just passed through north-western Europe and having left a trail of destruction after them.[20] Well, it is one way of explaining the text, but is does make three massive assumptions: first, that the exact time of Patrick's journal was just after them; second, that he landed in Gaul not Britain; and thirdly, that the marauders obliterated everything over a vast area and that Patrick and the crew were almost the first to arrive there after this devastation.

There are so many contradictions in what is written in the *Confessio*, and the whole account is so permeated by Patrick's assertions about providence and his experience of being tested by Satan and then delivered by Christ, that it is very difficult to know how much of this account is to be seen as historically factual and how much is to be seen as his memory explaining his life, to himself and others, as part of a pilgrimage of faith. All we can know with certainty is that he escaped by ship from Ireland and that he was eventually welcomed home by his family in Britain. The crew

20. Bury 1905.

were not Christians and were Irish (i.e. not Romans). How long the journey took, its route (i.e. from Ireland to Britain or from Ireland via Gaul to Britain), and the events along the way are questions for which we do not have sufficient information to give definite answers. So, given that the *Confessio* is a religious justification for his own life, can we see these stories as part of another narrative? The whole section of the *Confessio* is reminiscent of the 'Exodus experience' of the chosen people escaping from Egypt through water, to wander in the desert and be fed by God miraculously, but also to be tried there, prior to being brought to their homeland. This is a theme which was deeply ingrained in the minds of Christians in the early Church, for it was the theme that was used to explain the transformation of the individual and the community in baptism – and is possibly Patrick's analysis of his own experience. After a time of slavery in Ireland (equivalent to the time the Israelites spent in Egypt), he was rescued by God over water (equivalent to the crossing of the Red Sea) (*Confessio* 17). Then he wandered in a wilderness and had to depend on God for food (equivalent to the wandering for 40 years in the desert being fed with manna) (*Confessio* 19). And during that time his faith was tested, just as the faith of the Israelites was tested (*Confessio* 20).

Just before Patrick says that he reached home, there is a difficult little piece of the *Confessio* that relates another captivity (*Confessio* 21). When this second enslavement took place is unclear, and there is no solution to the problem that is wholly satisfactory. All we can deduce from it is that enslavement was an ongoing danger for anyone who was perceived as an outsider in the world in which he lived.

A bishop

There is a sense of relief both for him and his family when he finally reached home (*Confessio* 23), and while he immediately relates his call to return to Ireland, the cumulative evidence – which will be examined in the next chapter – suggests that he continued to live in Britain for quite some time. He could not have been a cleric when he arrived home and one has to allow many years – a decade would be a minimum – for him to progress through the various orders up to the time when he could be

ordained bishop. There is no evidence that he arrived in Ireland
prior to being ordained bishop and he refers to the time before he
was a deacon (*Confessio* 27). Since Muirchú's time there has been
much speculation as to where he trained – usually this is given as
somewhere in Gaul – and by whom he was ordained. However,
with the exception of his statement that if he went home to
Britain, he could then easily visit the brethren in Gaul (*Confessio*
43), there is nothing to indicate how and where he studied or was
ordained. In all likelihood, he learned how to be a cleric – the
notion of a specific training is anachronistic – in the region where
his family lived, and it was there that he was ordained to the
various orders. All we know is that when he tells us of his work in
Ireland we are to assume that he is already a bishop. However,
given his statement in *Confessio* 43, there is nothing implausible in
stating that at some time between his escape and return to Ireland,
he visited some part of Gaul and met with clergy there. As to the
content of his training, all we can say is that for most clergy until
well into the Middle Ages, training consisted in being mentored by
other clergy as to how the liturgy was to be celebrated, and what
comprised the customs of the Church and its law, supplemented
by whatever reading was available to them.

Missionary in Ireland

Patrick's account of his vocation to work in Ireland is the most
dramatic scene in the whole of the *Confessio* (*Confessio* 23–25). It
is a structured three-step call that is closely modelled on the call
of Samuel (1 Samuel 3). In a dream he sees a man named
Victoricus who comes from Ireland with innumerable letters asking him to return and then he hears a voice that sounds like that
of the people of the area of the wood of Foclut. When Patrick sees
what is written on the letters it is 'the voice of the Irish' (*Vox
Hiberionacum*) asking him to walk among them once more.
Incidentally, later tradition would turn this figure into an angel,
and in that form Victoricus appeared on the first Irish airmail
stamps – bearing letters on wings out of Ireland – and on the
stamps the angel carried the legend '*Vox Hiberionacum*'; few saints
can say that what they heard in a dream later inspired a Post
Office!

This missionary work is explicitly aimed at those Irish who are not Christians, and nowhere in the *Confessio* is there even a suggestion that he was to convert the whole island. He was to return to the island of Ireland, because there were people there who were not yet Christians. We have become so used to hearing – following Muirchú's lead – that Patrick converted Ireland, that we fail to see that he says nothing of the sort: he is called to a particular group of the Irish and it is with that group that he works – beyond where anyone has preached before (*Confessio* 51). He will work in the outermost parts, where no one else has preached, and by this preaching the gospel will finally reach everyone on the island. Far from conveying the impression that Patrick converted Ireland or that he introduced Christianity to Ireland, the text actually leads us to assume that he was the final missionary to Ireland, the one who went to mop up the last pockets of paganism so that Ireland could be wholly Christian, and through Patrick's work they might become 'a prepared people' (*Confessio* 51).

In this work Patrick knew that he would face many weaknesses and difficulties, but following the classic form of biblical vocation stories he is assured at the outset that he will be given divine support and his weaknesses will provide opportunities for the strength and consolation of God to be made manifest.

Travels

As the cult of St Patrick grew, he became associated with innumerable places throughout Ireland, from the mountain in Mayo that bears his name, to an island penitential site on Lough Derg in Donegal, to innumerable holy wells. All claim that at one point or another Patrick visited them, blessed them, or caused the well to spring up as a gift to the local people. Such associations are a key part of taking upon one's self a patron saint: the saint knows us and our locality, he is interested in this place, and his 'historical' links are the token/proof of this interest. We see this desire to link the patron with various places first explored in the work of Bishop Tirechán in the late seventh or early eight century, and until quite recently scholars have collected these stories in the hope that they would show where exactly Patrick travelled or worked in Ireland.[21] Alas, we have no evidence from the *Confessio* as to

21. See Shearman 1879.

where he went, and by the time that place-name and dedication evidence becomes available it is quite useless for reconstructing the area of the historical Patrick's operations, for that evidence cannot be shown to be any earlier than the rise of his cult as a patron of places in Ireland.

All we know is that Patrick did not see himself as attached to a particular community in one place – after the manner of most bishops – but as having a divine commission to wander from place to place seeking out those who had not yet heard the gospel. He moved about 'among the nations' (*Confessio* 48), met local rulers here and there and adapted his lifestyle to local customs (*Confessio* 49–51). He only mentions one specific event: the baptism, followed soon after by this woman's entry into what would now be called the life of a nun, of an Irish noble woman who, because of her decision to become either a Christian or celibate, faced opprobrium from her family (the exact cause – being a Christian or becoming a nun – is not clear in the text). Where this event took place is, however, unknown (*Confessio* 42).

Why and where did he write?

Patrick says at the end of the *Confessio* that he wrote before he died and had earlier stated that he was bound to remain in Ireland on his mission until death; we can therefore be sure that the *Confessio* was written in Ireland. The *Epistola* is an excommunication of Christian slavers who are operating among his converts and, since this slaving business is run by Picts and Irish, we can assume that his converts were living in Ireland and therefore that this text too was written in Ireland. As such, the two works by Patrick are the earliest documents that we can be certain were written on that island.

When we come to the motives that led Patrick to write the two works we face a more complex set of questions. The *Epistola* is, at first sight, a farce. It is a letter to a bunch of violent slavers from a bishop telling them that they are bad people and should desist. The idea of someone reading this to them and the letter having any other impact than amusement is ridiculous. So why did Patrick write it? The *Epistola* is a formal declaration of judgement on the 'apostates' and in telling them of the evil of their actions he passes judgement on them, and this judgement is heard by God.

By Patrick binding those soldiers on earth, the judgement against them is bound also in heaven (Matt. 16:19; 18:18). The condemnation is heard by God – the letter's ultimate intended auditor – and is given by Patrick by being written by him as a bishop. It is duly witnessed in the Church – and the soldiers are condemned as apostates from the Church – by the presence of clergy who act as its deliverers. It is this complicated set of audiences for this act of binding and exclusion from the Church that accounts for some of the shifts in emphasis in the letter: sometimes Patrick appears to be addressing the soldiers directly, sometimes it is other Christians, and sometimes it addresses God directly.

Patrick describes the crimes which call forth this letter of judgement upon them. Sending a priest to tell them of their crimes – a priest who is then laughed at – should not be seen as an example of Patrick's political naiveté. The pattern that Patrick is following is that of the parable of the evil tenants of the vineyard in Matthew 21:33–46 and Luke 20:9–16. There, after several warnings, the lord of the vineyard sends his son. It is when the son is not respected, as the owner expects, but killed, that the moment of judgement comes for those wicked tenants. Patrick sees himself in the place of the owner of the vineyard, and the priest is like his son (hence his insistence that it was not just an ordinary priest he sent to them, but one who was dear to him and whom he had instructed since he was an infant). Now, with his messenger rejected, the moment has come for the final judgement to be delivered against these evil men. Patrick as judge announces the true spiritual identity of the wicked soldiers: by their actions they have separated themselves from light and true life. It is interesting to see how Patrick viewed his ministry: he does not use images of a representative, but of a plenipotentiary ambassador. As Patrick sees it, to encounter him is to meet with Christ the judge.

The motives that caused Patrick to write the *Confessio* are more difficult to untangle. The occasion of the *Confessio* is Patrick's need to defend himself against detractors of his person and his mission. But, if this is the occasion for writing, Patrick does far more than answer criticisms or defend his actions: he wants to offer a testimony and acknowledgement for the work of God in his life such as has inspired many other works of Christian autobiography, most famously the *Confessiones* of Augustine of Hippo.

So it is a mingling of a defence and a declaration of divine good-ness. One cannot separate the two strands, though there are places where we can see that narrating the mighty works of God is the dominant theme and other places where an apologia for his own style of episcopate is dominant. Moreover, within the criticisms to which he wants to react there are at least two distinct elements. On the one hand it is a justification of his ministry or the style of his episcopate against other Christian critics. These were presumably bishops, but who they were and where they were located is not made clear. For those who have assumed that Patrick was a sole missionary to Ireland or that he was the first bishop in Ireland, the answer is obvious: they were bishops in Britain; but if we assume – as I have – that he was not such a figure, then these bishops, who criticised him could be other bishops in Ireland or bishops in Britain or a combination of both. On the other hand, there was definitely another specific charge against him as unworthy due to a sin which he committed in his youth 'even before I was a deacon' (*Confessio* 27), which he wishes to refute. This does not appear to be the main criticism of him that provokes the *Confessio*. It is quite possible that the criticisms of Patrick that provoked the *Confessio* were general concerns about his mission and style, and that this unnamed 'sin of his youth' was merely added by his detractors as further evidence of his general unsuitability. As we might expect, much ink has flowed speculating on what that early sin might have been, but Patrick does not tell us, and such speculation has tended to reflect the writers' own perceptions of what a serious youthful sin might be. In Chapter 5 we shall return to the possible concerns of those who criticised Patrick and his missionary agenda, but we will still be faced with the fact that has appeared again and again in this chapter: Patrick is not forthcoming on the sort of details that are the stock and trade of modern historians.

CHAPTER 4

❧❧

Patrick's Perception of
Space and Time

Personal perceptions

Given that we must reconstruct Patrick from the internal evidence
of his writings, we need appropriate questions to bring to those
texts in order to elicit information from them. This chapter is such
an attempt to see how he viewed his own life and location. In the
previous chapter I have tried to gather the outline of his life as it
lies openly in his texts, for example what he tells us of his background or his time as a slave in Ireland. Now I shall attempt to see
if we can find other, more personal, aspects of how he saw his life.
Then, in the next chapter, I shall build on this information to see
what we can discover about his theological perspective.

How do I see myself in space and time? This is not the sort of
question most people pose to themselves consciously; indeed
when space and time are thought of at all it is usually as sets of
impersonal co-ordinates that form a grid relating locations and
events. Time and space as an organising grid are all around us: an
entry 'meeting, room x' against a line in a diary; 'I will see you next
week'; 'In the fourteenth year of King Hezekiah' (Isa. 36:1); 'I live
near London'; 'In those days a decree went out from Caesar
Augustus that all the world should be enrolled ... when Quirinius
was governor of Syria' (Luke 2:1–2); or the interesting 'Paris and
London are less than an hour's flight apart,' where space is

measured by time. In these examples the time and space grids are assumed to exist independently of the observers forming an objective frame against which changes can be reckoned. The extreme form of this occurs when we locate places/events against a frame that has a 'given' quality: 'Dublin is 53°20'N 6°15'W'. Such frames can now become almost absolutes in our thinking – dividing a circle into 360 units and the Greenwich meridian make them into more 'facts' to be respected. Likewise we produce clocks that are tied as closely as possible to the regularities in nature, and 'what they tell us' – presumably time – is perceived as another 'fact', rather than a mutually agreed inference.[1]

However, there is another space and time within which we exist. Individual to each of us, this personal sense of time and place, of its nature, is not public even when many in a community or society share it. This is our private sense of *where* we are *now*. This private sense of time and space is often apprehended negatively. We have a sense of *how far away* certain events or places are from us. While we think of some events as long ago and almost forgotten, other events were 'pivotal', and some happened 'at the wrong time'. We think of certain places as our own or 'familiar' (an interesting choice of word), other places as distant, strange, even alien. These personal notions of space and time are very hard to tie down – often we are barely conscious of them and we only externalise them, in ways that others can glimpse, incidentally. Today they are frequently labelled 'mental maps' but the vagueness of the term is witness to the problems inherent in ascertaining these aspects of an individual's thought.[2] This is tantalising to the historian or biographer, as any glimpse will help in understanding their subject, but this insight can only be had by assembling

1. The contrast between modern and early medieval views of time is explored in O'Loughlin 2000, pp. 166–84.
2. Cf. Gole 1993, which reproduces an anonymous map intended to portray the world of the 'Sloane Ranger' that captures the essence of 'private space': what is important equals what is significant within my world of values, contacts and prejudices. On the question of how space is a personal phenomenon before it is a public, 'objective' one, cf. the collection of essays by Smith 1978. The notion of 'mental map' has generated a vast literature, but two older works still provide the best introduction: Lynch 1960, and Gould and White 1974; while the collection of essays in Cosgrove 1999 gives several examples of how the concept has been taken over by other branches of the humanities.

numerous little pieces into a pattern, without a guarantee that the pattern is the correct sum of the parts. The best sources for these reconstructions are personal documents, where public space and time do not predominate. Letters are the most common source, but autobiographical materials – diaries and the like – are perhaps those most likely to yield detailed results. If this is so, then Patrick's writings are an obvious target for examination: the *Confessio* is explicitly autobiographical (even if we cannot be sure who is intended as the ideal reader: God, bishops in Britain, Christians in Ireland, or a combination) while the *Epistola militibus Corotici* is not only personal, but autobiographical, in that Patrick is a central actor in the events which give rise to the letter and the threats it contains.

Normally, personal senses of space and time are things very secondary to the historian – if they are mentioned at all. The ambition is to locate persons and events within a frame of space and time that is external to the actors, and as objective to the modern observer as possible. But there is a great irony here regarding Patrick: while in terms of the normal historical quest we have no certain dates or locations, the sources do contain many clues as to his personal sense of time and place. So, on the one hand, the information that is usually the easiest to obtain is here beyond reach but, on the other hand, that which eludes us in so many medieval sources is, in Patrick's case, at hand in relative abundance.

A stranger

The most obvious clue to how Patrick saw his location is that it was 'among strangers'. Repeatedly he declares that he is away from home and an alien in Ireland. This sense of being apart appears as something quite acute: he does not belong to this place or its people, and his home is not just across the sea in Britain but it is *far* away. The *Confessio* opens with a statement of where home is: Bannavem Taburniae. This is a place he knows well and identifies with, his family have deep roots there as members of the decurion/clergy class, and he expects the reader likewise to know the place, and recognise his family's social status. Taken from home he suffers the consequences of not studying his own language and of having to express himself in 'an alien tongue'. But this suffering is justified by its end: for he has been, and is, prepared 'to hear the opprobrium of being a foreigner' (Sir. 29:30) in order that he preach the gospel (Mark 13:10) to the Irish.[3]

This juxtaposition of scriptural texts, Sirach and Mark, is interesting for understanding him as a 'foreigner for the gospel'. Sirach 29:28–35 sets out the primary needs of a man for life and happiness. Basic to a happy life is living in one's own home with one's own family. Sirach asks, 'What are a man's first needs?' and replies that they are 'Water, bread, clothing, and the safety of a *home*.' Indeed, the poor man with a home is better than one living in the presence of splendour without one. The little man dwelling in his own home is far better off than the stranger wandering from house to house accepting hospitality. It is a bitter thing to be homeless and it invites one to be reviled. As long as you are *with your own people and in your home* (my emphasis is an attempt to reflect the force of Patrick's words) you do not have to hear the hatred that is heaped on the stranger. Sirach captures the sense of alienation felt by so many who have had to live as exiles or immigrants in a society which does not welcome them, and at the same time promotes the notion of home found in the rhyme: 'Be it ever so humble there's no place like home.' This whole passage from Sirach, not just the line Patrick quotes, seems to capture his sense of being a stranger where he is.

When, moreover, Sirach is read in combination with the statements of Christ on preaching from Mark, Patrick's self-portrait seems complete. In Mark, the preacher of the gospel has to abandon home, brothers, sisters, mother, fathers, children, and his own fields (Mark 10:29); he suffers insults and is dragged before his own religious leaders in the synagogues and before foreign[4] kings and rulers (*praesides*) where he has to bear witness to Christ (Mark 13:9–10). So for Patrick to be a preacher is to be cut off

3. Patrick says that he came 'to preach the gospels to the Irish peoples' (*ad Hibernas gentes euangelium praedicare*) (*Confessio* 37) while Mark 13:10 reads that 'the gospel must be preached to all the nations' (*in omnes gentes primum oportet praedicari euangelium*). The change from the passive to the active voice may be significant given, as we shall see, Patrick's overall sense of fulfilling what is commanded about preaching in the gospels: Jesus spoke about what has to have taken place before the eschaton; Patrick is setting out to help in accomplishing this result.

4. This is implied in that the preacher is also brought before the rulers of the synagogues.

from home and family, to have the lot of the suspect stranger, and to suffer the extremes of homesickness, for he has no home in Ireland. In *Confessio* 37, Patrick's presentation of his experience seems to fit with this reading of the scriptures down to the last detail: grace (here presented as equivalent to the divine will), not himself, sent him to Ireland to preach, so he lives among strangers, endures insults from aliens (unbelievers), is taunted as a foreigner, treated as a prisoner, has heard hatred uttered against him, and endures many persecutions.

But this theme of suffering as a stranger is a recurring one. He repeatedly notes that he has left his parents,[5] those he would like to have as friends, and his homeland (*patria*) for the sake of the gospel.[6] Indeed, he has given up his own estate (*uillula*) for his mission, which echoes those in Mark 10 who have given up their own fields (*agri*) for the gospel. He has been held in contempt, has had to forage for food and been despised[7]: these are the dangers Sirach sees facing the foreigner. He has been betrayed by those close to him, has had plots hatched against him, has been brought before his own religious leaders and rejected, and brought before foreign kings and judges[8]; all these problems are consistent with what is foretold in Mark 13 for the preacher. And having been taken, in his youth, as a captive to an alien land, he again takes up that slavery – and with it exile – in response to a divine call.[9] The gospel's task alone, he tell us, explains his spending his life far from home and family, for as a young man he was told to go home from there and later told to go back to preach (i.e. leave home once more). Implicit in these directions is that Ireland is an alien place and that Patrick dwells there among 'the nations'.[10] In the *Epistola* this being without his home is presented as a basic quality of ministry founded directly on the teaching and experience of Christ: 'A prophet has no honour in his own land' (John 4:44).[11] While he quotes John, he has in mind an image of this text that is based on all the uses of this theme in the gospels (cf. Matt. 13:57;

5. See *Confessio* 23, 43 and *Epistola* 1.
6. See *Confessio* 43 and *Epistola* 1.
7. See *Confessio* 1, 22 and *Epistola* 1.
8. See *Confessio* 26–7, 29, 32, 35, 52–3.
9. See *Confessio* 37, 43 and 61 and *Epistola* 10.
10. *Confessio* 48.
11. *Epistola* 11.

Mark 6:4; Luke 4:24) for Patrick reads the phrase in its Synoptic context of rejection from homeland and family, and with it the duty to live as a stranger. This passage in the *Epistola*, when read against the related passages in the *Confessio*, shows Patrick as viewing his sense of alienation from home as part of the configuration of his own mind to the mind of Christ: being a stranger is part of the ministry imposed upon him.

We do not know how Patrick imagined the physical world, but we sense that he thought of Ireland and Britain as far apart. Certainly, the actual place of his captivity as a youth is very far from his home: it is a long journey from the Western Sea to where one can sail home, and then there is the barrier of the sea. But if he thinks of these islands as far apart, Britain and Gaul seem very close. A journey to Britain is a major step and one he is unwilling to take once he has returned to Ireland, despite its personal benefits. But if he were to go to Britain, then a stay in Gaul with those he desires to see would be one of the added benefits which could be had without difficulty.

Distances for an individual's travel are as much a matter of imagination as geography: being in Ireland is dwelling far out from the centre and where all the people who matter personally to him live, and returning there again at the time when he is writing involves what we could call 'excessive travel costs'. It seems that from Ireland to anywhere in the Roman world is a major journey over obstacles and frontiers; but any journey within the Empire is just popping into the neighbours. Britain and Gaul are imaged as very close together; Britain and Ireland as very far apart.

An old man

My question here is how did Patrick *view* the Irish episodes within the events of his life. That the two periods in Ireland, first as a slave to a man, then as a slave to the gospel, form the pillars structuring his life's story as presented in the *Confessio*, there is no doubt. However, how they relate to one another within his personal sense of time is another matter.

The first period begins in youth, about sixteen, and is presented as having all the folly of youth in attendance.[12] Patrick gives us a

12. See *Confessio* 1, 2, 9, 10 and 12.

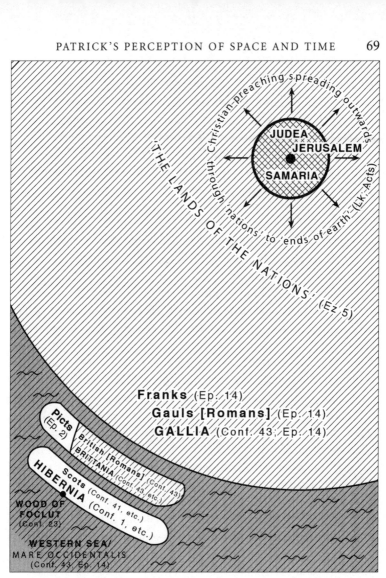

The insular world as a late Roman Christian might have imagined it

little information about the length of this first Irish episode: 'Shortly after that I took to flight, left the man with whom I had been for six years, and journeyed ...' However, we should note that when we take this as referring to the whole period of his time as a captive,[13] it assumes that he had only one master. But it is most

13. E.g. Salway 1981, p. 462.

probably the whole length of his stay, for this would accord with the way he introduces the Victoricus visitation: 'Again after few years I was in Britain with my parents.'[14] He presents it as a period of learning and growing to know 'the true God', so that when he travelled home he was one who prayed and was aware of the workings of the Spirit within him.[15] He saw the early years as being a time of probation and initiation: that he could then leave Ireland is equivalent to a graduation.

Matters become more complicated when it comes to his second trip to Ireland. The sequence of events as noted in the *Confessio* presents his call to go back to Ireland as taking place very soon after his return from slavery, and we imagine that this trip to Ireland was not too long after that again. However, he assumes that we know that there was a very long period – at least several decades – between the two Irish episodes. The evidence can be set out like this. The *Confessio* appears to be written in what he considered to be his old age, though we cannot quantify what he considered 'old age' to mean. In *Confessio* 10 he contrasts the time of his writing with that of his youth and describes it as 'in my old age', and this coheres with his statement at the end of the work that he writes his declaration before he dies. But this second Irish episode is presented as having begun much later.[16] Similarly, in an earlier place he noted it was 'after many years had gone by' that his mission began.[17] And this sense of many years fits with what he says about the sin confessed before he became a deacon, and thirty years before any accusation was made against him.[18] Granted he was sixteen when taken captive, and spent (at least) six years in Ireland, then the earliest he could have been ordained deacon is twenty-two.[19] So the earliest

14. *Confessio* 23.
15. *Confessio* 1 and 44 provide examples.
16. *Confessio* 28.
17. *Confessio* 5; his statement that 'after many years he was taken captive again' (*Confessio* 21) does not help us for all this tells us that there was a long period between his youth and this event.
18. *Confessio* 27; that there was a lengthy span of time between his two periods in Ireland is corroborated by the fact that there was a major development in Patrick's understanding of his being taken captive aged sixteen: the young Patrick saw it as a punishment and recalls that understanding, but Patrick at the time he wrote the *Confessio* appears to see the matter as an essential preparation located within God's providence.
19. It is tempting to try to be more precise by examining the 'canonical ages' for

age at which an accusation could be made is fifty-two, and he wrote some time after that. In fact, we could add some years on to this, and imagine that when he set out for Ireland as a missionary he may have been in his forties or fifties.

However we might construe his incidental remarks, one point seems clear: his life has two significant periods, one in youth, the other in mature age, both in Ireland.[20] From his perspective at the time of writing the *Confessio*, the rest of his life, even though it seems to be longer in quantity of time, is less real, no more than duration separating the times in Ireland. His real life is in these two periods. It appears as if he saw himself as a part of the structure of a greater history (the history in which the Word is made known)[21] while he is serving (either a human master in the time of probation, or a divine master during his mission) in Ireland. Hence these periods stand out in his own perception of his personal history. And events before Ireland, or between Irish visits are only incidental; they are not important, even if others in criticism of him might think so.

While Patrick's omission of details about his time outside Ireland might frustrate the historian – or even a hagiographer like Muirchú – it does reveal part of his humanity. For when we recall our own past, without deliberately attempting to recall events in the manner of a historian, as when, for example, we are compiling a c.v., we notice that some periods and events stand out from the rest of life as its times of significance. The rest of the time can appear as if the person is standing still with time passing behind them as a backdrop. This selection of the important periods of one's life is personal time at its most real.

ordination to the diaconate. However, this is useless for two reasons: first, and most importantly, since he claims that the sin took place before he was made deacon it had to have been between when he returned from Ireland (at twenty-two) and whatever age he was made deacon, so all we can say is that he was at least fifty-two when the accusation was made; second, appeals to such documents as the letter of 385 ('*Directa ad decessorem*') of Pope Siricius to Himerius of Tarragona (P.L. 67, 236–7) which mention the ages for promotion to the various orders assume that there was a variety of practice in this matter.

20. See Dumville 1993, pp. 25–8.
21. This becomes clearer when we look at how he saw a connection between the preaching of the gospel and the eschaton.

In the uttermost parts

One of the phrases that recurs in Patrick is that he is in 'the utter-most part of the earth' or similar expressions.[22] These phrases, which for Patrick locate the position of Ireland, are taken from the New Testament. In Luke 11:31 (= Matt. 12:42) Christ tells of the 'Queen of the South' who came from the ends of the earth (*a finibus terrae*) to hear Solomon's wisdom. In Acts 1:8 and 13:47, both of which are in Patrick's mind at the opening of the *Confessio*,[23] 'the ends of the earth' are linked to the preaching of the gospel: the Spirit will make the apostles witnesses to Christ in Jerusalem, the surrounding areas, and right out to the end of the Earth (Acts 1:8: *usque ad ultimum terrae*), and thus the apostles are set up as light for the salvation of the nations out to the very end of earth (Acts 13:47: *usque ad extremum terrae*). Moreover, the notion that the gospel is heard at the ends of the earth (*in fines orbis terrae*) is also found, but with a different focus, in Romans 10:18, which quotes Psalm 18:4: 'Their voice [the heavens' pro-clamation] goes out through all the earth, and their words to the ends of the world.' So Scripture provides a framework to locate where Patrick finds himself located by the will of God. He has been sent to the last place among all the lands, to the furthest out nation, first by a divine judgement and latterly by a divine commission.

22. *Confessio* 1, 34, 38; *Epistola* 9.
23. The text of *Confessio* 1 reads:
    ... *et Dominus 'induxit super' nos 'iram'* [Isa. 42:25] *'animationis suae et dis-persit nos in gentibus'* [the concept of dispersal among the nations as a divine punishment for infidelity is found in many places in the Old Testament, but especially in the prophets where it is presented as a just reward of the people: Lev. 26:33 and 38; Deut. 4:27; Ps. 106:27; 1 Chr. 16:35; Jer. 9:16; Lam. 1:3 and 2:9; Hos. 9:17; Zech. 10:9; Ezek. 4:13; 5:14; 6:8; 11:16; 12:15–16; 20:23; 22:15; 25:10; 29:12; 30:23, 26; 32:9; 36:19; 39:28; and it is found in Joel 2:19 and 3:2 – a prophet is echoed in the next section – and in Tob. 13:4–7, which seems to be reflected in several ways by Patrick in this section] *mul-tis etiam 'usque ad ultimum terrae'* [this final phrase is taken from Acts 1:8: *sed accipietis uirtutem superuenientis Spiritus Sancti in uos et eritis mihi testes in Hierusalem et in omni Iudaea et Samaria et usque ad ultimum terrae*; how-ever, it follows on *gentibus* and so picks up the memory of Acts 13:47: *sic enim praecepit nobis Dominus posui te in lumen gentium ut sis in salutem usque ad extremum terrae*].

In Luke/Acts we have the story of the early preaching which presents the message of Jesus spreading through Jerusalem (preaching to Jews); next, through the apostles, to the surrounding areas (also Jews); and then, through the journeys of Paul, reaching 'the nations' (Gentiles) within the Roman Empire. Luke makes clear that this is a three-stage process.[24] This can be represented as a message spreading through three concentric circles. But as Patrick sees it, the limit of the preaching up to his time was the boundary of the empire in the west, but there were a few places even beyond that. Now he has gone out there to the very end, to the nations that are beyond the reach of everyone until then. He is with the nations that are in the furthest west to carry out this commission to teach the nations.[25] Indeed, he has gone beyond where people live, right out to the shore of the Western Sea.[26]

The probability is that Patrick thought the world to be something like this.[27] Towards the centre of the great land-mass of the earth was the city of Jerusalem, and around it the Promised Land. Around this were ranged the nations (cf. Ezek. 5:5), and their lands stretched out to the Ocean. Most of this land-mass was held by the Romans, but out on the fringe was at least one place outside both the orbit of Rome and Jerusalem: Ireland. It was in the land of the west, and its location destined it to be the outer limit of preaching, and thus one extreme of the *catholica* – the whole community of Christians – for from there to the furthest east, people were summoned to the Lord's banquet.[28] That Patrick is

24. Luke 24:47 and Acts 1:8; and note that the same theme can be found in Acts 2:14–32.

25. See *Confessio* 39–40 and *Epistola* 1; and cf. Matt. 28:19, which is quoted in the *Confessio* and alluded to in the *Epistola*.

26. See *Confessio* 23 and 51.

27. This is explicitly how Isidore of Seville (d. 630) viewed the world. However, while Isidore is very different to Patrick -- not just in time, but as a bookworm who loved to create synthetic overviews of topics -- he drew on the same biblical notions for his basic vision, and on the same general Christian ideas about the action of the body of Christ in the world that Patrick is drawing upon. On the background to Isidore on this question, cf. O'Loughlin 1996 and 1997.

28. The notion that the eschatological Eucharist, the perfect offering, will involve people from the extremes of the earth, from the east to the west, and that this will constitute the whole of the Church is common among the Fathers: the following texts are central to the image: Ps. 106:3; Isa. 49:12;

thinking in this structural way about his location is confirmed by the way his memory silently conflates Matthew 8:11 with Luke 13:28–9 so as to mention the earth's four 'corners'[29]: 'I tell you, many will come from east and west, and south and north, and sit at table with Abraham, Isaac, and Jacob in the kingdom of heaven.'[30] And the particular people being called, through him, to the banquet is 'from the extremity of earth'.[31] Patrick is someone operating out on the final frontier. An attempt to portray graphically how Patrick imagined his location can be found opposite.

Through his work the message of the Gospel, which originated at the centre and had been carried to the nearby nations by the first apostles as recorded in Acts, was brought out to the very last piece of land (*ad ultimum terrae*).

On the edge of the eschaton

If Patrick imagines his location as being on the edge, the borders, the last place, of the lands, he has a similar view of his place in history: he belongs to the last times, and the End is imminent. Indeed, the End will not be delayed very long after the completion of his own work in Ireland. He develops this theme in the central section of the *Confessio* by seeing a direct relationship between the preaching of the gospel and the close of human history.

The theme is announced by Patrick thanking God for the task he has been given in 'the last days' (*in nouissimis diebus*). The basis for his belief that he lives in the final times is that God has promised that he would 'announce his gospel before all nations before the world's end'. Now, Patrick is the instrument of this proclamation and, with his fellow Irish Christians, he bears witness to it at the very limits of the inhabited world (*ubi nemo ultra est*).[32] So we presume that since everywhere has now heard the Gospel, there is

---

59:19; Mal. 1:11; and Matt. 8:11; and note that it is developed in the Eucharistic Prayer texts in the *Didache* 9 and 10.

29. The notion of the Earth having four corners is found in Isa. 11:12; 41:9; Rev. 7:1; 20:8.
30. *Confessio* 39 and compare *Epistola* 18.
31. *Confessio* 38; he presents this as the fulfilment of a prophecy in Jer. 16:19; and then returns to the Lukan theme of the gospel spreading from Jerusalem by quoting Acts 13:47.
32. *Confessio* 34.

THE EAST
(Matt. 8:11; C39)

THE NORTH	Jerusalem	THE SOUTH
(Matt. 8:11; C39)	(Acts 1:8; C1)	(Matt. 8:11; C39)

Israel   :   Judea and Samaria
(Matt. 10:23)   (Acts 1:8)

The lands of the 'Holy Romans' (E2; 14)
where the first apostles preached

Gaul (C43)
Britain (C43)

Ireland
final nation (Acts 1:8; 13:47; Matt. 24:14; C1; 34; 38; 40)
last inhabited place (C34; 51)
more than 200 miles in extent which he
thinks of as a great distance (C51)
where Patrick preaches (Matt. 28:19; C40)

The Western Sea
[The Ocean] (C23)

THE WEST
(Matt. 8:11; C39)

This diagram of Patrick's mental map has been built up from
the references he makes to places, which he takes for granted
as the common co-ordinates known to all his readers.

nothing to delay the end, so it is now close at hand! This reason-
ing becomes clearer when he restates his position a little further
on.

Having announced repeatedly that he has preached the gospel
at the ends of the Earth, and how thus a prophecy is fulfilled,

Patrick turns to the basis of all his work: Christ's command to preach.[33] He strings together three roughly parallel[34] texts: first, Matthew 28:19–20 ('Go therefore and make disciples of all nations, baptising them in the name of the Father and of the Son and of the Holy Spirit, teaching them to observe all that I have commanded you; and behold, I am with you all days until the consummation'), second, Mark 16:15–16 ('Go, therefore, into all the world and preach the gospel to every creature; whoever believes and is baptised will be saved; but whoever does not believe will be condemned'), and finally Matthew 24:14 ('This gospel of the kingdom will be preached throughout the whole world, as a testimony to all nations; and then will come the end'). As Patrick read these verses they conveyed a single structure: preaching followed by completion, preaching followed by judgement, preaching followed by the End.[35] As he reads these verses, the second event – the final judgement that marks the end of the age – is the direct consequence of the completion of the task of preaching. Put simply, once everyone has heard the gospel then there will be no further reason to delay the End. Patrick sees this as a plan in the divine mind for the period between the Ascension and the return of Christ in the Last Times.[36] Moreover, this vast plan for the history of the world is something that addresses and

---

33. *Confessio* 37–40.
34. Most synopses (e.g. Huck-Greeven 1981, or Throckmorton 1949) do not present any of these verses in parallel, as they are not verbally alike; however, this should not obscure the fact that they do share a common structure and context within the synoptic tradition. Matt. 24:14 and 28:19–20 can be seen as a couplet: the command to preach is announced, and then repeated at the decisive moment at the end of the gospel. Mark 16:15–16 belongs to the longer ending that was added to Mark and which is based on Matthew: in this case the context is supplied by Matt. 28:19–20 but the language echoes Matt. 24:14. The command to preach in Luke (24:47 to which we have already referred) is linguistically distinct from Matthew, but falls in the same position within his text as Matt. 28:19–20 in its text. We can therefore conclude that a command to preach (in some form) was part of the double tradition and was handled differently according to each writer's theological perspective (eschatological in the case of Matthew; the message spreading to the ends of the earth in the case of Luke); and, Mark is derived from the Matthaean form. While Patrick sees the links between these verses through a very different optic, the actual combination is a sound one.
35. See Charles-Edwards 2000, pp. 215–6.
36. *Confessio* 35.

involves him in a particular way. He is the one who is preaching in the very last place on Earth to the very last nation to hear the message. As such, Patrick sees himself as the final preacher in a chain going back to the apostles. He has had a unique task given to him, for when he has finished his work in Ireland, then the preaching phase of history is finished. With history complete, the universe enters the next stage in God's plan: the End. And in the very next sentence (*Confessio* 41) Patrick announces the state of history: the gospel has reached Ireland, the outermost place, and those who had only known idols are now 'the prepared people' (Luke 1:17) of the Lord and the children of God.[37] Although Patrick never quotes the verse, he seems to have Matthew 10:23 ('When they persecute you in one town, flee to the next; for truly, I say to you, you will not have gone through all the towns of Israel, before the Son of man comes'), or something like it, in mind in formulating his theory. There is a fixed quantum of time before the End, this is determined by the need to preach everywhere, and it is not as great as the length of time needed to get around all the towns of Israel. In any case, there is no need for more time as the given task is completed.

When we reflect on Patrick's humility[38] we should remember that he presents himself as having a singular place in bringing about the consummation of creation. And, with this knowledge we are in a better position to understand the urgency he must have felt when he referred to living in 'the last days'.[39] This may also throw light on his expansion of the credal statement, 'who is to come again' (*et iterum uenturus est*), to the more pointed: 'and whose coming we look for soon' (*expectamus aduentum ipsius mox futurum*).[40]

Conclusion

Constructing mental maps from literary remains is a process of interpretation that yields results with a low index of certainty.

---

37. *Confessio* 41; here I follow White's edition (*quomodo nuper perfecta est plebs Domini et filii Dei nuncupantur*); while this appears to be the *lectio difficilior*, by echoing Luke it makes the purpose of the whole sentence clear.
38. *Confessio* 1 and 55 for example.
39. *Confessio* 34 and *Epistola* 10.
40. *Confessio* 4.

This fact alone raises questions as to the utility of the endeavour. Yet such pictures of one's place in space and time are part of our human consciousness; hence, at the very least, asking these questions – whether they can be answered to any appreciable extent – is justified. In Patrick's case we can be certain of this much: he saw himself as a stranger in Ireland working on the fringes of human space and time. His work of evangelisation belongs to the final, and most difficult, phase of a process that began with the sending out of the apostles by Christ to the whole world (Matthew), starting with Jerusalem and reaching out to every nation to the very ends of the Earth (Luke/Acts). He, Patrick, has carried out successfully his part in this work, so his finishing his work coincides with the completion of the whole apostolic task. The completion of this task ushers in the completion, the judgement, the coming of the Son of Man in glory. So the return of the Christ at the End, foretold in the scriptures and confessed in the creed, cannot be far, in external time, in the future.

❧.❧

CHAPTER 5

Patrick's View of his Ministry

Patrick and his critics

In Chapter 3 we noted that Patrick saw his *Confessio*, at least in part, as an answer to Christian critics of his ministry, his episcopal style, and his worthiness for office. In the last chapter we tried to tease out from his two writings how Patrick perceived his location in time and space, noting that he believed himself to be a man on the margins: he was in the outermost parts and he was close to the end of time. The return of Christ was not going to be long in the future and Patrick had a special role as one of the final evangelists whose work heralded the beginnings of the End times. Although he never quotes the passage, this verse seems to lie just beneath his perception of his own work: 'When they persecute you in one town, flee to the next; for truly, I say to you, you will not have gone through all the towns of Israel, before the Son of man comes' (Matt. 10:23). Patrick will get to the last of the towns – or if not 'towns', the places where people dwell – out on the edges of the Western Sea, and then it cannot be long before the Son of Man returns. Patrick saw himself as the final missionary.

So, what of these criticisms to which he alludes, but without giving their nature, in the *Confessio*? It is the purpose of this chapter to argue that Patrick had taken the notion of the imminence of the End so totally into his personal agenda as a missionary that he was reprimanded for this by his fellow bishops – probably in both Ireland and Britain – as standing outside the normal preaching of the Church in regard to the closeness of the Second Coming. However, before looking in detail at the texts that support this view, we should remember that the image of Patrick as anything other than a model bishop-missionary is one with a long pedigree. When Muirchú wrote his *Vita Patricii* he carefully presented Patrick not only as Ireland's first active and successful bishop (he presented Palladius as a failure), but also as one who was similar to Moses, Samuel, John the Baptist, and all the apostles. There was no hint in the *Vita* that Patrick had been criticised in his own time, nor indeed that there was anything in his life, work, preaching or liturgy that was at variance with the expectations of a bishop as that task was understood in the late seventh century. His education was with a noted saint in Gaul who had opposed heresy, and his work in Ireland was formally authorised and recognised by the clergy of the whole Church, including the Bishop of Rome. Indeed, at about the same time that Muirchú wrote, the beginnings were being made in Ireland – by clerics with whom we know Muirchú was in contact – of what would be the West's earliest systematic collection of canon law, the *Collectio canonum hibernensis*.[1] The first book of that collection is devoted to the nature, ministry and lifestyle of bishops, and it is fair to say that the portrait of Patrick's work and teaching in the *Vita*, and that emerging from the *Collectio* are almost identical. As Patrick was taken by successive generations of clergy as the patron and apostle of Ireland, there was never a doubt that not only was he holy, but that he was orthodox in every respect. Even after the Reformation, when there were competing orthodoxies seeking to have the warrant of antiquity for their vision of the Christian Church, each side found the exact churchmanship in his works that they needed. For Roman Catholics, there was Patrick's saying 'if you be Christians, then you are Romans', which stressed the link in their eyes with the See of Peter; for Anglicans he arrived in Ireland without a papal mandate and so was an adherent of the theory of 'diffused authority': but in neither group was there any suggestion that he was theologically at odds with the bishops of

---

1. For an introduction to this collection of law, see O'Loughlin 2000, pp. 109–27.

his time. More recent writers on Patrick have usually stressed his simplicity and the personal transparency of his writings, with the implication that 'abstract' theological questions were not part of that intrepid missionary's concerns.

But these approaches to Patrick's theological stance still leave the question as to why his contemporaries were critical of him. The most common reply is that this was some sort of clerical envy of Patrick's courage in doing something new – in going beyond the Empire's frontiers – or a vendetta pursued over some sin in Patrick's early life to which he alludes in *Confessio* 27. Other writers, often Irish, have seen these criticisms as little more than 'British' carping at anything that is successfully happening in Ireland. However, these criticisms were significant enough for Patrick to believe he had to defend his work in the face of them, and so we cannot simply ignore them. And, we must bear two points in mind as we puzzle over them: first, that it is just as likely that Patrick's critics were in Ireland – hence his justification for his staying there rather than returning to Britain with its personal attractions for him (see *Confessio* 43) – as in Britain; and, second, those critics, presumably church leaders (i.e. bishops), knew far more about Patrick and his work than we do. So, unless we *assume* that this was a carping jealously, we should take those contemporaries' worries seriously and seek in Patrick's writings hints as to what those complaints were. After all there is no shortage of cases from other places in the West at the time where a group of bishops called one of their fellows to account for what they saw as erroneous preaching.

This would be a simple task if Patrick had said something like: 'you have accused me of X, and this is my reply', but he does not. Our question has, therefore, to take this form: are there any places in the *Confessio* where Patrick appears to be pleading his cause or any hints where he makes his point in a way that is distinctive of normal Christian preaching at the time? If so, then these may be the very points on which he was been criticised.

An operative theology

However, is it fair to ask Patrick to justify his 'theology'? Going back to the nineteenth century and the work of Ernest Renan there has been a common assumption that insular, or 'Celtic', writers – including Patrick, though he would not have thanked us for denying his Roman identity – had little time for theology, being far more 'caught up' in the reality of the life of the Spirit.[2] This view is simply Romanticism using the past as a screen for modern concerns: there is no shortage of theological writing of one sort or another from the region and period.[3] So it is best to unpack the notion of 'theologian' and of 'theology' as it applies to a person like Patrick.

Our notion of a theologian is that of a professional academic speculating on the structures of Christian belief and practice and functioning as a teacher or writer, and whose ministry is, in most cases, visibly different to that of bishops as leaders or local clergy as pastors. No such academic cadre existed prior to the ninth century and the common image of the theologian emerged even later. In the early Church what we have is a body of teachers (some of whom wrote and some of whose writings have been preserved), almost all of whom were bishops (non-bishops are the exceptions). So the very fact that Patrick was a bishop puts him into the company of a body of preachers and teachers who were expected to know the Christian faith, to have studied its scriptures, to have reflected on its implications, and to have been willing and able to communicate that in homilies, sermons, instructions to catechumens (i.e. those preparing for baptism), and possibly in letters (the equivalent of our pamphlets) or books. Clearly, when we look at a 'theologian' in this sense – bishops like Ambrose (c. 339–397) and Augustine (454–430) would be the most famous examples, while men like Germanus of Auxerre (c. 378–448), Eucherius of Lyons (d. c. 449) or Caesarius of Arles (c. 470–542) would be closer in time, culture and stature to Patrick) – Patrick fits neatly in the frame. We know that he claimed a deep knowledge of the Christian faith, parts of which came to him by revelations. He had studied the scriptures in depth, for he can quote widely from them to support his position; he tells us of his preaching and of his instruction of catechumens and he quotes the creed he would have used; he had thought about how to communicate with his audiences; and he even shows an ability to write letters in support of his mission. Thus, in the

2. See Sims-Williams 1998.
3. See O'Loughlin 2000.

sense that we are happy to use the term 'theologian' of St Augustine or St Caesarius, then we can use it of Patrick, allowing that from Patrick we have far less surviving evidence (just the *Confessio* and the *Epistola*) upon which to assess his teaching.

Similarly, we think of 'theology' as an abstract body of ideas, the name of an academic discipline, or a category for a certain kind of book in a religious bookshop; and in these terms Patrick did not produce a theology. However, 'theology' has a second meaning: the covering term for the particular understanding by individuals or groups of what constitute the essential structures of Christian faith. In this sense we can speak of 'South American theology' or 'liberation theology' today, or of 'Roman Catholic theology' or 'Lutheran theology' now or in the past. It is clear that prior to Patrick's time there was 'Augustine's theology' and that there was a reaction to that view of the Christian message, which is linked to southern Gaul and has been given the derogatory label 'Semi-Pelagian theology'. In this sense it is possible to assert that there was 'Patrick's theology' – and he was aware that he was doing new things due to his new understanding – but whether or not we can recover this from the two works is a distinct question.

We should also distinguish between 'published theology' and 'operative theology'. By 'published' I do not mean books, but any publicly announced theology: in creeds, sermons, lectures, and perhaps books. This is what an individual or group says they believe about God and the mission of the Church. Then there is the way that groups or individuals actually work to promote their vision of the Christian faith or the Church's work and this may be based on a very different notion of God and faith. A classic case of this dissonance would be to preach a God rich in mercy and forgiveness as opposed to a divine punitive lawgiver, yet to work within society to establish a set of penalties for departures of the law that imply a belief that the universe works in a different way to the way one claims in one's preaching. So, for example, many Christians today reject the notion of a punitive legislator as a fit image for the divine – that is not the sort of creator they preach, yet they may equally believe that the death penalty is necessary and would act to retain or introduce it; here there is a clash between a published theology (the claims they make about the sort of universe God created) and an operative theology (how they actually act and what they also claim is necessary in the universe). Likewise, the Catholic Church embraced in its published liturgy in 1970 a view of the Eucharist as 'the prayer of thanksgiving' which recalled the Last Supper in the 'institution narrative' (a change in terminology for those sentences which were formerly called the 'words of consecration'), and clearly distanced itself from the notion that the quotations from Jesus were the sacred words for effecting the action of consecrating bread and wine so that there would be Holy Communion for those who were fit to receive it. However, most Catholic priests have continued to speak these words in the old style – slowly uttering the sacred formula while gazing at the objects in their hands – so their operative theology still relates to the rite of 1570 not 1970. Such dissonance between published and operative theologies is inevitable: human beings are not perfectly consistent creatures and, we must all still take deeper into our lives the lesson of Matthew 5:23–4: 'So if you are offering your gift at the altar, and there remember that your brother has something against you, leave your gift there before the altar and go; first be reconciled to your brother, and then come and offer your gift.' It means that someone may not recognise that what they are doing may be at odds with the Christian message, and that an individual or group may be criticised by other Christians as having missed the point without their recognition that the criticisms are valid. This is a distinction that can help us understand why Patrick may not have recognised what it was in his work and preaching that was causing such fluster to his fellow Christians.

The End is close at hand

There are a few details in what Patrick writes which would have caused an average bishop in the fifth century to pick his ears up and ask for more clarification on what Patrick meant. Let us begin by listing these in the order they appear in his writings. In the *Epistola* he notes how he has been 'set up as a bishop by God', that he is a wanderer and he is charged to teach even though he is held in contempt (*Epistola* 1). This would suggest that other Christians were asking by what authority he was living as he was, wandering about, and were questioning his right to teach. This theme is picked up again when Patrick points out that he is not going beyond his authority for God appointed him to teach at the very ends of the

Earth (*Epistola* 6). This theme of being on the edges surfaces again when he presents himself as one of those 'hunters and fishers' who it was announced 'would come in the last days' (*Epistola* 11).

There is also a curious phrase near the beginning of the *Epistola* when Patrick says: 'I gave birth to many in God and I have "strengthened" them in Christ as well' (*Epistola* 2). This could be an unproblematic phrase meaning that he baptised many people ('gave birth to them in God'), and then that he stayed with those people and built up their relationship with Christ as Christians ('I strengthened them in Christ') through encouragement, admonition, and example. Or, it could be that the two phrases 'I gave birth' and 'I strengthened' form a rhetorical doublet emphasising one act: that Patrick has established a paternal relationship with those new Christians through baptising them. One possibility that can be excluded is that this refers to the rite now known as 'confirmation' – that word only came into use much later, and the post-baptismal anointing would not be separate in this case where it was a bishop who was baptising, and would be linked in thought by Patrick with the Holy Spirit not Christ. In view of what we shall look at in the *Confessio*, another possibility appears: Patrick not only baptised as the final missionary, thus establishing the Church in the outermost places as part of the final preaching of the Gospel, but he also performed another rite which he believed prepared people for 'the day [of the Lord] drawing near'.[4] The 'Day of the Lord', the 'Day of Jesus Christ', the 'Day of Judgement' was the name given by many in the early Church for the time when this world would cease, Christ return, deliver the saints and cast the wicked to their doom.[5] Patrick may have believed that now that the End was upon them, Christians needed some special final preparation which would enable them to endure – that is to be found worthy by Christ the judge – in the day of trial. If that were the case, then who had authorised him to preach in this way and to set off to work in those places would become urgent questions for his fellow bishops. He would have been considered to have 'gone off message' and to be operating outside communion with

4. Heb. 10:25.
5. The theme is found in many places in the New Testament and with 'the day' named in many ways; here are some examples: Acts 2:20; Rom. 2:5; 1 Cor. 1:8; 2 Cor. 1:14; Eph. 4:30; Phil. 1:6; 2 Thess. 2:2; Heb. 10:25; 1 Pet. 2:12; 2 Pet. 2:9; 1 John 4:17.

them, and no doubt in the ears of Patrick's critics these lines from
Paul would be ringing:

> As to the coming of our Lord Jesus Christ and our being
> gathered together to him, we beg you, brothers and sisters,
> not to be quickly shaken in mind or alarmed, either by spirit
> or by word or by letter, as though from us, to the effect that
> the day of the Lord is already here. Let no one deceive you in
> any way. (2 Thess. 2:1–3)

Someone preaching imminent doom is to be viewed as a deceiver,
disturbing the lives of Christians, pretending to have a secret
knowledge from God not given to the rest of the Church. That
Patrick was convinced that the End was nigh seems clear from
what we have seen in the last chapter, and that he believed he had
a special commission to prepare Christians for that 'day' becomes
clear as we turn to the *Confessio*.

The *Confessio* was written with one audience clearly in mind:
those of Patrick's contemporaries who were criticising him and
his work in Ireland. Posterity was not intended as its audience and
it appears to us to jump around without justification. Sometimes
we can suppose that his critics were in Britain when he says that
he replies from where he now lives (Ireland) to those critics
among whom he lived as a youth[6]; at other times he seems to
explain himself to those who are very close to where he now
works.[7] Moreover, he does not appear to be answering a single
charge but three different accusations of his impropriety as a bishop.
In order to make this situation more consistent we might suggest
that unworthiness to be a bishop is the basic charge laid against
him, and the three criticisms are simply three distinct blocks of
evidence. But it could equally be the case that there were various
criticisms levelled against him over the years by various groups,
and the *Confessio* is a general defence against all of them. He says
in *Confessio* 32 that there was an enquiry at which a 'friend' (who
revealed the sin he committed as a fifteen-year-old[8]) spoke in his
favour, and we are to understand that this enquiry was held some
time before the present, yet he was writing in the present to reply

6. *Confessio* 48.
7. *Confessio* 49–51.
8. *Confessio* 26–27.

to current attacks upon him. Let us begin by noting that there was a time when this son of Calpornius the deacon and decurion, and grandson of Potitus the priest, was a fully accepted brother bishop in Britain.[9]

There appear to be three different grounds for complaint. The one most clearly mentioned is the sin committed when he was about fifteen and which, when he was about forty-five years old, was published by a close friend to whom he had mentioned it in confidence. What that sin was we shall never know, but Patrick does not consider it to have been too serious for he is sure that God has forgiven him, and indeed his friend had agreed that it was not something too significant. We should bear in mind that in the fourth and fifth centuries the Latin church went through a pastoral crisis with regard to sins committed after baptism and that for the more serious sins the only solution was a long and arduous public penance.[10] For Patrick and his friend this sin was not in that category, and it appears that while it was the friend who told others about the misdemeanour, he also spoke for Patrick at the enquiry held about the matter. Moreover, this past 'sin' would not explain the other accusations Patrick appears to want to counter in the *Confessio*.

There are several references in the *Confessio* to money and to how Patrick's ministry in Ireland was financed. He first says that he refused gifts from those to whom he preached and whom he baptised (*Confessio* 37). He repeats this later by saying that when his converts gave him gifts and ornaments he always returned them (*Confessio* 49), that he never charged someone for ordaining them and that he did not get even the cost of his shoe leather (*Confessio* 50). This amounts to a very clear rebuttal of any charge that he was engaged in his ministry for financial gain or that he was engaged in simony (selling sacraments or claims to Christian holy 'power' for money). But Patrick does not tell us how his ministry was financed; if it had been supported by existing churches in Ireland or Britain this could have been known to his accusers or Patrick could simply have pointed it out. Yet, it is clear that Patrick was spending money: he admits that he gave presents to 'kings' and that he paid their sons to form a retinue for him

9. *Confessio* 32.
10. See O'Loughlin 2000a.

(*Confessio* 52). This would make perfect sense for anyone, especially a stranger, who wanted to work in non-Christian Irish society, where gifts between local rulers were part of the structure of society and anyone who travelled without a retinue would have simply been ignored as being of no importance. Patrick also points out that he had to pay another group, 'judges', in order to remain on his mission (*Confessio* 53), but still does not say where that cash came from. It is quite possible that when other Christian leaders heard what he was doing they believed he had 'gone native' and that his whole mission was corrupt. We should note that Roman Christians had a distain for barbarians – a word Patrick himself uses for those among whom he works in *Epistola* 1 – which manifested itself in a rejection of non-Roman customs as non-Christian. Among the British Christians there also seems to have been a rejection of the notion of evangelising their non-Roman-background neighbours. Thus, they may have seen Christianity in Ireland as being confined to a minority, possibly with slaves and ex-slaves as its core group, and have viewed any effort to reach the larger society with suspicion as 'casting pearls before swine' (Matt. 7:6). In that scenario, Patrick's fundamental crime is his vulgarity and his style is attacked under the guise of his base motives for financial and social self-aggrandisement. Such a scenario would explain why Patrick is at pains to show that his missionary endeavour is being done at divine command (for example, *Confessio* 40) and an essential part of the Christian task. But we are still left wondering how Patrick financed his work!

There is still a third theme of accusation reflected in the *Confessio*. Patrick seems to protest his orthodoxy and the authority for what he does in Ireland just too vigorously. He cites a creed in its entirety as that which he believes (*Confessio* 4). Why bother if his beliefs, or his 'take' on the Christian message, were not in question? He points out that he has been called in a proper vision, modelled on the call of Samuel, to work in Ireland (*Confessio* 23–25), that it was God who appointed him even if men do not think him worthy (*Confessio* 13), and that his continuing work is guided by revelations (*Confessio* 17, 21, 29). However, looking closer at Patrick's statements about the success of his work we find a theme emerging that we have already noticed in the *Epistola*: Patrick's belief in the imminent Second Coming in

Judgement and that he had been given a unique role in ushering in the End.

The first indication of this comes with the addition of a single word to the text of the creed that he quotes and, no doubt, used in his teaching.[11] Most Christian creeds have two future-looking statements about the Second Coming and the life of the world to come. The text linked with the Councils of Nicaea and Constantinople is typical: 'He is the one who is to come again in glory to judge the living and the dead'; and it then concludes: 'We look forward to the resurrection of the dead and the life of the world to come.'[12] Patrick writes: 'And we look to the coming in the very near future – *mox futurum* – of him who is the judge of the living and the dead and who will repay each according to their deeds' (*Confessio* 4). Patrick's Christ is a just judge and is very close to returning, closer certainly than other Christians confess him to be. The coming of the Day of Judgement is again a pressing feature for him in why he wants to set out the truth of his case (*Confessio* 6, 7 and 8). What, for Patrick, the Lord wants is preaching to the multitudes and the ordination of clergy to baptise and preach (*Confessio* 40), then in the Last Days the Spirit will inspire people to visions (*Confessio* 40) and all will be able to prophesy (*Confessio* 41). Ireland seems to be a case in point: not only was he himself the recipient of visions, but those who are coming to him for baptism are recipients of divine communications (*Confessio* 42). The present is the time of pain and suffering as witnessed by what people are undergoing at the hands of slavers, but it is also the time when God is witnessed in the midst of 'every nation under heaven' (*Confessio* 3). Through Patrick's work, Christianity has now reached the very ends of the Earth and there is nowhere left which needs to have a preacher sent to it. But has Patrick prepared for this in any other way?

In *Confessio* 38 he tells us that many peoples were reborn, out

11. See O'Loughlin 2000, pp. 41–2.
12. This has two forms in Latin: *Ex expecto resurrectionem mortuorum et vitam venturi saeculi. Amen* (And I look to the resurrection of the dead and the life of the coming world. Amen) and *Expectamus resurrectionem mortuorum et vitam futuri saeculi. Amen* (We look forward to the resurrection of the dead and the life of the future age. Amen). These differences are not important for all oral texts change in this way, but note how the variants do not contain a variant like Patrick's.

at the ends of the earth in the last days (*in novissimis diebus*) (*Confessio* 34), and were then 'brought to completion' (*consummarentur*) and that he ordained clerics. In *Confessio* 51 he more or less repeats this and says that, having gone beyond where anyone lived, he baptised and also ordained clerics and 'completed' a people (*populum consummaret*). And in *Confessio* 41 we read that those to whom Patrick preached have become the 'prepared people of the Lord'. These statements when taken together, and we have already seen a similar expression in the *Epistola*, suggest that Patrick was so convinced that the End times were upon the creation that it became central to his whole vision of Christianity, and that everything that happened was offering him further confirmation that the Second Coming was simply awaiting his work in Ireland. Moreover, in the same sentences in which he speaks of baptising and ordaining – two basic sacramental actions by which the Church continues its life on Earth – he speaks of 'bringing to consummation' or 'completing' not just individuals, but entire groups. What he means by this phrase – and searching other roughly contemporary writers for similar expressions draws a blank – is wholly obscure. The only usage that may throw some light on it is in the Latin text of Matthew's gospel. At 10:23 the twelve disciples are told by Jesus that they would not have gone through all the cities of Israel before the Son of Man comes. But in Latin it can be read slightly differently, for what we render as 'gone through' reads *non consummabitis civitates* (literally: you will not have finished with the cities), and could be interpreted as 'You will not have completed the cities of Israel until the Son of Man comes.' This seems to be echoed in 24:14 when Jesus says that when the gospel is proclaimed throughout the whole world as a testimony before all peoples then will come the End, which is rendered in Latin: *et tunc veniet consummatio*. This is a verse used by Patrick in *Confessio* 34 and 40. Then at 13:39–40 there is reference to the *consummatio saeculi* (the completion or end of the age) when the angels will come to sort the good from the wicked, and in the 'command to preach' text, 28:20, used by Patrick at *Confessio* 40, Christ promises to be with the disciples 'until the close of the age' (*usque ad consummationem saeculi*). From these uses, all echoed in the *Confessio*, it could be that Patrick was focused on the End, which he referred to as 'the *Consummatio*', and it was his task to 'bring about the finishing' or to get a people 'ready for the finishing'. Such a notion would explain the passages in the *Confessio* and that in the *Epistola*. But what did he do 'to finish' these people? Well, obviously he would have preached that the End was close at hand, but he might also have had some sort of final sacrament which he offered people – perhaps a 'final' pardoning of their sins, a sort of a renewal of baptism, after which they were to remain 'ready for the End'. We can only guess at the details, but clearly there was something with regard to the End that made Patrick stand apart. It raised the suspicions of his fellow bishops that he was one of those who were claiming secret knowledge of the End and preaching its imminence. They criticised him for it just as bishops elsewhere had preached against similar harbingers of the End times, and he justified his orthodoxy and ministry in the face of the criticisms.

The extent of the mission

If the focus of Patrick's preaching was on those places which had not heard the Gospel – so that there would be no place unevangelised and holding up the Second Coming – then we can see why from the text of the *Confessio* one could get the impression that he was the first missionary in Ireland. Patrick did not see it as his role to stay within the community where he was appointed bishop, but to go to where there were no Christians in response to a call from God (*Confessio* 23–25). There is no contradiction between stating that there were communities of Christians in Ireland before his time and saying that there were places that were first evangelised by Patrick – it was those very places in Ireland, not Ireland as such, that he sought out as his particular territory. However, we have no indication of how widespread that area was. In all likelihood, it was quite extensive. He says that he was a wanderer, he mentions moving around from place to place, he kept a retinue and he had to offer gifts to several local rulers and 'judges' – all this indicates a roving ministry whereby he baptised, ordained clergy, 'completed people', and then moved on. This moving on was probably inherent to his whole vision as he had to search out the last pockets of the land which still had not heard the Gospel. If he was the one appointed to finish the preaching, then he had to stay on the move, always checking out the next valley to ensure that they had been evangelised! But while we know that when he started there were parts of Ireland that had never heard of Christianity, we do not know whether there were still such places at the time of his death.

It might seem surprising that having left a community for this roving ministry, he does not make more defence of his actions – for a bishop to leave his diocese was seen in the early Latin church as a species of the crime of divorce – but this may simply be implicit in his whole defence of his ministry. Why bother to defend oneself for leaving a diocese when it is the whole of the ministry after that event that has to be defended? If God called him to what he was doing, then permission to leave his diocese was implicit in that call. Patrick's casual statements about ordaining clergy (*Confessio* 38, 40, 50, 51) may strike modern ears as strange: clergy are viewed as professionals who need special training, but this is simply anachronistic. Clergy were a well-defined sub-group in the church by Patrick's time, an *ordo*, but there were only halting and half-hearted attempts to impose such demands as a minimum age on them. Until well into the second Christian millennium there was only one real test for clergy: did the bishop deem that he needed that man for the maintenance of his church? If so, then the man was ordained and presumably shown how to perform his duties. Patrick would simply have appealed to the example of Paul in Acts 14:23: 'And after they had appointed presbyters for them in each church, with prayer and fasting they entrusted them to the Lord in whom they had come to believe.'

Who appoints prophets?

St Jerome, writing in the early fifth century, in a work that would become a standard work for the West, had addressed himself to the question of who appoints prophets in an attempt to have categories that could distinguish between true and pseudo-prophets.[13] He had these four categories: (1) those made directly by God of Christ, and not through man or by man, such as Isaiah or St Paul; (2) those made by God through man as when God commissioned Joshua through Moses; (3) those made by man, not by God as in the case of those appointed by the churches; and

---

13. In his *Commentariorum in epistolam ad Galatas* (*Patrologia Latina* 26, 312); on its use in the West see Contreni 2002, p. 39.

lastly (4) those who are self-appointed, and into this category fall all the pseudo-apostles and pseudo-prophets. This neat little system helps us to understand Patrick, if his fellow bishops believed that he had 'lost the plot' and was no longer preaching with them but thinking that he alone knew the vast plan of history until the End. If those bishops were criticising his mission and preaching as his own thing, rather than as the teaching of the Church, then Patrick would have no alternative but to assert in defence of his ministry that he – if he were a true prophet – fell into the first category. Patrick had to assert that his mission and message were a direct appointment and inspiration by God. That this is the case is suggested by the number of times that he states that his ministry in Ireland was the result of divine 'revelations' (see *Confessio* 17 for example) or that his actions resulted from divine visitations in dreams (and there are many such examples in the *Confessio*). Indeed, on no fewer than twenty-two occasions he points out that his work in Ireland is based on his dependence on God and his appointment (see *Epistola* 5 or 10 for example). But to claim such appointment is a lonely road within the Christian Church for it is tantamount to saying, 'You are all out of step except me.' Moreover, taking this line would probably not have silenced his critics but merely convinced them that they were correct in their judgement that Patrick was a bishop operating 'on his own', without the judgement of the churches seen in their bishops. By the fifth century the local synod/council was already a favourite means of establishing 'the mind of the Church' right across the Roman world – we have volumes of synodal decisions from Gaul and Spain alone for the fifth century – and one of their key features was pointing out teaching by individual bishops that was wide of the mark. Patrick's case, for all we know, may have come up at such a meeting and they took a strong line on whether or not the last times were upon them, they criticised him, and the *Confessio* was his reply. However, as with all letters of reply to queries or criticisms – those of Paul being the most famous example – we have only one side of a dialogue: it is as if we can only hear the replies given by someone in the same room as us answering questions on a telephone: from what we hear we can only guess what questions are being asked. If these were the criticisms of Patrick's fellow bishops, then we can state that his fellow bishops were indeed right – the world did not end after

Patrick's ministry, but without their criticisms and his trenchant replies we would not know of Patrick's work in Ireland!

Patrick and the bishops

Patrick clearly wanted to be in communion with the other bishops (or he would not have written) and believed himself to be wholly orthodox (hence his citation of a creed and numerous other references to his dependence on God), but his operative theology was based on his own sense that the final times had arrived, the age of visions and prophecy, the age when the testing would occur – all prefigured in his own life – and that he had a unique task to accomplish in Ireland before the coming of the Son of Man in the very near future. Such a theology of the End, that it is a function of the preaching of the Church, or that there is a preparation that can be imparted by a bishop as the preliminary to the End, puts Patrick at odds with the mainstream of Christian teaching. Such teaching and practice would justify his investigation and correction by fellow bishops, just as others both before and after Patrick – what we would now call 'millennarians' – have called forth condemnation.

Taken all in all, Patrick must have been a considerable annoyance to his fellow bishops. He was operating at large with his own style and message, seemingly in possession of an insight into the future that was unique to him but which no doubt was causing commotion even among their congregations. He had a dodgy track record, which no doubt led many who heard of his preaching to ask what more could be expected from such a character. And, there was always the question of how this preaching of 'the End is nigh' was being financed.

Since the time that Muirchú wrote the *Vita Patricii,* the image of Patrick has been one of a bishop solidly in line with the tradition and one who could be looked up to as a model of ecclesial rectitude. In this chapter I have tried to show that that image does not do justice to what we can see in his surviving writings. Viewing Patrick as the insular, fifth-century analogue of a modern American television preacher who claims to know the countdown to the end of the world may seem equally bizarre, but we must take account of what he saw as his unique mission and position within the whole history of Christianity. Moreover, unless Patrick had some personal view of the Christian message that impelled him to stand aside from his fellows, then he would probably have spent his entire life within the community where he had been first appointed bishop, and we would never have heard of him.

❦

CHAPTER 6

The Patrician 'Dark Age'

'Dark Ages'

If we assume that Patrick worked and died in the later fifth century, and date Muirchú's *Vita Patricii* to the closing decades of the seventh century, then we have 200 years when we barely hear of Patrick. The concept of a 'dark age' is one that historians of the early Middle Ages instinctively flee, as it conjures up a notion that usually says more about our lack of understanding than it characterises a period. Usually, it is an underhand way of saying that the period was one of whose values and beliefs we do not approve: 'enlightenment', or an age of light, usually means that the period is seen as one that anticipates or prepares for our modernity. However, when we are left with a period of which we know little and must therefore speculate as to what happened during that time which may have laid the basis for what came later, then it is hard to avoid the term. And it is an appropriate term for the history of the cult of Patrick between his time, remembering that for that time we have only his own writings, and when he emerges as the great apostle of Ireland.

During that time we have many well-informed writers whom we would expect to know the situation in Ireland or between Britain and Ireland, yet they never mention Patrick. The British writer Gildas (mid-sixth century) gives an account of the work and suffering of the British churches, yet does not even allude to a mission in Ireland. The Irish theologian and missionary

Columbanus (*c.* 543–615) is conscious of his origins and the connections between the churches on the periphery and those on mainland Europe, but he never mentions Patrick in what is the largest body of writings from a single Irishman in the period. Many other documents from Ireland, for example dealing with saints, simply do not mention Patrick. Moreover, just after that period, from the year 731, we have the *Historia ecclesiastica gentis Anglorum* (literally: 'the history of the Angles as a church') by Bede (*c.* 673–735). This work has much to say about the churches in Britain before the Anglo-Saxons and has much information on Ireland, but never mentions Patrick, despite the fact that one of its aims was to trace the lineages of the churches as they impact on Bede's peoples. How can this silence be explained? While it is always dangerous to build an argument from silence, this silence seems so great as to say something about this man who by the 690s had emerged as a central figure in the history of the Irish as a church, and who was also the patron of Armagh – a place that was then emerging as the leading church centre in Ireland.

What evidence do we have?

We must start by noting that when Patrick died, whenever and wherever that was, there were communities that looked to him as their spiritual father. To these communities he was a teacher who was illustrious and 'had left a mark' and among whom his memory was cherished and celebrated.[1] Without such communities who owned his memory, Patrick's memory would have been like those of so many others of the early bishops (possibly including Palladius), and we would know nothing about him. The proof of this continuance of memory is the survival of two of his letters. Our earliest manuscript of the *Confessio* is found in the Book of Armagh and dates from the beginning of the ninth century.[2] We know that the author of the hymn *Audite omnes* – which we will examine shortly – had a copy, and so too did Muirchú when he wrote. Our earliest manuscripts of the *Epistola* are considerably later, but we know that Muirchú had a copy when he wrote. However, for both these patrician documents to have

---

1. The notion of 'leaving a name' – and so being one of the 'illustrious teachers' within the tradition goes back to Sir. 44:1—50:24.
2. See Sharpe 1983.

survived at all means that they were being copied between Patrick's death and the time of our first evidence of their existence (when the hymn writer and Muirchú were using them). So, in Ireland, probably for the greater part of the sixth century and certainly for much of the seventh century, there was at least one community which looked back to Patrick and viewed him in much the same way that he presents himself in those documents: their evangelist. For them, Patrick was the one who had been the first to preach to them, had converted them to Christianity, and had established a clergy to continue the life of their church.

Our question about the silence regarding Patrick can now be seen in a slightly different light: does our evidence or the lack of it help us to establish just how widely Patrick was seen as the father of churches during the sixth and seventh centuries? Writing in 1929, James Kenney, the great bibliographer of early Christian Ireland, summarised the problem and the extent of our evidence for this 'dark age' thus:

> Patricius died in 461.[3] His name was kept in honour in the diptychs[4] of the church of Armagh[5]; the entries in the annals show that some records of him and his disciples were preserved in calendars and paschal tables; he was invoked in the colophon to the Book of Durrow which may preserve the words of Columba of Iona; Cummian's paschal epistle of about 633 refers to his Easter reckoning; Ultán of Árd-mBrecáin (d. 657) had a book containing early memorabilia regarding him; the so-called Hymn of Secundinus in his praise was probably written in the fifth or sixth century; and it seems certain that there was, at least throughout Leth Cuinn,[6] considerable popular and traditional knowledge of

3. He accepted the earlier traditional date for Patrick's death, see Chapter 3 above; but that date does not affect the evidence he presents here.

4. The name given to the lists of names of saints included in the celebration of the Eucharistic Prayer.

5. Kenney assumes that because this later became the chief church of Patrick it had continuously been such – but the evidence for the Armagh link comes from the period when Patrick's cult was growing rapidly as a cult for the whole island, over which Armagh was then claiming primacy.

6. Literally 'Conn's half'; however, there is no certainty about what part of Ireland this terms refers to (see Charles-Edwards 2000, p. 569); it may mean Leinster or Ulster and Kenney seems to take it as referring to Ulster.

the saint, and a number of distinct legends preserved in prose and verse. Patricius was not entirely forgotten, but such evidence as we have regarding the two hundred years following his death seems to show that his memory had slipped into the background of old and far-off things. Neither Columbanus, nor Jonas the biographer of Columbanus, nor Cogitosus in his Life of Brigit alludes to him in any way. Adomnán and Bede, to whom were particularly available the earlier records of Irish and English Christianity, make no mention of Patricius in their great historical works.[7] Zimmer has shown that, on Adomnán's testimony, the position in the commemoration of the mass, as celebrated by Colum-cille, which, had the Patrick Legend been accepted, it might be expected would be held by the name of Patrick, was occupied by that of Martin of Tours, and that likewise Martin's name is found where Patrick's would be looked for in an obituary notice of Colum-cille, written, Zimmer thought, just after the saint's death, by an Irishman in Gaul.[8]

In this passage Kenney was trying to square the circle. On the one hand it seeks to maintain the case that the memory of Patrick was a significant factor in the churches in Ireland at the time, while, on the other hand, it shows just how little material there is from this period which relates to the bishop who would later be claimed as the sole father in faith, indeed the apostle, of the Irish. It is worth looking at the positive evidence for Patrick's memory in the period point by point.

a. The colophon to the Book of Durrow

The Book of Durrow is one of those great copies of the four gospels, some of whose pages are continually being reproduced in books on Christian art in the early Middle Ages.[9] It contains a

---

7. At this point Kenney adds a footnote: 'In the second preface to his Life of Columba – which possibly may be of later composition to the rest of the work – Adomnán alludes to St Mochta as a disciple of "the holy bishop Patricius". This reference will be examined later in this chapter.

8. Kenney 1929, p. 324.

9. Meehan 1996 is a very convenient introduction.

remarkably pure and accurate text of the Vulgate, along with an elaborate scholarly apparatus. Therefore, unlike gospel books which were intended mainly for the eye as beautiful artefacts – artistic monuments to the 'word of God' as a book, such as the Book of Kells – this is a book whose marginal additions render it most suitable for use in formal exegetical work by a theologian.[10] However, there is no agreement as to where or when it was produced. Many scholars are prepared to link it in some way with a monastery with some connection to Iona, but dates – all based on comparisons with the style of writing and decoration in other Gospel books – vary from between 650 to the early years of the eighth century, and a good 'working date' would be the last decades of the seventh century.[11]

At the end of the work there is a colophon – a little message from the scribe who wrote it – which reads:

> I ask your blessing, holy presbyter Patrick, that whoever shall hold this little book in his hand may remember the scribe Columba who has written this gospel book for himself in the space of twelve days; by the grace of our Lord I have written. Pray for me my brother, the Lord be with you.[12]

In this colophon 'holy Patrick' (s[an]c[t]e patrici) clearly refers to St Patrick, but one wonders just how much that scribe knew of the saint when he refers to him as a 'presbyter' (praesbiter), when Patrick so vehemently pointed out that he is a bishop (episcopus).[13] Moreover, it is no longer (given that we date the Book of Durrow to fifty years later than did Kenney) evidence for the cult of Patrick in the 'dark age' because by 700 we know that the cult of Patrick had not only 'taken off', but the most famous early document of that cult (Muirchú's Vita) was already in circulation.

---

10. See O'Loughlin 1999.
11. See Meehan 1996, pp. 17–22; earlier scholars such as Kenney thought it belonged to the period before 650.
12. This is the translation given in Kenney 1929, p. 631; the Latin text can be found in Meehan 1996, p. 26 with a facsimile of the colophon on p. 78.
13. In late-seventh-century works from Ireland the word sacerdos is sometimes used of both presbyters and bishops, Adomnán's De locis sanctis being an example, but the precise names 'presbyter' and 'episcopus' were never used interchangeably.

b. The Paschal Letter by Cummian

Of the disputes that took place among the churches in Ireland none is more famous than that about how to calculate Easter – it is famous because of the amount of coverage given to it by Bede as the background to the meeting that took place in Streanaeshalch (usually now assumed to be Whitby) in AD 664.[14] The dating of Easter was a problem because no calculation system (known as a *computus*) in use in the Middle Ages was accurate in the long term, and by the seventh century those in use in Ireland were out of harmony with those being used elsewhere, in places such as Rome and Alexandria. Some churches in Ireland were moving to newer systems, while others were retaining their familiar methods. One of the disputants was Cummian. We know nothing with certainty about this man except that he wrote a letter to Ségéne (abbot of Iona between 623 and 652) in 632-633 to encourage Ségéne and his monks to adopt the new manner of calculating the date of Easter.[15]

In that letter Cummian refers to the many different ways he knows of calculating Easter, including one that he believed was of great age within the Irish churches as it was the one brought by Patrick, whom he refers to as 'our father' (*papa noster*). Thus wrote Cummian's editors:

> This is the first reference in any seventh-century Irish text to St. Patrick. As such it has a unique importance, not least because it refers to Patrick as *papa noster*, and in a non-tendentious tone which contrasts vividly with the later seventh-century claims on behalf of the saint made by the *paruchia* of Armagh.[16]

So for this churchman, wherever he was in Ireland, Patrick is not only a saint with a living cult, but the one who is recalled as their father in faith, the one who founded their church, and he is the one who gives the authority of antiquity and origins to what they have done. We can take at face value what Cummian says about

14. *Historia ecclesiastica gentis Anglorum* 3, 25.
15. See Walsh and Ó Cróinín, 1988, pp. 3-15.
16. Walsh and Ó Cróinín 1988, pp. 29–30; for the full Latin text with a translation, see pp. 83–5.

Patrick having brought to them a *computus*: for in introducing Christianity in any place Patrick would have had to introduce a liturgical year, and since that year was built around Easter he would have had to give them a table for its celebration and teach his clergy how to operate the calculation system.[17] And, in a manuscript containing many computistical pieces compiled about 658 we have another reference to a *computus* linked with Patrick for it says: 'Patrick, in his prologue [to a *computus*] says ...'[18] However, while Patrick would have had to have a *computus*, whether or not any extant early *computus* claiming a link to him was the one he actually would have used must remain an open question.

These two references to Patrick may be explained in a scenario like this: in the early to mid-seventh century there were several churches in Ireland that looked back to Patrick as an authority figure – for whatever *computus* they had in their possession which they considered to be their most ancient practice they linked it with Patrick's name.[19] Even though these churches now wished to embrace newer methods for dating Easter, they were aware that there was an older method which they linked with their earliest times as Christians – and those times were connected in their memories with the time when they were under the direct teaching of Patrick. On this basis we could assume that wherever Cummian came from, it was one of those places where Patrick had evangelised.

c. The book of Ultán of Árd-mBrecáin

Bishop Tírechán wrote his 'Collection of Memories of Patrick' (the *Collectanea*) probably between 670 and 700. In the opening line of his work Tírechán says that he gathered his material from the 'mouth and book of Bishop Ultán whose pupil and disciple he was'; and he later states again that he got information from his foster father 'Bishop Ultán son of Connor'. From other sources we

17. This may surprise many today, but it should be recalled that even copies of liturgical books intended for lay use (e.g. *The Book of Common Prayer* or Catholic lay missals) printed before the 1930s often had a complete *computus* section in their opening pages.
18. See Walsh and Ó Cróinín 1988, pp. 31–2.
19. See Dumville, 1993, pp. 85–88.

know that Ultán was bishop in Ardbraccan, near Navan, Co. Meath, and that he died in either 657 or 663. Moreover, Muirchú also refers to having obtained written information about Patrick from Ultán. Ultán may have had an interest in gathering materials on several Irish saints; there is a later tradition that he gathered material on Brigit,[20] and from what Muirchú and Tírechán tell us we can be certain that he wrote something on Patrick – but the book itself has not survived. From this meagre evidence we can assert that he was one of the first of the group of later seventh-century Irish churchmen who were committed to the cult of Patrick in the generation immediately before Tírechán and Muirchú. However, the fact that Ultán's book disappeared may indicate that when he wrote his book, this cult was not yet as significant as it became later in the seventh century.

d. The hymn Audite omnes amantes ascribed to Secundinus

In the 'Antiphonary of Bangor', a liturgical book dating from the end of the seventh century, we have the first major composition that can be included in the dossier of Saint Patrick.[21] It is a hymn of twenty-three verses (each verse beginning with the next letter of the Latin alphabet of twenty-three letters) wholly devoted to praising Patrick and presenting him as the great apostle of Ireland. For us there are two questions. First, when was it written? Second, how does it present Patrick in comparison with the later cult?

The hymn's age has been the subject of controversy for over a century because in a ninth-century work it is attributed to St Secundinus (known in Irish as Sechnall) who was then believed to be one of Patrick's immediate disciples. This gave rise to the theory that it was contemporary with Patrick and indeed written while he was alive and that it was presented to him. It may seem incredible that scholars as skilled as Bieler[22] or Curran could have advanced these arguments, but such was the desire to have material going right back to the age of Patrick that the same old arguments were rehearsed time after time. The arguments were that the hymn was 'sober' in its language while later writers were less so (read it and see if saying someone is perfect in every way

20. See Kenney 1929, pp. 362–3 and 368.
21. See Curran 1984, pp. 35–46.
22. Bieler 1953a.

can be considered a 'sober' comment). Secondly, that some pre-Vulgate scriptural readings could be detected beneath its text.[23] However, this ignored the fact that such reading remained in use for centuries after the time of Jerome and that until the ninth century such 'contamination' was commonplace. And, lastly, that the hymn was contemporary because it speaks of Patrick in the present tense and as alive! This last argument I find most bizarre of them all, as it wholly ignores the fact that a hymn is a liturgical composition and that all the saints are not only alive now in the moment of the community praying, but they are now more alive in heaven than they were in their time on earth. With regard to anyone whom Christians view as a saint then, the present tense is an essential expression of belief, and it is the normal tense of liturgy. So if we see the attribution to the time of Patrick as part of the later cult – which then attributes the existence of the cult of Patrick to the very earliest times, when was it written? The latest date is the date of the earliest manuscript (late seventh century) and we know that Muirchú knew the hymn for he makes several attempts to explain obscurities in it. It has been suggested that it was written by a man called Colmán Elo who died around 612, but there is no convincing evidence.[24] It does make elaborate use of biblical allusions and this is a style that can be found in other seventh-century authors, and it belongs to a time when the cult of Patrick had already gained some currency, so I would opt for a date some time in the early or mid-seventh century. Many have judged the hymn by the standards of Latin poetry and found it wanting. However, as Orchard (1993) observed, that is to mistake its purpose and to ignore the real skill in using biblical and other written materials that the author displays.

The hymn presents Patrick as the sole converter/evangelist of the Irish. It does not admit any competitors or equals – but then one would not expect such admissions in a composition of praise. Secondly, he is the great teacher of the faith and made the equal on several occasions of Peter and Paul. There is no hint of any shadow over Patrick and he is an ideal bearer of the Gospel. The hymn is also our earliest evidence for the notion that Patrick is not only a patron but a special intercessor for his people, and that he

---

23. Burkitt 1902 first drew attention to these pre-Vulgate readings.
24. Orchard 1993.

has been granted apostolic status. Wherever the hymn was produced there was already a most elaborate cult of Patrick and one
that felt free to set Patrick's cult apart in many ways from that of
other saints. It is significant that this first full-blown item in the
dossier is not a para-liturgical text such as a *vita*, but something
that is taken directly from the liturgy itself. And, perhaps more
importantly, its presence in the 'Antiphonary of Bangor', which is
roughly contemporary with Muirchú, shows that he was not
writing in a vacuum, but elaborating what was already a
widespread and distinctive cult.

e. The second preface of Adomnán's Vita Columbae

In this *vita* dating from the end of the seventh century we have a
reference to 'holy bishop Patrick' as the master of Mochta (a pilgrim from Ireland to Britain) who made a prophecy concerning
Columba many years before the latter's birth. The *Vita Columbae*
presents its hero as being born in the early sixth century, and thus
presents Patrick as belonging to the mid-fifth century. This cannot
be taken as evidence for the date of the man Patrick, but it does
show us that Patrick's cult had reached Iona by Adomnán's time,
and that indeed the sort of chronology for Patrick that we find in
Muirchú was already accepted there.[25] The reference to Patrick is,
therefore, part of the process of establishing links between all
those who were considered the 'great saints' of Ireland – a *de facto*
apostolic tradition – in the later seventh century.

f. The Vita Geretrudis

St Gertrude, the daughter of Pippin, died on St Patrick's Day, 659.
How long after that her *vita* was written we do not know with any
precision, but in the *vita* it is said that 'blessed bishop Patrick' is
waiting to receive her soul into heaven.[26] This is one of the earliest references to Patrick from the continent, but we cannot take it
as evidence for his cult earlier than the late seventh century.
Indeed, it may not even indicate that there was a vibrant cult of
Patrick in the region, but simply that Gertrude died on 17 March

25. On the links between Adomnán and Muirchú, see O'Loughlin 2000, pp.
    87–108.
26. Richter 1999, pp. 129–30.

and the hagiographer, on consulting a calendar, found Patrick's name there and so wrote that he 'along with chosen angels of God were ready to receive her'. Therefore, despite arguments that this *vita* might indicate a cult of Patrick brought to France by Fursa *c.* 630,[27] it could simply be that there was already a calendar similar to Willibrord's – and the exchange of memorial dates between calendars is one of the more common and simple of exchanges of information between churches in the period.

g. A poem by Abbot Cellanus of Péronne

There is a short poem in a manuscript linked with Abbot Cellanus – but of his dates we are none too sure and he is usually dated by assuming that he was in contact with the Anglo-Saxon writer Aldhelm who died in 709. Here is the poem:

> This hall perpetuates Patrick's fame,
> Whom humbly we revere, as is his due.
> He bathed us in the sacramental bath,
> He taught us how to worship God in heaven,
> Brightening our darkness with the light of faith,
> Calpornius's son, in Britain he was born,
> Gaul reared him, happy Ireland gave him rest.
> The heaven's blessing shines on either land.[28]

If Cellanus lived in the later seventh century, then this is good evidence that the cult of Patrick as the one who baptised Ireland was not confined to Ireland but was being taken overseas by Irishmen. The information in the poem, especially about Gaul rearing Patrick, does not indicate direct knowledge of Patrick's writings but rather with the basic story line found in Muirchú. So, as with Adomnán's second preface, the poem points to the vigour of the cult of Patrick among a wide range of Irish clerics at the end of the seventh century. The poem also has another significance: it is the first case of Irishmen taking the memory of Patrick abroad as part of their own religious memory and identity.

---

27. Richter 1999, p. 130.
28. This translation is that of Dr Michael Richter; see Richter 1999, pp. 131–3.

h. The Calendar of Willibrord

Willibrord (658–739) was a Northumbrian and went to the Irish monastery of Rath Melsigi in 678. He left there in 690 and went to Frisia and later founded the monastery of Echternach (just inside the Luxemburg border with Germany).[29] In his liturgical calendar there is found this entry for 17 March: 'St Patrick: Bishop in Ireland.' No doubt this feast day entered into Willibrord's liturgical consciousness while he was in Ireland – at the time when we have the greatest concentration of evidence for the growing cult of Patrick. However, the form of the entry in Willibrord's book probably came from an earlier calendar and it is significant that Patrick is simply described as a 'bishop in Ireland'. Patrick is not claimed as the first bishop or as the bishop at some point in the past, nor is he linked with a particular place in Ireland that was considered as his see. It is possible that this notice reflects a time, before Willibrord, when Patrick was remembered as a bishop who was linked with various places on the island who recalled him as the missionary who preached to them.

i. The Dicta Patricii

In the 'Book of Armagh' (early ninth century) are preserved 'sayings' (usually punctuated by scholars into three sayings) of Patrick, and over their authenticity there has been much debate.[30] The second is not problematic as it is a quotation from Patrick's *Epistola*. The first, if genuine, would imply that Patrick did visit Gaul, if not Rome itself, at some stage. That is not inherently problematic, as Patrick mentions the possibility that if he were to leave Ireland, then one of the benefits would be being able to visit Christians in Gaul. So it could be that this is a genuine memory of what Patrick said, but we have no way of verifying it. The third saying has been problematic not simply with regard to Patrick, but because it has been part of the denominational rivalries in Ireland since the Reformation over who 'owned' Patrick. 'If you be Christians, then you are Romans' was read in terms of loyalty to the Roman Pontiff; consequently, there were benefits in seeing it

29. Ó Cróinín 1984.
30. See Gwynn 1975, for the background to the *dicta*.

as genuinely Patrick or else a later imposition by the 'Roman party' in the later seventh century. However, if the saying is Patrick's, then it would mean no more than that anyone who had adopted Christianity was also becoming part of the larger Roman world – a world to which Patrick was very conscious that he belonged. The argument usually deployed to urge that it must be later than Patrick is based on the date for the introduction of the *Kyrie* into the Eucharistic liturgy in Rome, but this fails to note that the *Kyrie* was already part of the prayer formulae of Christians long before it had a fixed place at the Eucharist, and in the 'saying' it is being exhorted for use as repeated prayer for continual use. Indeed, if the saying was composed after the *Kyrie* became a fixed part of the Mass liturgy, then the 'saying' makes far less sense. So, on balance, given that neither saying 1 nor 3 can be shown to be later than Patrick, and saying 2 is genuine, I am inclined to view all three as being a part of a tradition of memory that goes back to Patrick himself.

So, in some communities there was a living link that remembered Patrick and some of his words even when these were no longer directly meaningful to their situation. Muirchú remarks that he was able to garner stories of Patrick orally, and it could be that this is part of that oral memory. It may be that they were written down and preserved in writing long before the 'Book of Armagh', but we have no way of knowing.

j. 'Laws' attributed to Patrick

There is a sizeable body of legislation in both Latin and Irish that lays claim to Patrick as its author and hence its authority. However, our earliest evidence for these laws and decisions are all from after the period when Patrick's cult had become well established. They therefore provide evidence for how his full-blown cult manifested itself rather than evidence for the surviving memory of Patrick in the 'dark age'.

k. Irish saints 'before' Patrick

The last piece of 'evidence' I wish to examine with regard to the time when Patrick was not yet seen as the great single converter of the Irish and the island's special patron stands apart from the above in that it is, firstly, more strictly an 'argument from silence', and secondly, the materials involved are problematic as to their historical worth and their dates of composition.

There is a tendency in hagiography to bring saints into alliances with other saints and present them as supporting one another, teaching one another, and being authorised within the tradition by earlier more renowned saints – and, indeed, to show that they were in such harmony in their lives and work on Earth as they are now in heaven. Thus, many writers – including most Irish hagiographers after the time when Patrick's cult is established as preeminent – engage in a kind of celestial 'networking' for their subjects: Saint X was visited by Saint Y, ordained of Saint Z, and so forth – and dates are bent to match the network being formed. We have already seen a small instance of this tendency in the case of Adomnán's second preface, which gently presents Columba as the third or fourth generation after Patrick, but with a definite tradition of authorisation being shown: Patrick to Mochta to Columba. However, there is a group of saints whose lives claim them as very early in Irish history and which are not linked in any way with Patrick: Declan of Ardmore, Ailbe of Emly, Ciaran of Saigir, Abban of Moyarny, and Ibar of Beg-Eri.[31] Moreover, Cogitosus – whom Muirchú claims as his model in writing a *vita* – wrote a life of Brigit some time in the seventh century (at least a generation before Muirchú) and does not link her with Patrick. And there are later traditions of other missionary bishops – Auxilius, Iserninus, and Secundinus – working at an early date in Ireland, but by this time these traditions were written down they are firmly linked to Patrick as his assistants.

There have been many attempts over the years to explain this phenomenon, the most common being that they might have been working as missionaries in Ireland before the time of Patrick – which, of course, cannot be verified. Moreover, most of them are presented not as preachers of the Christian faith, but as the founders of monasteries. A simpler solution is to explain the absence of any reference to Patrick as being the result of these various cults growing up in places in Ireland where at the time Patrick's cult was virtually unknown, or at least was no more significant than that of any other saint. This silence about Patrick,

31. See Kenney 1929, p. 311 as a starting point.

therefore, does two things. First, it suggest that his cult spread slowly in Ireland and only in the later seventh century was it beginning to assume the form we see in Muirchú. Second, it puts the silence of Columbanus and Bede in perspective – neither of these mention Patrick, probably because the cult was not significant in their localities: not in Ireland at the beginning of the seventh century in the case of Columbanus, nor in Northumbria in the early eighth century in the case of Bede.

Reviving a memory

What particular churches remember and forget from generation to generation is central to how they, as active tradition bearers within a historical religion, define themselves as Christians, give form to their practice of their religion, and express their beliefs in liturgy and works of doctrine. The twentieth-century theologian Karl Rahner once expressed it as 'the church is always remembering and always forgetting.' There is no automatic 'storing' of all the memories: some are active and important, others only known vestigially or through books. In the early Middle Ages one of the key ways that Christians expressed their group identities was through the cults of saints – a method of defining themselves and holiness that is now foreign to most Christians – and so who was remembered and made the focus of much religious practice changed with places and times. The growth of the cult of St James in Spain is an example of a cult that later spread all over western Europe. Similarly, in later medieval England we find the cult of St Thomas Becket at Canterbury, or the burgeoning cult of St David in Wales from the later eleventh century. When each new cult emerged, others faded into greater or less obscurity. The evidence we have looked at in this chapter shows a similar process at work in Ireland in the seventh century.

Patrick, after his death, was remembered by few: by those churches that he founded and, probably, by very few outside those churches – hence the 'dark age' and silence about him in many writers where, with hindsight, we might expect to find him mentioned. During the seventh century there was a change in this situation, whereby his cult spread more widely, and this led to more mentions of him and the production of new items within his cult such as the hymn *Audite omnes*. These, in turn, bolstered and extended his reputation. By the end of that century his cult had eclipsed other memories of saints, had spread even beyond the boundaries of Ireland, and was developing an entire 'history' of that Christian people, where Patrick was central to their past and so to their identity as one of the 'baptised nations' – a process we see in full flower in Muirchú's *Vita Patricii*. And to this document we must now turn.

ʍuirchú and the Crystallisation of the Legend

Seventh-century Ireland: hagiography and society[1]

By the last decades of the seventh century we can observe three significant phenomena in Ireland that affected both church and society. First, we have a new density of material relating to Patrick. Apart from the *Vita* by Muirchú, there is a collection of memories about Patrick by Bishop Tírechán, and another text known as the *Liber Angeli* whose tone can be appreciated from its opening words:

> The highest angel of the Lord handed on to the holy bishop Patrick what was wisely spoken to him by God on the reverence due to [Patrick's] apostolic see [in Armagh] and the honour due to his heirs there from all the Irish.[2]

Tírechán was probably writing at the same time as Muirchú and had much the same sources, although they do not appear to have known one another's works. He preserves bits and pieces about Patrick, miracles stories similar in form and content to those in Muirchú, lists of clerics which enable churches to link themselves

---

1. For a summary of hagiography in early Christian Ireland, see Hughes 1972, pp. 217–47; McCone 1989; Herbert 1996; and Herbert 2001.
2. See Bieler 1979, pp. 184–91 for an edition and translation.

into the genealogy of Patrick, as well as lists of places he supposed were linked with Patrick and which would want to claim that link in the late seventh century. His work is called the *Collectanea* and we might render this 'the compilation' for it is diverse pieces of material without a narrative structure and, as is the wont with such works, it grew in bits and pieces between its time of composition and the time of its oldest manuscript witness – the Book of Armagh in the early ninth century.[3] So, by 700 the cult of Patrick has generated all that it needed in terms of cult material to be a major cult – i.e. one that spreads over many churches and which dominates local cults – and is claiming the whole island as its area. The 'area' of a saint was expressed in terms of that area over which he exercised special protection and hence was its inhabitants, patron/intercessor in the heavenly court.

Second, at this time there appears to be a major realignment of ecclesiastical networks in Ireland: older structures seem to have been passing away and new ones establishing themselves. We see this in synods that were held, legislation that was promulgated and codified, and in the new importance of particular groupings such as the '*familia*' of the monastery of Iona,[4] and most of all in the claims of the see of Armagh to be the 'first church' in Ireland and to exercise a jurisdiction of sorts over the others.[5] And, thirdly, there were important changes taking place within the secular power structures of the island, and, in particular, with the rise to power over a large area in the northern half of the country of the Uí Néill dynasty.[6]

It should be obvious that while we can identify these three themes, they were in reality closely intertwined: the development of Patrick's cult, the rise of Armagh and the Uí Néill – are all part of the one human tapestry. And, for more than half a century, historians of early Ireland have studied the three phenomena in just this manner: hagiography pointed to the political situation among ruling families and the rise of particular churches and cults

3. See Bieler 1979, pp. 122–67 for an edition and translation of Tírechán; and pp. 166–79 for an edition and translation of the 'additions [to Tírechán]' (*additamenta*).
4. See Herbert 1988.
5. On church structures in Ireland in this period, the key work is Etchingham, 1999.
6. See Charles-Edwards 2000, pp. 8–144; 416–585.

reflected the interests of the ruling families. These historians have made extensive use of the documents of the cult of Patrick as evidence for the politics, both secular and ecclesiastical – to the extent that these can be separated in the period – of Ireland.[7] A good example of this is the use made of Tírechán's work as an expression of the growing power of the Uí Néill, and seeing the motives for Tírechán in the advancement of the Uí Néill cause.[8] Likewise, the rise of Patrick's cult and the rise of Armagh to pre-eminence are inextricable as part of the social history of the church at the time – a fact witnessed in that all our earliest documents relating to Patrick survive in a manuscript for Armagh provenance.[9] Moreover, just as a theology is reflected in a saint's life, so too are other aspects of the world of its author, and many scholars have mined saints' lives for appropriate information relating to their concerns.[10] However, here my focus is slightly different: I wish to focus on the *idea of Patrick within the memory of Christians in Ireland at the period* in so far as it reveals their 'operative theology' and their understanding of themselves as Christians. This is a much more restricted aim, and an abstraction from the more general image of the past presented by historians of Ireland at that time. This more restricted view belongs properly to the history of theology and spirituality, rather than to the history of Ireland. However, the results of this more limited focus may contribute some elements to the larger picture which otherwise may escape notice. This has two practical implications for this chapter. First, I shall not attempt to draw a picture of Ireland in the later seventh century in which to locate the cult – there is already an excellent 'tour' of Ireland in the seventh century in the work of Prof. Thomas Charles-Edwards.[11] Nor shall I attempt a general description of the ecclesiastical structures of the period, as this can be found with far more precision than could be accomplished as a section of this book in the work of Dr Colmán Etchingham (1999). Second, I shall only examine one of the products of the cult of

---

7. See, for example, Etchingham 1999, pp. 148–67.
8. See, for example, Swift 1994; and Charles-Edwards 2000, pp. 15, 37 and 445–6.
9. See Sharpe 1982; and Sharpe 1983.
10. See Doherty 1982.
11. In Charles-Edwards 2000, the opening chapter is entitled: 'Ireland in the seventh century: a tour.'

Patrick in this period: Muirchú's *Vita Patricii*. My reason for passing over the two other works of the cult upon which historians
have laboured, namely Tírechán and the *Liber Angeli*, is that contained in Muirchú we have all the central themes that go to make
up the idea of Patrick at the time, such that, from my perspective,
these other works only add further instances, parallels, and particular applications of the cult to the church life in Ireland at the time.
If I were writing a history of the period, or of the Church in general at the time, such an omission would be unpardonable, but in
a work devoted to the structure of the memory of Patrick within a
community, their omission may help us see 'the wood for the trees'.

My rationale for concentrating on Muirchú is, in the first place,
that as a *vita* it has a narrative running through it that not only
makes it accessible in reading, but as a piece of Christian hagiography it can be located easily within the tradition of such
writing.[12] It can be related and compared with how other saints'
cults grew in the Latin churches and how other communities
formulated their history of who they were as Christians both in
vitae and in works devoted to their origins which are usually
entitled 'histories'. The pursuit by Christian communities of their
particular origins was a major concern of churches from the very
beginnings of Christianity until, at least for western Europe, quite
recently. And in early Christian Ireland this search for *auctoritas* in
their 'fathers' (and through them ultimately to the apostles) took
the form of hagiography and is a theme in virtually every *vita* we
possess. Second, because the *Vita* has a narrative structure with
many distinct tales, each intended as an 'example' of some virtue or
practice in one way or another, it is a very good source for studying theological concerns. It is worth recalling that the basic source
for the genre of the *vita* is the gospels, especially Matthew and
Luke: a series of episodes, wonders and teachings given narrative
form around the sequence of genealogy, birth, youth and entering
ministry, mature ministry and some of its events and teachings,
and then death and its aftermath. We see this influence in the
opening words of Muirchú where he adopts the opening words of
Luke as his own. This modelling on the gospels was more than a
convenient writing convention; it was based on the assumption
that the life of the saint had been patterned upon, and assimilated

---

12. See Bieler 1962; Bieler 1975; Bray 1983; and O'Loughlin 2000b.

to, the life of Christ; therefore, the pattern of the two lives (Jesus in the gospels, the saint in his/her *vita*) is the same. This has an important value for us as scholars, but one frequently not recognised by those writing on hagiography, for it allows us to extract the theology of the tales and the whole narrative, using the techniques developed for the gospels. A collection of 'bits' only allows us to look at the theological perspective of this or that bit, but once these are arranged in a narrative we can both study the pieces and see how they relate to the overall editorial slant of the narrative, as well as seeing how the narrative as a whole advanced a perspective on the question 'What is Christian belief?' With the exception of one brilliant item in Tírechán, this sort of analysis is only possible with Muirchú, for there miracle stories, accounts of 'events', and other snippets of 'information' are combined in such a way that we can see not only the religious content of the pieces, but the larger agenda and theological style of the author/compiler/editor.[13] Third, the image of Patrick that becomes standard for the period between the eighth century and the end of the nineteenth century has as it basis the story of Patrick in Muirchú. Later *vitae* in both Latin and Irish harmonise other stories, from Tírechán for example, within Muirchú's narrative structure, and this process only reached its finality in John Healy's work of 1905 which 'may be described as representing the final stage in the evolution of the Patrick Legend: all the traditional material is gathered together and harmonised into a connected narrative.'[14] This is not surprising, as what survives best in the memory is not collections of information, but narratives – and it is these recalled narratives that structure the parts wherever they are encountered.

Muirchú: the man, his work, and his sources[15]

Details of Muirchú's life are as elusive as those of other seventh-century writers of early Christian Ireland.[16] Apart from what we

13. The exception in Tírechán's work is the creed text he preserves; this is translated and commented upon in detail in O'Loughlin 2000c.
14. Kenney's judgement (Kenney 1929, p. 320) on Healy 1905.
15. In this chapter I have tried to draw together and develop what I have written on Muirchú previously: O'Loughlin 2000, pp. 87–108; O'Loughlin 2002b; and O'Loughlin 2003.
16. See Lapidge and Sharpe 1985, n. 303; Kenney 1929, pp. 331–4; and Bieler 1979, pp. 1–35.

can learn from the *Vita*, we have only one item of contemporary information about him: he was present at the Synod of Birr in 697 as one of the guarantors to the *Cáin Adomnáin*.[17] This indicates that at the end of the seventh century he was an important Irish churchman.

His tribal name *moccu Machthéni* has usually been taken to indicate that he belonged to the Túath Mochtaine, whose lands were in the Mag Machae ('the plain of Armagh'), an area roughly south of Armagh. Because of this, since Kenney, scholars have linked him to Armagh as one of its clerics. This seems a reasonable inference as he clearly identifies his hero with Armagh, and such identification makes most sense if he were an Armagh cleric writing for an Armagh audience about their patron saint. However, it makes it very difficult to understand how Aed of Sleaty could command him to write the *Vita*. So I am predisposed to seeing what other evidence there might be as to his origins.

From the Prologue to the *Vita* we learn that Muirchú considered himself to be following in the footsteps of Cogitosus who earlier in the century had written a *vita* for Brigit. He refers to him as his 'father', which is best understood in terms of discipleship.[18] Muirchú also tells us that he composed the work at the request of 'Aed, Bishop of the city of Sléibte' (Sleaty)[19] and he dedicated the work to Aed.[20] We know little of Aed except that he placed his diocese under the protection of Patrick (i.e. Armagh) during the time that Ségéne was bishop (661–688). We know also that Aed was, along with Muirchú, one of the guarantors at the Synod of Birr, but had already relinquished office by 692 (for in that year his successor as bishop died) in favour of an anchoritic life, and in all likelihood he died in 700.[21] So the *Vita* was certainly composed prior to 700, and some scholars see its purpose, in part, as fostering the assimilation of Sleaty within the jurisdiction of

17. See Ní Dhonnchadha 1982.
18. See O'Loughlin, 2000d.
19. This is the present parish of Sleaty on the west bank of the River Barrow, in Co. Laois, about 1.5 km north-west from the outskirts of Carlow Town. There are the ruins of a medieval church there and some early Christian crosses; the site is marked on the 1:50,000 Ordnance Survey of Ireland Series (1997) and can be located on the Irish Grid at S716792.
20. Prologue 1 (p. 62).
21. See M. Ní Dhonnchadha, loc. cit., p. 192.

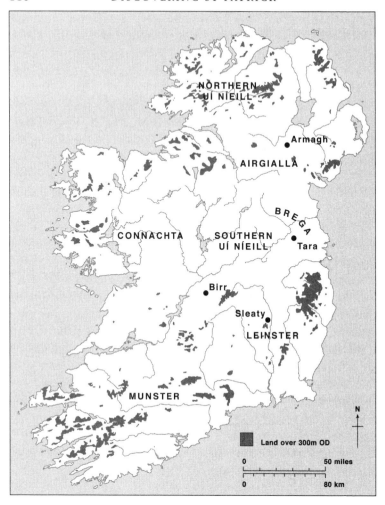

Significant places for Muirchú's *Vita Patricii*

Armagh, and so place it before 688 (as we know that the incorporation had taken place by that date). Our only other piece of
information is from a ninth-century calendar which mentions a
'Murchon' as having a feast day on 8 June. It is possible that this is
our Muirchú, and in its favour is that it would link him with a
family group near Wicklow.[22] Hence, he could have a connection

22. So argued John Colgan, the father of Irish hagiography, in the seventeenth
century, see Kenney 1929, p. 332.

with the same region as Sleaty, and also be easily aware of the growing cult of Brigit in Kildare and the work of Cogitosus. However, all these arguments are built on only a slim base of solid evidence. Like his subject Patrick, we can know far more about Muirchú's theological vision than his biography.

While among Christians today there is not a great taste for reading medieval hagiography – it is seen as embarrassing child-ish lies and superstitions – we should try to move through the 'pain threshold' and see what appealed to earlier generations of Christians and note that these works were seen as elegant within their own time and context. Muirchú's *Vita* is very typical of hagiography of the period – he would take this as a great com-pliment – and uses all the standard commonplaces found in earlier lives in Latin. He was conscious that he was doing this and is quite prepared to use this obliquely to praise Patrick: seeing the heavens opened is a commonplace, but only St Stephen in Acts and Patrick see them opened in this way! As with the nature of the *vita* it begins with Patrick's birth and ends with his death, but between those points the material is arranged in a particular way. Throughout the *Vita* and at every juncture when Muirchú wants to make a point – virtually in every chapter – there is a miracle or vision story. While we might like to prune the *Vita* of this element, to do so would denature it: it would no longer be a witness to the beliefs and world of the seventh century. These divine inter-ventions in the narrative indicate and prove, for Muirchú, the holiness of Patrick, his power as an intercessor, and the divine authority with which he worked. The work can be divided into three parts (see page 120), and from the way he writes it is clear that he thought of it as a work in three sections or 'books'.[23]

So what sources did Muirchú have to work with in building his picture of Patrick? Muirchú was aware that he did not have as much material on his subject as had many other writers of saints' lives. Already there were many details that were obscure to him, and at times we see him trying to make sense of things as best he can and at other times admitting that he does not know exactly where places were that are mentioned by Patrick. He had access

23. This can be seen in the translation given here; that other great work of hagiography from this period, Adomnán's *Vita Columbae*, is also in three books, although Adomnán is far more explicit than Muirchú in his ration-ale for a division into three books.

	Content	Themes
Part 1	Preliminaries	
	Birth Early life Slave in Ireland Escape Training Mission First few days in Ireland First Easter in Ireland and the 'trial of divinities' at Tara	Why Patrick is a saint; his authority as one commissioned by God; the origins of the Irish church in that the Irish 'nation' is baptised and so become one of the 'chosen nations' making up the whole Catholic Church.
Part 2	Dealings with mortals in Ireland	Patrick as a teacher of humanity; examples of how to behave as a Christian; and of how to honour Patrick as patron.
Part 3	Dealings with divine beings (visions and angels) during his life	Demonstration that Patrick is part of the court of heaven; that he is the intercessor of this 'chosen nation'; that his present cult – with
	Death Post-mortem wonders and cult details	its major focus in Armagh – has divine recognition.

to both the *Confessio* and the *Epistola*, and he tells us that he had the work of Ultán, and stories handed down to him. In addition, we can see that he had a copy of the *Audite omnes*, and a few other writers are echoed in his work: John Cassian (the standard work on holiness at the time); Vincent of Lérins's *Commonitorum* (a basic textbook of theology at the time); and Isidore of Seville's encyclopedia, the *Etymologiae*. From closer to home he must have seen the *Vita* of Brigit by Cogitosus, and he had a copy of Adomnán's *De locis sanctis*. Whether or not he had a copy of the *Vita Columbae* cannot be known, but he must have had other saints' lives for he shows real familiarity with the genre. Such a library would not have been out of the ordinary in his sur- roundings – indeed, we would be justified in assuming he had much more, but such works are not echoed in the *Vita*. However, he had two other sources that outweighed all these books and from which he derived models not only of what a saint should be, but to show how the work of conversion should be understood: the Christian scriptures and the liturgy. It is the integration of these last two sources that really drive his work and it is within a liturgical framework – the *Vita* was to be read within such a context – that we should understand the work and how he used his sources.

Why did Muirchú write his *Vita*?

The most common answer to this question is that he wrote as part of the propaganda of Armagh to become principal church in Ireland, or that it was indirectly to bolster the dynastic ambitions of the Uí Néill, in whose territory Armagh lay. Indeed, in some cases this motive has been so unquestioningly cited, that it is sug- gested that without the dynastic claims no one would ever bother to write such a text. This view rather cynically thinks of all reli- gious writing as somehow propaganda, and as such it must be in the service of power understood in terms of *Realpolitik*. However, while this could explain compositions such as the *Liber Angeli* or attributing a body of synodal legislation to Patrick (as happened), it does not take account of the wider motives that led to the pro- duction of *vitae* both in Ireland and in churches elsewhere. Just before the end of the first section of the *Vita*, as the finale to the Tara event, Muirchú quotes the final lines of Matthew's gospel: 'Go teach (*docete*) all the nations (*gentes*), and baptise them ... ' (Matt. 28:19). We read this verse in terms of individuals: make individuals into disciples and baptise those individuals, but Muirchú read it far more literally: nations were to be taught, and it was nations that were to be baptised. So that is Patrick's greatest feat: he taught the Irish *gens* and he baptised it on the hill of Tara. The *Vita*, when written by a member of the *gens* for others who belong to that *gens*, is as much about the identity and Christian origins of that people as it is about Patrick.

In Muirchú's world the human population is made up of 'nations' or peoples – a notion that he derived from the Old Testament – and each of these receive the message of Christ and collectively form the universal Church. In this process each nation becomes a 'chosen race (*genus*), a royal priesthood, and a holy people (*gens*) (1 Pet. 2:9). This way of thinking was confirmed by the way that the notion of the nations is used in other passages in the New Testament which speak of the spread of Christianity out-side of the people of Israel. The history of the world, as perceived by the Christian Muirchú, is one of nations, which are then bap-tised, and then form part of the final people. This final gathering was imagined in terms of the times when the mountain of the Lord would be the highest mountain and all nations would stream to it (Isa. 2), that would be in the New Jerusalem set in the midst of the nations (Ezek. 5) when will be gathered the saints from every tribe, tongue, people and nation (Rev. 5:9).

So the Irish have to be presented as a single people who already figure in the providence of God. This is achieved by thinking of the nation of the Irish as all the inhabitants on the island – Muirchú is the first to use this concept, which would be a back-bone of Irish nationalist thought a millennium later – who are distinct as a people, as a religion, and as a language. The island and its inhabitants had been thought of in this way by people from elsewhere already; Muirchú was one of the first Irish people to think of his fellow islanders in this unified way.[24] So he presents the Irish as a unified kingdom, with their own learned class, and with an appreciation of the movement of time so that they know they are part of some vast historical plan. Then Patrick comes and it is a trial of two belief systems, two priesthoods, two kingdoms: the nation's eternal destiny is at stake and the true God triumphs. The result is the nation's baptism and Patrick's great moment. This is really all that we hear about what Patrick did to preach in Ireland; this is all we hear about his evangelisation. When the story is told about Patrick's baptising the bandit Macc Cuill, the focus of the story is not on a pagan accepting Christianity, but rather a tale of the morality of repentance: Macc Cuill is every

24. See Freeman 2001; and O'Loughlin 2001c.

bandit who needs to do penance, not a pagan who embraces Christianity. Indeed, Muirchú makes a little slip in this pastoral theology that drives this point home. By the late seventh century infant baptism was the norm in Ireland, hence baptism and penance were functionally separate realities: baptism belonged to infants, penance to adults. And in the case of repentant adults the performance of a penance was essential to the forgiveness – thus, in the story, Macc Cuill has to take on a penance; but if Muirchú had checked the law he would have noted that baptism was unique in not requiring a penance! His own pastoral situation and the need to produce a repentance tale caused this usually careful writer to make a rather serious blunder!

The baptised nation now had a history as part of the people of God, and this history is the continuation of the history of the Church that can be found in the Acts of the Apostles. That book had contained the first accounts of the churches among the nations, then came other histories, and now Muirchú has added his account of a new church among another people. We see this desire to have an account of how one nation became grafted into the larger plan of history in works from before Muirchú's time: Gregory of Tours's *Historia Francorum* (*History of the Franks*) is the outstanding example, and after his time in Bede, *Historia ecclesiastica gentis Anglorum* – the history of the *gens* of the Angles as a church. For Ireland, the apostolic origin story and the account of the grafting into the unity of the whole Church is supplied by this text. In each case the nation has its own history and its own imperfect religion, it then encounters missionaries, the nation's rulers speak for the whole *gens*, and its history is fitted into a history that reaches back to the division of the world into the nations after Noah's flood.[25] In the work of Gregory of Tours this is made explicit in his opening chapters; in Bede it is divided between the *Historia* and his commentary on Genesis; in Ireland it is divided between Muirchú and the annals.

Conversion as performance

So what did Muirchú know about the process of the Christianisation of Ireland, or of Patrick's part in that work,

---

25. See Jones 1969; and Barnard 1976.

whether significant or not? Despite living far closer in time to Patrick than we do, Muirchú probably had only the same direct information on Patrick (his writings and Prosper) as we have, and less circumstantial information (for example, from archaeology) than we have. So, if even then there was so little to be known about Patrick, why was it that his cult grew up as the story of the Christianisation of Ireland? Such a question is, to an extent, meaningless, because what has happened has happened, and at no point in time is there a whole range of options clearly seen which allows someone to pick between one and another. However, there was one factor that surely helped Patrick's cult to grow as the account of the origins of Christianity: he had left writings that spoke of a time in Ireland when faith was spreading to a people who up till then had never heard of Christ. Put another way, as the Patrick cult grew, one of the great 'selling points' of that cult over that of other Irish saints' cults, was that there were writings from him that seemed to speak about the origins of the Irish – all of them – as Christians: Patrick arriving in Ireland seemed to be equivalent to Paul arriving in Galatia. We can assume that other early Christian leaders in Ireland – whether they were revered as saints after their death or not – must have written to one another or compiled sermons or something, but not one line has survived. So as the Irish churches sought to tell themselves the story of their beginnings as a church, they had to use the writings of Patrick or else have nothing that seemed to come from the earliest period. As the matter stood in the time of Muirchú, they had to take the *Confessio* and *Epistola* as their earliest records, and yet still they had almost nothing to go on as to the sequence of events that took place in their conversion. In order to fill this gap, Muirchú engaged in a form of composition that can be found in many places in the Christian scriptures: producing as history what is an ideal theological form. So, first, knowing the theology of baptism, second, knowing that his audience understood this theology through its expression in their liturgy, third, knowing the fact that Ireland has become Christian, and, fourth, that Patrick had a hand in this – he proceeds to weave a tale about how any people should be converted and particularises it by adding touches of local colour such as place names and personal names. So, for example, the story line of the Tara event is found in the Book of Daniel, as read and used in the Easter Vigil liturgy, and as understood in the context of baptisms in the liturgy, but the 'emperor' is now called Loíguire rather than Nebuchadnezzar (*Nabuchodosor*) and the scene is the Plain of Brega rather than the Plain of Dura (Dan. 3:1). At this point it is important to note a major difference between most modern readers and Muirchú's target audience: experience of liturgy. We interpret what we hear (Muirchú expected that his work would be experienced by the ear, with the reader being the lector; we come to know it as a written text[26]) in terms of what we already know; this prior structured knowledge shapes how we take on board the new information and what significance we give it. Muirchú and his audience both knew the Easter liturgy as part of the high point of their year and appreciated it in a particular way, and the Patrick story dipped into this prior common experience, and that experience gave the tale its significance.

Muirchú knows that the conversion of a people is an act of baptism, and for him baptism has three stages prior to the beginning of the new Christian life. First, there is the period of preparation, then comes the encounter with the minister of baptism who presents a series of challenges in the form of questions which force a decision to reject Satan and then to assert belief, and then comes the ritual of water. The words of the Irish wise men and the early life of Patrick form the first stage, the trials between Patrick and the magicians represent the second stage, and then there is the acceptance by the people involved and finally their baptism – those who reject baptism are simply left behind by history and Muirchú points out how they leave the script of Irish history. And when is the perfect moment for a baptism? The Easter Vigil – so that is when Ireland would be baptised by a perfect apostle!

The Easter Vigil is now almost peripheral to the Christian churches. Most of the churches of the Reformation have simply dropped it, a few Anglican churches have revived it but it is not common, and even in Roman Catholicism it is a minority event today, where even in a populous parish it is only attended by the very devout. Moreover, it is disliked by clergy and so usually trimmed to the very bone in terms of its content, and the result looks very similar today to an evening Mass. However, to appreciate Muirchú it is worth reading the text of that Vigil to see its context, and to recall that for his community it was an all-night

26. See Achtemeier 1990.

affair that began round a great bonfire and continued in the flickering light of candles for several hours as readings and ceremonies took place. If you want to see the basic range of images that were conveyed, the best text to read is the *Exultet* – which would have been heard each year in Muirchú's church.[27]

Easter night was (and technically still is) the central moment in the whole annual cycle of the liturgy.[28] It was primarily the celebration of Christ's movement from death to new life, and so from the tomb to glory. But that movement was understood in terms of a whole series of other 'movements' that were seen as anticipating or explaining the 'movement' of the resurrection. This was, in the first place, the movement of Israel across the Red Sea, which was the movement from slavery to freedom. It was also the movement from the 'Old' to the 'New Adam', which was the move from old life to new life, and this world to the world to come. It was the movement of Daniel from serving a pagan to a believing king, and this was seen as foreshadowing the transformation of the nations with the coming of the Christ. These movements were then ritualised as the old people becoming the new people, darkness giving way to light, and death giving way to life. The whole mosaic of images was there to underscore baptism, for baptism was the moment of all these transitions, both for individuals and groups. So if Patrick baptised Ireland – and this is Muirchú's 'basic' fact, then all the aspects of a baptism were present and it would take place in the way the drama of the liturgy recalls it: hence the great scene at Tara. The conversion of the nation is presented as a liturgical drama where everyone in the audience is fully familiar with the basic plot. We think of Muirchú as one of the great early hagiographers, but we could justly also think of him as the first Irish dramatist.

Pagans and Christians

One of the features of Muirchú that comes as a surprise to those whose knowledge of Christianity has been influenced by the doctrine of all denominations in the aftermath of the Reformation is

---

27. An updated text can be found in the 1970 Roman Missal; other translations of the Missal contain the older form of the text.
28. See Talley 1991, pp. 1–78 and 163–230.

his attitude to pre-Christian religion. From the sixteenth century until very recently, Christians have presented the difference between Christians and 'pagans' (i.e. non-Christians) as one of X and not-X, and it became equivalent to the 'saved' and the 'damned'. For Muirchú the situation is far more complicated because the non-Christians living after the time of Christ who have not yet heard of the Gospel are seen as equivalent to those who lived in a covenant with God before the time of Christ. And, as the coming of Christ, the world's 'sixth age', was the culmination of centuries of preparation for the Gospel, so too among those peoples who heard the Gospel later – such as those in Ireland who did not hear of it until Easter 432 – their own past was to be seen as a preparation leading to a culmination: the preaching of the Gospel by Patrick.

So there was a 'natural law' that showed people how to live, and if they lived in its accord they did not suffer with the damned but waited until the fullness of time when 'Christ would be all in all' (Col. 3:10). The just of all the ages of the world could look forward to the moment when Christ would put all his enemies under his feet (1 Cor. 15:25) and then all would be alive in Christ (1 Cor. 15:22). So in the *Vita* we see righteous, just 'pagans', who would eventually reap the reward of their justice, and equally blind 'pagans', who would reap their reward in punishment. In this way of presenting the fate of those who had not heard the gospel and who were his own ancestors, Muirchú was following a line on 'natural law' and natural goodness that could be traced back to Paul's Letter to the Romans as interpreted in some of the works of Augustine, and which was being echoed in other writings from the seventh century that mentioned the 'law of nature' as a source of law for Christians.

The advent of Jesus had been, in the view of Luke, both in the genealogy in his gospel (3:23–38) and in the story of Paul in Athens in Acts (17:15–34), something that had been prepared for from the very beginning, not only among the people of Israel but among all peoples. This had become a major theme of Christian apologetics and preaching (for example, in the work of Eusebius of Caesarea at the end of the fourth century), so that Christianity did not present itself as a break with the pre-Christian past, but rather as its fulfilment and completion. Unknown to the nations, the Spirit was at work preparing them for the final moment of full daylight when they would hear the gospel: then, and only then, would they understand themselves and their history, and appreciate the true parts and genuine prophecies of their own religion. For Luke in Acts this preparation comes with 'the altar to the unknown God' – the implication being, for exegetes until very recently, that Greek religion had advanced so far in its reflection on the nature of the divine that it recognised that there must be a god beyond all those gods whom they worshipped by name. Then the climax of that history comes about when Paul arrives there and exclaims:

> What therefore you worship as unknown, this I proclaim to you. The God who made the world and everything in it, being Lord of heaven and earth, does not live in shrines made by man, nor is he served by human hands, as though he needed anything, since he himself gives to all men life and breath and everything. And he made from one every nation of men to live on all the face of the earth, having determined allotted periods and the boundaries of their habitation, that they should seek God, in the hope that they might feel after him and find him. (Acts 17:23–7)

And then he goes on to quote one of their own poets to make the point that they should be expecting him (v. 28–9), and that 'The times of ignorance God overlooked, but now he commands all men everywhere to repent' (v. 30).

This is the exact structure that Muirchú knows must have been followed in Ireland, and therefore he imagines it. Their own wise men in 'their books of learning' – a little conceit since books came to Ireland with Christianity – had known that some new faith was coming, had predicted it in poetry, and some were ready for it when it arrived. Moreover, the whole liturgy of the 'pagans', as Muirchú imagines it, was built around an annual fire, and so they are all assembled for the great 'trial of divinities' when the Paschal fire of the Easter Vigil will flame up while the flame of the pagan liturgy will die down. This is a particularly nice touch as we know that in the later seventh century there was no moment in the whole year over which there was more controversy than fixing the night of Easter – yet, the 'pagans' could even get their ritual to fall on the same night! Not surprisingly, the notion that Easter night and the night of the 'pagan' annual festival falling on the same night (the implication being for Muirchú that God was preparing the 'pagans' for the perfect liturgy by giving them a calendar that meshed with the Christian calendar) is not original to him: Eusebius had noted that in AD 68 the date of Easter had fallen on the same day as the festival of Serapis.[29] The Irish nation had been undergoing a period of preparation, and when that had reached a climax within the whole span of history, Patrick arrived. Through him they became a Christian 'nation' and all that was best in them was relocated in the true home of goodness: the Church. We may not share Muirchú's beliefs, nor his attitude to the legibility of time, but one still has to admire the scale of his vision.

This picturing of the past by Muirchú, in terms of what would make the ideal preparation for the gospel, has, of course, an important impact on the usefulness of his work for those who are seeking the content and religion of the pagans to whom he refers. He shows no signs of any knowledge of the actual pre-Christian religion of Ireland. All his pagans are closely modelled on the pagans he read about in the Old Testament, mainly in the Books of the Kings and the Book of Daniel. Just as the great 'city' of Tara is based on what he read about Babylon, so his pagan wise men are based on Persian *magoi* (he always uses the Latin word *magus*), rather than 'Celtic druids'!

Muirchú's image of Patrick

Muirchú's method of showing Patrick's holiness is through comparisons: sometimes explicitly as when he says 'Like Moses, Patrick ...'; sometimes implicitly as when he gives a quality to Patrick that the listener is to connect with and notes the similarity between Patrick and one of the apostles or other saints. An example of this process can be seen in that at the end of the *Vita*, when Patrick's age is given as one hundred and twenty years: the listener should know that that was Moses's age when he died and is the ideal age for mortal men: Patrick is an ideal and 'like Moses'. However, the overall picture, while more detailed, is virtually identical with that found in the *Audite omnes* – Muirchú did not

---

29. Although the route by which Muirchú could have garnered this item of information is not clear.

promote his subject beyond what he already found in the tradition and the liturgy. So Patrick, the sole converter of Ireland, is made equivalent to the apostles – and indeed given apostolic powers at the final judgement. Patrick is a prophet who can see into the secret thought of human hearts, know things without being told, and foresee the future. Patrick is a law-giver who can determine cases, announce the true law, and whose judgements stand in both this world and the next. Lastly, Patrick is a salvation-bearer: through him the grace of God is made available and it is demonstrated with mighty acts of power.

Patrick, like the prophet Elijah, can stand for the whole faith in the Christian God, and can enter a trial which demonstrates to all not only that the divine power resides with Patrick's God, but that Patrick is his representative and agent on earth.[30] However, as befits this high status, Patrick has to be without blemish, and so any hint of disagreement between Patrick and other bishops is silently omitted from the picture. In Muirchú, Patrick has not only become a prophet, apostle and evangelist, but the very model of a seventh-century bishop.

Unfinished business

The *Vita* was not intended to be the last word on Patrick: Muirchú was aware that there were stories that he did not have and his desire would have been that by giving a guide to the cult of Patrick, the cult itself would develop. In this aim, his work has succeeded beyond what he could have dreamed. The *Vita* became a spring used by generation after generation to find the elements to re-invent Patrick. However, while that particular mining of the work has probably come to an end, there is still much to be found in it for understanding the development of Christianity and theology in Ireland.

30. See O'Loughlin 2003.

❦⠂❦

CHAPTER 8

Patrick the Icon

17 March: Contrasts

On the seventeenth day of March in some unknown year in the late fifth or early sixth century, somewhere in Ireland, an elderly Romano-British bishop died and was buried. He was remembered by those to whom he ministered. He was probably seen as somewhat eccentric in comparison to other clerics. We do not know whether he believed his work was a success or a failure, or whether right up to the end he believed that he was the final missionary heralding the Second Coming. His communities held his memory, but probably only in a subdued way: we do not know (apart from later traditions) where his grave is, nor have we any record of his relics until much later. These were embarrassing gaps in the cult and may explain Muirchú's inclusion of a miracle story to show that one should not disturb his grave. For many of his fellow Christians in Ireland, his passing may have been something of a relief for they considered him to be a self-proclaimed prophet disturbing the churches, and no doubt they were less than anxious to ensure his memory or message survived.

If we roll forward to the year 700 we have a different scene. In the church in Armagh, 17 March is the central patronal festival – joyfulness breaking out in the midst of Lent to celebrate the founder of this church. Likewise in Sleaty, where the liturgy almost certainly included the *Audite omnes*, this was a great feast for an 'apostle' and for the church of the Irish – their 'nation' being made part of the 'catholica'. And in numerous other churches on the island this was a feast of a local saint, which rivalled in its liturgical stress the greatest saints' cults from the rest of the Church: Patrick in Ireland was ranking with St Antony of Egypt, St Martin of Tours, and the apostles Peter and Paul in Rome. On that day, 17 March 700, we know that his cult had spread beyond the shores of Ireland. In the monastery of Iona, no doubt with Abbot Adomnán presiding, this was a feast of the first rank, not only of a local saint but of one now believed to have a connection with their own holy founder. In Peronne, then called *Peronna Scottorum* ('Peronne of the Irish'), Patrick was being celebrated as one who had moved between lands just as had its own monks. Out on the edge of the then Christian world in Echternach the feast was also being celebrated. The liturgy, the great engine of memory within the community, was transforming the obscure bishop into a prominent member of the heavenly court. Patrick had already passed into the memory of western Christians as a saint, a missionary and a patron.

If we roll forward to 2000, then on 17 March there seems to be no end to the remembering of Patrick. It is a day of 'Irishness' in every shape and form, but preferably in shamrock shapes and tones of green. From Dublin to Australia this memory is a generator of street theatre, and as good an excuse for a party as one can find. Shamrock becomes a token of Irishness, old loyalties, a willingness to party, and, incidentally, some obscure doctrine – as a theologian I would rather pass over that last bit: 'explaining' the Trinity smacks of rationalist blasphemy or heresy. On special beer mats in a local pub I can read the question 'What does the shamrock mean?' and am relieved to find that it means 'We're all going have a great time with ...' And yes, even today there is a liturgical memory within the Christian churches, but it seems peripheral – as if religion were once more cashing in on a festival. But, even there, there are some nice touches: having fought since the sixteenth century over who 'owned' Patrick, I recently heard two clerics, an Anglican and a Roman Catholic, agree that if Patrick were to return on Earth he would not understand what were the differences between them. I was tempted to add that he might be dumbfounded that the Second Coming had not yet occurred and that the idea of a party would probably have shocked him as being very far from the sobriety commanded in

1 Peter 5:8 where the devil is prowling around looking for someone to devour. We do live in different worlds.

Patrick now belongs to a special small group of Christian saints – along with St James in Spain and St Nicholas of Myra ('Santa Claus') – whose cults have grown far beyond the boundaries of liturgical memory and intercession among Christians, to become icons of identity and indeed commodities within our most general cultural memories. He is now a cultural marker that has become linked to 'craic' and friendliness. In the past he was the marker of other identities: to poor Irish emigrants his name was a muted marker of their own distinct cultural and religious identity. But that seems all over now: it's 'cool to be Irish' on St Patrick's Day! The cult rolls on and on, mutating and growing in volume. Muirchú would be shocked by the success of what he helped start. But this development of the cult and its transformation is not the concern of this book. If the basic and original inspirations of the cult have been examined – the basis of *the origins of the idea of St Patrick* – then I have done my task.

Interacting with the past

However, if the world of today, even its religious imagination for those who are Christian believers, is so distanced and changed from that of 700, much less the time of Patrick, is there any value in looking at that past except for historical curiosity? Firstly, historical curiosity is a basic human pursuit – and as an historian I need no further justification for searching out all that can be known about the distant past than that there is surviving evidence. Many who link research and scholarship to economic generation in the present might be shocked by this and describe such research as 'ornamental', but it is a fact that humans like knowing about other humans long dead and far away. And it is a great human achievement that historians have evolved a methodology for research that allows them to tease out details of the past and understand it from the most meagre of evidence. Secondly, the Patrick phenomenon continues to fascinate in the present and to be a major element in many cultural identities in the world today. Therefore, the study of the origins of that phenomenon contributes to human and cultural understanding. And this is a worthwhile project that needs no further justification. However, there is a third group who look to the past and do so from a very different standpoint: Christians for whom the Patrick event is part of their own story and identity. Has it any value for them?

Until a few hundred years ago there would have been no need to even pose this question. To seek to know more about the saints was to know more about the community of Christians of whom the saints and the living Christians were both members in different ways. To know about the saints was simply to know more about Christianity: the saint's life was a basic part of the tradition/transmission of the faith. Patrick was alive now and was active in human life now as patron and protector – to hear more about him, to seek out additional information on him was analogous to attending an evening course in one's local church nowadays to find out 'What Christianity means today.' Christians wanted to know about Patrick, but they interacted not with the information but with the saint. They asked for his intercession, they believed they received his help, and when they recalled him on his feast day, he was recalled as someone still present in the community.

Consider this little scene, which could be duplicated in almost every part of Ireland and in most parts of Europe with other saints: 4.5km east of the town of Tinahely in County Wicklow lies a little area called Toberpatrick (literally: Patrick's well). It is not even a hamlet, but just beside the road – and it is very much a 'back road' – lies a little well which long ago was built into a shrine and has now been restored as part of a local heritage initiative.[1] This well provided clean water to those in its immediate vicinity, and was reputed to cure various ailments and so would have attracted people in need from a wide area, and it was a focus of local community ritual from time to time. The well's existence there was perceived as Patrick's gift to them of clean and convenient water, its healings were not seen as due to some inherent quality in the water, such as might attract people to a spa, but due to the ongoing care of the patron, and it was part of belonging to that locality to celebrate at that well on its feast day. Patrick seemed intimate to the community, to be active within it, and so knowing more about him was the most natural thing in the world.

1. On the Ordnance Survey of Ireland 1:50,000 series (1995) the area and the well are marked and named: Irish Grid T081725.

And, since that well is less than 50km from Sleaty along a natural corridor between hills, there is every possibility that that cult site to Patrick may go back to the time of Muirchú or even earlier.

In more recent centuries interest in the Christian past and the saints has had a harder time in justifying itself as a worthwhile activity. Saints should be those who provide moral examples or whose writings 'inspire' us. Patrick has thus become a model for foreign missionaries – or, at least, for those Christians for whom missionary activity is morally acceptable – and a model of perseverance and peace making. However, all such inspirational interpretations tend to rely on the sanitised general image of the saint rather than the specifics. Most of the missionaries, for example, who invoke Patrick as a model would not like to be linked to 'evangelists' who are predicting the end of the world on religious TV. As for the cult documents, nothing written by Muirchú would today be found inspiring as moral example. Recently, someone wrote on Patrick as the 'patron for the environmental movement among Christians', but on closer examination this turned out to be based on the fact that Patrick is linked with the colour green (a result of his use within Irish nationalist movements in recent centuries), and environmentalists are 'greens'. Saints, unless they deal with our great issues, seem to be redundant.

Today, when questioned as to the value for Christian theology or spirituality of engaging with these ancient memories and of reading these texts, I try suggesting the following – and it applies equally to all ancient texts from the Christian tradition, not just the dossiers of saints. I can only understand myself when I come into contact with some other human being; I can only understand my own or my culture's appreciation of Christianity when it comes into contact with another's image of the Christian. Here lies a paradox at the heart of human understanding, and I believe especially of religious understanding: I only know and appreciate what is close to me, through confronting that which is most alien to me. This confrontation can take three forms. There can be a clash whereby anything that is different from me is declared deviant. This has been the dominant mode in which different groups of Christians have met one another for most of their history: difference equals the enemy and sectarianism and self-righteousness follow closely behind. It has also been the mode in which most encounters between Christianity and other religions have occurred in recent centuries. The second mode of confrontation is that the 'other' is seen as irrelevant and is simply ignored. This policy ignores the experience of other living groups as having anything really worthwhile to contribute to self-understanding, but similarly there is nothing that is worth getting upset over. There is no need for the other because I and my group or period know all we need to know about our religions or our pursuit of Christian discipleship. Dialogue with living groups in this mode is no more than civic courtesy, while interaction with past groups is no more than a curious background filler of anti-quarian interest. This mode may appear a much better option that the mode of clashing with the other in terms of avoiding religious or cultural imperialism or worse, but as a theological strategy it is just as isolated. Unless I engage with the other, I remain unknown to myself; a group that does not engage with other groups forgets that it lives in a culturally conditioned box and cannot discover the limits of that box. History is littered with Christian cultures that were so unaware of what really constituted 'Christian' action that we stand aghast at what was done in the name of religion, Christ or God. Self-awareness of our beliefs is not a given in human societies, and self-critical awareness is not automatic for Christians; to remove our blinkers requires dialogue with the other, facing hard questions, and making painful adjustments. We can quickly see the blinkers of the past – we saw that Muirchú's Christianity had no difficulty with slavery – but we must acknowledge that we are not the first generation without limitations, itself a painful realisation in our culture.

If to see what I really believe, I need another, and if in hard dialogue with that other I see limitations on both sides, then that other can be a culture different from my own today or a culture in the past which is different, even if I see myself and my own group as the modern descendants of that past. Dialogue, if it is to be as embracing as possible, must take place not just with the past 'other', or with today's living 'other', but with as many others as possible. Each dialogue has its own difficulties, each its own benefits, and here lies the value of studying the foreign world of Patrick, the world of the early insular Christians, or the world of the hagiographers. Even if one has no sense of being their spiritual descendants or successors, they show us an experience of the

Christian faith that can bring our own into relief. There is no ideal church, of which the human churches are copies of varying perfection, there are only the real groups that have treasured the memory of the Christ and been empowered by the Spirit, and because of this, to study any 'other' Christian experience is to consult more widely across the whole tapestry of what it is to be Christian. The very alien church world of Patrick is as much a part of the 'Christian thing' as is our own. When we struggle in these dialogues we are enriched as we try to understand a different world of belief, for we understand our own a little more clearly.

Part 2

❧❧

CHAPTER 1

The *Confessio* of St Patrick[1]

The translation is based on the edition of White (1905) but it takes account both of the edition of Bieler (1952) and the work of Howlett (1994). It has also been compared with other translations and studies to see where their notes might add to an understanding of the text.

1. The common title of Patrick's longer work; while the work does not have this title in some early manuscripts, we can consider it an authentic description of what Patrick wanted to write, as he uses the term at the end of the work: 'And this is my declaration (*confessio mea*) before I die.' The meaning of the title, in Latin, is also problematic. Our first instinct is to think of it as a 'confession' in the sense of a reply to his critics – an autobiographical work which fulfils a function somewhat like John Henry Newman's *Apologia pro vita sua* – and such a reply to critics does appear to be part of Patrick's motivation in writing. Another way of looking at the work has been to interpret *confessio* in the sense of a declaration or confession of faith (*confessio/professio fidei*). Again, the expression of his Trinitarian faith lends support to this way of understanding *confessio*. However, neither of these understandings of *confessio* addresses the fact that many events are retold by Patrick simply as they deserve to be known for they are seen by him as significant in that they testify to the work of God in his life and deeds. When we look at various uses of the term *confessio* in the scriptures in Latin, a different view emerges. It is a praise of the Lord for his strength (Ps. 95:6) and of his majesty and righteousness (Ps. 110:3). It involves telling of the glory which he shares with his people (Ps. 148:14). A confession is a song of God's works, his mighty deeds, and of his mercies towards his people (Ps. 88:2). It is part of the duty of the disciple to offer thanks and acknowledge publicly the gifts of God, that one is in his debt, and that one belongs to him and seeks to do his will in one's actions (Ezra 10:11). This sense is made even more clear in some passages in the New Testament. Confession is part of holding fast to

It has long been recognised that Patrick used written materials, besides the scriptures, in this work.[2] And recently, this realisation has led to a massive study of possible sources, or at least parallels, of the ideas found in Patrick.[3] However, the concentration here has been on adding a biblical apparatus in order to show the extent of Patrick's familiarity with the Christian scriptures.[4]

Patrick's declaration of the great works of God

[1][5] I am Patrick. I am a sinner[6]: the most unsophisticated of people; the least among all the Christians[7]; and, to many, the most contemptible. I am the son of the deacon Calpornius, as he was the son of the priest Potitus who belonged to the village on Bannavem Taburniae. Indeed, near it he had a small estate from where, when aged about sixteen, I was taken captive. I was then ignorant of the true God and, along with thousands upon

---

the work of Christ as the high priest who has made all nations acceptable to the Father (Heb. 4:14), and this activity of confession is testimony to Christian hope (Heb. 10:23). It is an aspect of fighting the good fight of the Christian to testify to Christ's saving work in the presence of others (1 Tim. 6:12), and in this the Christian imitates Christ, who testified to God's power in the presence of Pilate [cf. John 18:37] (1 Tim. 6:13). If we look on Patrick's account of what God did through him in this light, then his *confessio* is but another part of his own service of God, which is the preaching of the gospel to those who have not heard it (cf. Rom. 15:16; 1 Cor. 9:12–3).

2. For example, Bieler 1953, p. 15, wrote: 'It would certainly be a gross exaggeration to say that he knew no other book than the Bible. There is evidence of his acquaintance with the writings of Sts. Cyprian and Augustine.'

3. Conneely 1993.

4. While every edition and translation of Patrick has provided some biblical apparatus, that of Conneely far outstripped them. Conneely has been used extensively, but selectively, here, and other references have been added. In every case, the biblical numeration followed is that of the LXX/Vulgate. While this is inconvenient, especially with regard to the Psalms, the alternative would have burdened the text with additional notes, as many of Patrick's biblical allusions can only be understood in relation to the Vetus Latina or Vulgate versions.

5. The division of this work, and the Letter to Coroticus, into sections is the work of White 1905, and has been followed in all subsequent editions and translations.

6. Cf. 1 Tim. 1:15; 1 Tim. 1:9; 1 Cor. 15:9.

7. Cf. Eph. 3:8.

thousands of others, was taken into captivity in Ireland. This occurred according to our merits for we had pulled back from God[8]; we did not keep his commandments[9]; and we did not listen to our priests[10] who kept on warning us regarding 'our salvation'.[11] And 'so' the Lord 'poured upon' us 'the heat of his anger'[12] and dispersed us among many peoples[13] right 'out to the very ends of the earth',[14] where now my smallness[15] is seen among these men of an alien land.

[2] And there the Lord 'opened my understanding to my unbelief',[16] so that however late, I might become conscious of my failings.[17] Then remembering my need, I might 'turn with all my heart to the Lord my God.'[18] For it was he who 'looked on my lowliness'[19] and had mercy on the ignorance of my youth,[20] and who looked after me[21] before I knew him and before I had gained wisdom or could distinguish between good and evil.[22] Indeed, as a father consoles his son,[23] so he protected me.[24]

8. Cf. Deut. 32:15.
9. Cf. Gen. 26:5.
10. Cf. Dan. 9:4–6.
11. The Latin, *qui nostram salutem*, echoes the Nicene Creed (*qui propter nos homines et propter nostram salutem*).
12. Isa. 42:25.
13. The concept of dispersal among the nations as a divine punishment for infidelity is found in many places in the Old Testament, but especially in the prophets where it is presented as a just reward of the people: Lev. 26:33, 38; Deut. 4:27; Ps. 106:27; 1 Chr. 16:35; Jer. 9:16; Lam. 1:3; 2:9; Hos. 9:17; Zech. 10:9; Ezra 4:13; 5:14; 6:8; 11:16; 12:15–16; 20:23; 22:15; 25:10; 29:12; 30:23, 26; 32:9; 36:19; 39:28; and it is found in Joel 2:19 and 3:2 – a prophet is echoed in the next section – and in Tobit 13:4–7 which seems to be reflected in several ways by Patrick in this section.
14. Acts 1:8; and cf. Acts 13:47.
15. Cf. Jer. 45:15 (and Obad. 2).
16. A conflation of Luke 24:45 and Heb. 3:12.
17. Cf. Ps. 24:16–18.
18. Joel 2:12–3.
19. Luke 1:48; and cf. Ps. 24:16–8.
20. Cf. Ps. 24:5.
21. Cf. Ps. 24:7.
22. 1 Kings 3:9; Gen. 3:5.
23. Cf. Luke 11:11–13.
24. Cf. Wisd. 4:17.

[3] So it would be neither right nor proper[25] for me to do any-thing but to tell you all of the many blessings and great grace which the Lord saw fit to give me in the land of my captivity.[26] I tell you these things because this is how we return thanks to God,[27] that after being corrected and having come to an aware-ness of God,[28] that we glorify and bear witness to his wonderful works[29] in the presence of every nation under heaven.[30]

[4] For there is not, nor ever was, any other God – there was none before him and there shall not be any after him[31] – besides him who is God the Father unbegotten: without a source, from him everything else takes its beginning. He is, as we say, the one who keeps hold of all things.[32]

And his Son, Jesus Christ, whom we profess to have always existed with the Father. He was spiritually with the Father before the world came into being; begotten of the Father before the beginning of anything in a way that is beyond our speech. And through him all things were made, all things visible and in-visible.[33] He was made man, and having conquered death was taken back into the heavens to the Father.[34] 'And [the Father] has bestowed on him all power above every name in heaven and on earth and under the earth, so that every tongue may confess that [our] Lord and God is Jesus Christ'[35] in whom we believe. And we look forward to his coming, in the time that is soon to be, when he will be judge of the living and the dead, 'who will repay each one according to his works.'[36]

And '[the Father] has plentifully poured upon us the Holy Spirit',[37] the gift and pledge of immortality, who makes those who

25. Cf. 2 Cor. 12:1.
26. Cf. 2 Chr. 6:36–8 (this phrase is also found in Jer. 30:16 and 46:27).
27. Cf. Ps. 115:12; 1 Thess. 3:9
28. Cf. Eph. 4:14.
29. Ps. 88:6.
30. Acts 2:5.
31. Cf. Isa. 43:10–11.
32. Cf. Col. 1:17.
33. Cf. John 1:3; Col. 1:16.
34. Cf. Mark 16:19.
35. Phil. 2:9–11.
36. Rom. 2:6.
37. Titus 3:5–6.

believe and listen into 'sons of God' the Father 'and fellow heirs with Christ'.[38] [This is] who we confess and adore, One God in Trinity of sacred name.

[5] As he himself said through the prophet: 'Call upon me in the day of trouble; I will deliver you, and you shall glorify me'.[39] And elsewhere he said: 'it is honourable to acknowledge and reveal the works of God'.[40]

[6] But even if I am imperfect in many things I want my brothers and relatives[41] to know the sort of man I am, so that they may understand what it is to which I have committed my soul.

[7] I am not forgetting 'the testimony of' my 'Lord'[42] who testifies in the Psalms: 'You destroy those who speak lies'[43] and who elsewhere says: 'the lying mouth kills the soul'.[44] Again, the same Lord says in the gospel: 'I tell you, on the day of judgement men will render account for every careless word they utter'.[45]

[8] So with all my heart I dread, 'with fear and trembling,'[46] this sentence on that day,[47] which no one can evade or hide from,[48] when every single one of us shall 'render an account' of even the least sins 'before the judgement seat of' the Lord 'Christ'.[49]

38. The notion of 'sons' is found in many places in the New Testament (e.g. Matt. 5:9), as is that of 'heirs' (e.g. Gal. 3:29), but the passage behind this phrase of Patrick appear to be Rom. 8:14–19.
39. Ps. 50:15.
40. Tobit 12:7.
41. Cf. Luke 21:16.
42. 2 Tim. 1:8, the implicit statement is that as Paul, the prisoner, warned Timothy 'never be ashamed of your testimony to our Lord', so Patrick has taken the apostle's advise and is not ashamed of his testimony.
43. Ps. 5:6.
44. Wisd. 1:11.
45. Matt. 12:36.
46. Eph. 6:5.
47. Here Patrick echoes the theme of the great and terrible day of judgement which is found in the prophets, e.g. Isa. 24:21; Jer. 25:33, and again in the New Testament, e.g. Rom 2:16; Luke 10:12.
48. There is an echo here of Adam and Eve hiding in the garden (Gen. 3:10) and of Cain after murdering Abel (Gen. 4:9).
49. Rom. 14:12 and 10.

[9] For these reasons I have thought of writing this account this long while, but held back until now as I was afraid of the attack of men's tongues, and because I have not been a student like other men who in the very best manner have drunk equally in law and sacred letters.[50] They have never had to change their speech since infancy, rather they were always adding to the command of language and bringing it to perfection. My words and speech,[51] however, are translated into an alien language, and you can easily assess the quality of my instruction and learning from a taste of my writing. For as the wise man says: 'For wisdom becomes known through speech, and education through the words of the tongue.'[52]

[10] But what use is even a true excuse, especially when there is an element of presumption in it? Since now, as an old man, I desire to have what I did not acquire in my youth. Then my sins blocked me from gaining a firm grasp on what I had already read. But will anyone believe me if I repeat [the reason I came to proper learning so late in life]? I was young, indeed almost a speechless boy, when I was taken captive. And at that time did not yet know what I ought to desire and what I ought to avoid. So today it is with shame and very great fear that I lay bare my lack of expertise and polish. The situation is this: to the learned I am unable make my meaning clear[53] with the brevity my spirit and mind desire and the disposition towards which my understanding points.[54]

[11] But if I had been given the same chance as the rest, then without a doubt, 'for the sake of the reward,'[55] 'I' would 'not keep silent.'[56] And, if it seems to some that I am being arrogant in making my declaration – I with my lack of learning and my 'slow tongue'[57] – then note that it is written: 'The tongue of the

50. Cf. 2 Tim. 3:14–15.
51. Cf. John 8:43.
52. Sir. 4:29.
53. Cf. Qo 1:8.
54. This sentence, and especially the last part of it, is unclear; it baffled medieval readers, who in turn contributed to the bafflement of modern editors. It has been emended in several ways, none of them wholly satisfactory. What is given here is a rendering that seeks to reflect the overall direction of the sentence's meaning.
55. Ps. 118:112; and cf. Ps. 115:12.
56. Isa. 62:1.
57. Exod. 4:10.

stammerers will learn quickly to speak peace.'[58] So how much more then should we want this; we who are, as it says, 'the letter of Christ for salvation unto the uttermost parts of the earth.'[59] And, although this letter is not a learned one, it is 'one delivered' with strength,[60] 'written in our hearts not with ink, but with the Spirit of the living God.'[61] And again, 'the Spirit bears witness'[62]: 'For the Most High also created the things of the farm-yard.'[63]

[12] So at first, I was a rustic[64] and a wanderer[65] without any learning 'who knew not how to provide for what would come

58. Isa. 32:4 (This is a Vetus Latina/Septuagint reading).
59. This sentence is a conflation of 2 Cor. 3:2-3 and Acts 13:47.
60. The manuscripts are corrupt at this point having either *ratum* or *rata* and several editors have held that the text is beyond restoration. However, if the readings are corrupt, this does not put the text in doubt for clearly its meaning is linked to both 'the letter of Christ' and 'written in our hearts'. Patrick has combined two verses out of sequence: 2 Cor. 3:3 (*quod epistola estis Christi, ministrata a nobis, et scripta non attramento*) with 2 Cor. 3:2 (*Epistola nostra uos estis, scripta in cordibus*) to make his point. Hence *rata* in some manuscripts is a legacy of *ministrata*; and *ratum* in other manuscripts is a clumsy attempt to make some sense of '*rata*'.
61. 2 Cor. 3:2–3; Patrick's familiarity with the text of Scripture, as well as his competence in handling it, can be observed in this quotation, where the elements of Paul's argument are rearranged without loss of meaning, yet in a way which reinforced the exact point he wishes to make. The text of 2 Cor. 3:2–3 reads (RSV): 'You yourselves are our letter of recommendation, written on your hearts, to be known and read by all men; and you show that you are a letter from Christ delivered by us, written not with ink but with the Spirit of the living God, not on tablets of stone but on tablets of human hearts.'
62. Heb. 10:15, the notion of the Spirit bearing witness is found on several occasions in the New Testament (John 15:25; Rom. 8:16; and 1 John 5:7), but the usage here is a more specifically linked linguistically and theologically with Hebrews. Linguistically there is an echo of Hebrews (*Contestatur autem nos et Spiritus sanctus*) in Patrick (*Et iterum Spiritus testatur*); theologically, the Spirit's witness is used in an exactly parallel way: in both a christological point is witnessed to by the Spirit in that there is a text in the Old Testament to support it, which is then quoted.
63. Sir. 7:16.
64. Cf. 1 Tim. 1:13 in the Vetus Latina; cf. White 1918, p. 4.
65. This word, *profuga*, in most translations of Patrick is rendered as 'exile', I am rendering it as 'wanderer' as it seems that Patrick, in a foreign land away from his family as a punishment for his sins, is seeing himself as like Cain who in (the Vetus Latina version of) Genesis is send off to wander (Gen. 4:12); cf. *Epistola* 1.

later.'66 But I know one thing without any doubt and with the greatest of assurance: that 'before I was punished'67 I was like a stone lying in the deepest mire68; and then, 'he who is mighty'69 came and, in his mercy, raised me up.70 He most truly raised me on high and set me on the top of the rampart.71 So I ought to cry out with all my strength and render thanks to the Lord for his blessings are indeed great, here and in eternity, and beyond all that the human mind can imagine.

[13] So now, be amazed 'you both small and great that fear God'72 and all you learned ones, all you clever speakers, listen and examine what you hear. [Now tell me:] who was it that raised me up a fool from the midst of you who seem to be wise men and 'experts in the law'73 and 'powerful in word'74 and in every other matter? But indeed, [God] inspired me, the detestable of this world75 – if that is what I am, above others so that I should faithfully serve, 'with fear and reverence'76 and 'without blame',77 the people to whom Christ's love brought me,78 and to whom he gave me for the rest of my days should I be found worthy. In effect, that is that I should truly serve them with humility.79

[14] And so it is proper and right 'in the measure of faith'80 in the Trinity, to make clearly known 'the gift of God'81 and his 'eternal

---

66. Qo 4:13.
67. Ps. 118:67.
68. Cf. Ps. 68:15 and v. 2 of the same Ps.
69. Luke 1:49.
70. Cf. Ps. 114:14.
71. Cf. Ps. 112:7–8.
72. Rev. 19:5.
73. Luke 7:30 (and cf. Luke 10:25; 11:45; 11:46; 11:52; 14:52; Titus 3:13).
74. Luke 24:19 (and cf. Acts 7:22; 18:24).
75. Cf. 1 Cor. 1:20; 3:19.
76. Heb. 12:28.
77. This notion that one of the qualities of the holy people is living blamelessly is found in many places in the Wisdom literature (Wisd. 10:5; 10:15; 13:6; 18:21; Sir. 8:10) and in Paul (Phil. 2:15; 3:6; 1 Thess. 2:10; 3:13; 5:23).
78. Cf. 2 Cor. 5:14.
79. Cf. Acts 20:19.
90. Rom. 12:3.
81. John 4:10.

consolation'.[82] And, to do this 'without hesitating'[83] at the dangers involved. Likewise it is proper to spread abroad the name of God, trustingly and 'without fear',[84] so that even 'after my death'[85] I may leave something of value to the many thousands of people, my brothers and sons, whom I have baptised in the Lord.

[15] And I was not worthy[86] in any way for what the Lord was to grant to his servant after tribulations, many setbacks, captivity, and many long years. He gave me a great grace towards that people [among whom I had been captive]. This was something I had never thought of, nor hoped for, in my youth.

[16] But then, when I had arrived in Ireland and was spending every day looking after flocks, I prayed frequently each day. And more and more,[87] the love of God and the fear of him grew [in me], and [my] faith was increased [88] and [my] spirit was quickened,[89] so that in a day I prayed up to a hundred times, and almost as many in the night. Indeed, I even remained in the wood and on the mountain to pray. And – come hail, rain or snow – I was up before dawn to pray, and I sensed nothing of evil nor any other spiritual laziness in me.[90] I now understand why this was so, at that time 'the Spirit was fervent'[91] in me.

[17] And it was there indeed, that one night I heard a voice which said to me: 'Well have you fasted. Very soon you are to travel to your homeland.' And again, not long after that, I heard 'a revelation'[92] which said to me: 'Behold! Your ship is prepared.' But the

---

82. Cf. 2 Thess. 2:16.
83. Cf. Phil. 2:15.
84. Phil. 1:14.
85. 2 Pet. 1:15.
86. Cf. Matt. 8:8.
87. Cf. Phil. 1:9.
88. Cf. Luke 17:5.
89. Cf. Rom. 8:14.
90. Higgins 1995, has shown that this passage (from 'And more and more') was written in imitation of the Canticle of the Three Youths in Dan. 3:52–90.
91. Acts 18:25, and cf. Rom. 12:11.
92. Rom. 11:4 (this word *responsus* in Paul (NRSV: 'a divine reply') is used by Patrick (and later by Muirchú) as a technical term for what is said by God during or after a vision – in order to reflect this usage it is translated here,

ship was not nearby, but maybe two hundred miles away[93] where I had never been and where I knew nobody. Soon after that I took flight leaving the man I had been with for six years. And I travelled[94] 'in the power of God',[95] who directed my path[96] towards the good, and I feared nothing[97] until I arrived at the ship.

[18] The ship was about to depart on the very day I arrived and I said [to those on board] that I wanted to sail with them from there. But this was displeasing to the vessel's master who, with disdain, answered me sharply: 'No way can you ask to travel with us!' So having heard that I went away from them towards the hut where I was taking shelter. And on the way I began to pray. And before I finished my prayer I heard one of the crew shouting loudly after me: 'Come! Quickly! These men here are calling you.' So I turned back towards them at once and they said to me: 'Come on, we are taking you on faith. So show your friendship with us according to whatever custom you choose.' But on that day I refused to suck their nipples,[98] on account of the fear of God,[99]

and elsewhere it occurs, as 'a revelation.' When the uses of this word are drawn together a picture of its meaning appears: i.e. God is explaining what is happening to him in his life.

93. Cf. Rev. 14:20 where 1600 *stadia* (equal to 200 *millia passuum*) is given as an expression of a great distance; that 8 *stadia* made up a mile was common knowledge to anyone with even a basic Roman education and anyone growing up in a decurion's household would have known this in the way that anyone who grew up in the countryside until recently would have known its modern equivalent: 8 furlongs made up a mile.

94. The Latin reads: *Et ueni*, lit. 'And I came'; this use of 'I came', when the context requires 'I went', may be an echo of 1 Cor. 2:1: *Et ego, cum uenissem ad uos.*

95. 1 Cor. 2:5.

96. Cf. Tobit 4:20; 1 Thess. 3:11.

97. Cf. Ps. 22:4.

98. This phrase has troubled editors and translators of Patrick for centuries. In fact, 'to suck the nipples' is an Old Irish expression, and no doubt a symbolic practice as well, describing the appeal of an inferior for the protection and friendship of a superior. The significance of Patrick's refusal was that he did not want to enter into a formal agreement of protection with them, and thus deny them his intimate friendship, as they were pagans. It has been pointed out that the use of this Irish phrase indicates that Patrick sailed in a ship crewed by Irishmen. Cf. Ryan 1938. However, it could also be an allusion to Isa. 60:16 as it is found in the Vulgate.

99. Neh. 5:15.

but despite this I stayed with them for I hoped that some of them would come to faith in Jesus Christ – for they all belonged to 'the nations.'[100] And without any further ado, we got under weigh.

[19] We landed after three days and for [the next] twenty-eight days we made our way through a desert. And when their food ran out, starvation overcame them.[101] So one of the days the master asked me: 'So now Christian, you explain to us why were are in this mess. Your God is great and all powerful,[102] so why are you not able to pray for us? We who are on the very brink with hunger and it seems unlikely we will ever see another human being.' So I boldly said to them: '"Turn" in trust and "with your whole heart"[103] to the Lord, my God to whom nothing is impossible,[104] that today he may send food to satisfy you on your journey – for he has an abundance everywhere.'[105] And then, with God's help, it happened. Behold a herd of swine appeared before our eyes on the road,[106] and they killed many of them. They made camp there for two nights,[107] and, with their fill of pork, they were well restored[108] for many of them had dropped out[109] and had been left 'half dead' by the road side.[110] And after this they thanked God mightily, and I became honourable in their eyes.[111] From then on they had an abundance of food. As well as this they came across some wild honey[112] and 'offered some of it'[113] to me. Then

---

100. Patrick uses the word *gentes* in the biblical sense of what we call 'pagans'.
101. Cf. Gen. 12:10.
102. Cf. Deut. 10:17.
103. Joel 2:12.
104. Luke 1:37.
105. This is patterned on the Exodus desert experience, cf. Exod. 16:12.
106. This appearance of a herd of swine, on cue, for a demonstration of the power of God has echoes of the herd in the land of the Gadarenes in the Synoptic Gospels: cf. Matt. 8:28ff.
107. *Manserunt*; there is an echo here of the *mansiones*, the stopping places, of the people of Israel in the desert.
108. For the basis of this reading cf. Higgins 1995, pp. 130–1.
109. Cf. Matt. 15:32.
110. Luke 10:30.
111. This is a motif from several of the prophets (e.g. the Naaman story in 2 Kings 5) of the God of Israel showing his power, who was then thanked by the pagans, and his prophet held in honour.
112. Cf. Matt. 3:4.
113. Luke 24:42.

one of them said: 'This has been offered as a sacrifice'[114] But thanks be to God, I tasted none of it.

[20] That very night, while I was sleeping, Satan strongly tried me – I shall remember it 'as long as I am in the body'.[115] Something like an enormous rock fell on top of me and I lost all power over my limbs. But where did it come to me, for I was ignorant in spiritual matters, that I should call on Helias?[116] And at this point I saw the sun rise in the sky and while I called out 'Helia, Helia' with all my strength, behold the sun's splendour fell on me and dispelled immediately all the heaviness from upon me. And I believe that Christ, my Lord, assisted me and his Spirit had already cried out through me.[117] And I hope it will be so 'in the day of my distress'[118] as it says in the gospel: 'On that day' the Lord declares, 'it is not you who speak, but the Spirit of your Father who will speak in you.'[119]

[22][120] And as we travelled [the Lord] looked after us with food, fire, and dry-shelter each day, until after fourteen days[121] we came into human society. As I mentioned already, we journeyed for twenty-eight days through the desert and on the very night

114. Cf. 1 Cor. 10:28.
115. 2 Pet. 1:13.
116. This calling on Helias is one of the knottiest problems in this text: is he calling on the Sun as a god or as a divine sacrament (the Greek for Sun is Helios); or calling on Elijah ([H] elias in Latin) – some who heard Christ calling out on the Cross thought he was calling on Elijah (cf. Matt. 27:47).
117. Cf. Rom. 8:26.
118. Ps. 50:15.
119. Matt. 10:19–20.
120. In all the MSS n. 21 follows at this point, where it clearly does not belong as it interrupts the story of what happened on the twenty-eight days in 'the desert' from leaving the ship to reaching civilisation, hence some editors leave it in sequence but place it in brackets. However, it is clear that it belongs later than the days in the desert, but before Patrick received his mission to Ireland. Therefore, between 22 and 23 seems a logical place. An examination of the language adds some support to this. Having reached civilisation, 21 begins: *Et iterum post annos multos* ...; and then 23 begins: *Et iterum post paucos annos*, ... he is back with his family after his great tribulations.
121. Some MSS read: 'after ten days'.

we reached humanity, we had none of the food left.[122]

[21] And after many years, I was once again taken captive. But on the very first night I was with them, I heard a divine revelation[123] which said to me: 'You will remain with them for two months.' This is exactly what happened and on the sixtieth night 'the Lord freed me from their hands.'[124]

[23] And after a few years I was again with my parents in Britain who gave me a son's welcome. They, in good faith, begged me – after all those great tribulations I had been through – that I should go nowhere, nor ever leave them. And it was there, I speak the truth, that 'I saw a vision of the night'[125]: a man named Victoricus – 'like one'[126] from Ireland – coming with innumerable letters. He gave me one of them and I began to read what was in it: 'The voice of the Irish'. And at that very moment as I was reading out the letter's opening, I thought I heard the voice of those around the wood of Foclut which is close to the Western Sea. It was 'as if they were shouting with one voice'[127]: 'O "Holy Boy",[128] we beg you to come again and walk among us.' And I was 'broken hearted'[129] and could not read anything more. And at that moment I woke up. Thank God, after many years the Lord granted them what they called out for.

[24] And on another night, either in me or close to me – 'I do not know, God knows'[130] – I heard them using the most learned words. But I could not understand them, except what became

---

122. This coincidence of leaving the desert and running out of the food miraculously provided on the journey is modelled on Josh. 5:12 which declares that the manna ceased on the day the people entered Canaan.
123. Rom. 11:4.
124. Gen. 37:21.
125. Dan. 7:13.
126. Dan. 7:13.
127. Dan. 3:51.
128. Patrick's Latin reads *Rogamus te sancte puer*; the term *sanctus puer* is probable his rendering of his Irish nickname, given him as a result of people observing how often he prayed. I owe the suggestion that 'Holy Boy' is a nickname to Freeman 2004, p. 50.
129. Ps. 108:16; and cf. Acts 2:37.
130. 2 Cor. 12:2.

clear towards the end of the speech: 'He who "gave his life"[131] for you, he it is who speaks in you.' And at that point I woke up, and was full of joy.

[25] And on another occasion I saw him praying in me, and it was as if I was inside my body and I heard [him] over me, that is over 'the inner man'[132] and he was praying there powerfully with sighs.[133] And in my excitement and astonishment[134] I wondered who it could be that was praying in me? But towards the end of the prayer it became clear[135] that it was the Spirit. Just then I awoke and remembered what was said through the apostle: 'Likewise the Spirit helps the weaknesses of our prayers; for we do not know how to pray as we ought, but the Spirit himself intercedes for us with ineffable sighs which cannot be expressed in words.'[136] And again it says: 'The Lord is our Advocate,[137] he intercedes for us.'[138]

[26] And when some of my superiors challenged me coming up with my sins against my toilsome episcopate – for truly on that day 'I was struck' mightily 'so that I was falling'[139] here and in eternity – then did the Lord in his goodness spare the convert and the stranger 'for his name's sake'.[140] And he powerfully came to my aid in this battering so that I did not slip badly into the wreck-

131. Cf. John 10:11.
132. Eph. 3:16; and Rom. 7:22.
133. Cf. Rom. 8:26.
134. Cf. Isa. 29:9; and Acts 2:12; 8:13.
135. The same phrase is used in [24] and here: *ad postremum orationis sic efficiatus est.* In [24] I have rendered *oratio* as 'speech', but here as 'prayer'; this shift in words is to convey a nuance of developing awareness in Patrick: in the first case he seems unclear about what is happening except (*nisi*) for the final part; in the second case he seems clear that it concerns prayer, but he still had a question and (*sed*) it became clearer in the final part: it was the Spirit who was praying.
136. Rom. 8:26.
137. Cf. 1 John 2:1.
138. Rom. 8:27, 34.
139. Ps. 117:13.
140. Ps. 106:8, but while the notion of being delivered from trial for the Lord's name's sake is found in the Synoptics, it is the verbal form of Ps. 106 that Patrick has in mind: cf. Matt. 19:29; 24:9. Patrick sees himself in the tribulation prophesied in the gospel.

age of sin and into infamy. I pray God that 'it may not charged against them'[141] as sin.

[27] 'The charge they brought'[142] against me was something from thirty years earlier which I had admitted[143] before I was even a deacon. Once when I was anxious and worried I hinted to [my] dearest friend about something I had done one day – indeed in one hour – in my youth, for I had not then prevailed over [my sinfulness]. 'I do not know, God knows'[144] if I was then fifteen years old, and I was not a believer in the true God nor had I ever been,[145] but I remained in death and non-belief until I was truly punished[146] and, in truth, brought low by daily deprivations of hunger and nakedness.[147]

[28] Quite the opposite, when I went to Ireland, not of my own volition, I was nearly defeated. But this [captivity] was very good for me for I was corrected by the Lord; and, he prepared me for what I am today – a state I was then far away from – when I have the pastoral care, and many duties, for the salvation of others, but at that time I was not even concerned for myself.

[29] And so came the day when I was rejected[148] by those I have mentioned; and on that night: 'I saw a vision of the night.'[149] [I

---

141. 2 Tim. 4:16, Patrick sees himself as one opposed in a trial as 'Paul' says he was opposed by Alexander the coppersmith: 'Alexander the coppersmith did me great harm; the Lord will requite him for his deeds. Beware of him yourself, for he strongly opposed our message. At my first defence no one took my part; all deserted me. May it not be charged against them! But the Lord stood by me and gave me strength to proclaim the message fully, that all the Gentiles might hear it. So I was rescued from the lion's mouth (2 Tim. 4:14–17).
142. Dan. 6:5.
143. The text reads *confessus fueram* which has often been translated as 'I had confessed', but this is a false-friend as it suggests something like 'aural confession' or 'Confession' in later Catholic tradition; but any such formal interpretation would be anachronous.
144. 2 Cor. 12:2.
145. Literally: 'nor [had I believed] since my infancy'.
146. Cf. Ps. 117:18.
147. Cf. Deut. 28:48; 2 Cor. 11:27.
148. Cf. Ps. 117:22.
149. Dan. 7:13.

saw] a piece of writing without any nobility opposite my face, and at the same time I heard the divine revelation[150] saying to me: 'We have seen with anger the face of [our] chosen one with his name laid bare [of respect].' Note he did not say: 'You have seen with anger,' but 'We have seen with anger' as if in this matter he were joined to his chosen one. As he said: 'he who touches you touches the pupil of my eye.'[151]

[30] So it is that 'I give thanks to him who strengthened me'[152] in all things: that he did not impede me in my chosen journey, nor in my works which I had learned from Christ my Lord. On the contrary, I felt in myself a strength, by no means small, coming from him,[153] and that my 'faith was proven in the presence of God and men.'[154]

[31] And so 'I boldly declare'[155] that my conscience is clear both now and in the future. I have 'God as [my] witness'[156] that I am not a liar[157] in those things that I have told you.

[32] But I am very sorry for my dearest friend, to whom I trusted even my soul, that he merited to hear this [divine] revelation.[158] And I found out from some of the brethren that at the enquiry he fought for me in my absence. (I was not present at this, nor was I in Britain, nor did the issue arise with me.) He indeed it was who told me with his own lips; 'Behold, you are to be given the rank of bishop' – something for which I was unworthy. So how did he later come to the idea of disgracing me in public in the presence of all those people both good and bad, [regarding a matter] which earlier he had, joyfully and of his own volition, pardoned me, as indeed had the Lord who is greater than all?[159]

150. Rom. 11:4.
151. Zech. 2:8.
152. 1 Tim. 1:12.
153. The language and ideas reflect Mark 5:27–30.
154. Sir. 25:1; and cf. 1 Pet. 1:7; 2 Cor. 8:21.
155. Acts 2:29.
156. Rom. 1:9 (a phrase used on several occasions by Paul).
157. Cf. Gal. 1:20.
158. Cf. Rom. 11:4.
159. Cf. John 10:29.

[33] Enough said! However, I must not hide that gift of God which he gave us bountifully in the land of my captivity,[160] because it was then that I fiercely sought him and there found him and he preserved me from all iniquities.[161] I believe this to be so because of his Spirit dwelling in me[162] who has worked in me[163] until this very day.[164] This is something I will boldly repeat.[165] But God knows that if a man had said this to me, perhaps then I would have remained silent because of Christ's love.[166]

[34] And so I thank my God without ceasing who preserved me as his faithful one 'on the day of' my 'trial'[167] so that today I can offer a sacrifice to him with confidence. [Today] I offer my soul as 'a living victim'[168] to Christ my Lord who 'preserved me in all my troubles'[169] so that I can say: '"Who am I, O Lord"[170] and what is my vocation, that you have co-operated with me with such divine [power]?' Thus today I constantly praise and glorify your name[171] wherever I may be among the nations[172] both in my successes and my difficulties. So whatever happens to me – good or ill – I ought to accept with an even temper[173] and always gives thanks to God who has shown me that I can trust him without limit or doubt. It is he who 'in the last days'[174] heard me, so that I – an ignorant man – should dare to take up so holy and wonderful a work as

---

160. Cf. 2 Chr. 6:36–8.
161. Cf. Sir. 33:1; 2 Tim. 1:12; combine with a common scriptural expression: Lev. 16:21–2; Ps. 51:9; Ps. 130:8; Ezek. 36:33; etc..
162. Cf. Rom. 8:11.
163. Cf. 1 Cor. 12:11; Phil. 2:13.
164. This is a common scriptural expression, e.g. Josh. 16:10.
165. Cf. Acts 2:29.
166. Cf. 2 Cor. 5:14.
167. Ps. 94:9; and cf. Wisd. 3:18.
168. Rom. 12:1.
169. Ps. 33:5–7.
170. 2 Sam. 7:18.
171. Cf. Ps. 33:4; 45:11; Sir. 33:10.
172. This notion is found in many places in the scriptures (e.g. Ps. 17:49; Isa. 12:4; Ezek. 20:9; Mal. 1:11; Rev. 15:4; etc.), but Patrick may be thinking especially of 2 Sam. 7:23 as this part of 2 Sam. is used a few lines earlier.
173. Cf. Job 2:10.
174. Acts 2:17.

this: that I should in some way imitate those men[175] to whom the
Lord foretold what was about to occur when 'his gospel [of the
kingdom will be preached throughout the whole world,] as a testimony to all nations' before the end of the world.[176] And this is
what we see: it has been fulfilled.[177] Behold! we are [now]
witnesses to the fact that the gospel has been preached out to
beyond where any man lives.[178]

[35] To narrate in detail[179] either the whole story of my labours
or even parts of it would take a long time. So, lest I injure my readers, I shall tell you briefly how God, the all-holy one, often freed
me from slavery and from twelve dangers which threatened my
life, as well as from many snares and from things which I am
unable to express in words.[180] Moreover, I have God as my
authority – he who knows all things even before they happen –
that he frequently warned me, a poor ignorant orphan, through
divine revelations.[181]

[36] So where did I get this wisdom?[182] It was not in me: I neither
knew the number of [my] days[183] nor cared about God. Where
did I later get that great and health-giving gift that I might know
and love God, albeit that I had to leave my country and parents?

[37] And many gifts were offered to me with sorrow and tears.
And I offended them and went against the will not only of some
of my elders, but, under God's direction, I refused to consent or
agree with them in any way. It was not my grace, but God who

---

175. This notion of sanctity/discipleship as imitating models of holiness is a
theme in Paul, and a particular theme in Patrick's understanding of holiness, cf. *Confessio* 42, 47 and 59 (where there is a fuller comment on the
theme).
176. Matt. 24:14 (he paraphrases the final phrase using a word from Matt. 24:13;
there is also an echo of the notion of 'the ends of the earth' from Acts 1:8).
177. Jas. 2:23; and cf. Matt. 24:14.
178. Cf. Acts 1:8.
179. Acts 21:19.
180. Cf. Rom. 8:26.
181. Rom. 11:4.
182. Matt. 13:54.
183. Cf. Ps. 38:5; Job 38:21.

conquered in me and who resisted them all that I might come 'to the Irish nations to preach the gospel'[184] and put up with insults from unbelievers, that I might 'hear the hatred of my wanderings,'[185] [endure] many persecutions even including chains,[186] and that I be given my freedom for the benefit of others. And, indeed, if I be worthy I am ready to give my life right now[187] 'for his name's sake.'[188] And, if the Lord should grant it to me,[189] it is there [in Ireland] I want 'to spend freely'[190] my life 'even until death'.[191]

[38] Truly, I am greatly in God's debt.[192] He has given me a great grace, that through me many peoples might be reborn[193] and later brought to completion;[194] and also that from among them everywhere clerics should be ordained [to serve] this people – who have but recently come to belief – [and] which the Lord has taken [to himself] 'from the ends of the earth.'[195] He thus fulfilled 'what he once promised through his prophets'[196]: 'to you shall the nations come from the ends of the earth and say: "Our fathers have inherited nought but lies, worthless things in which there is no

---

184. Cf. Mark 13:10. Patrick says that he came 'to preach the gospels to the Irish nations' (*ad Hibernas gentes euangelium praedicare*) while Mark 13:10 reads that 'the gospel must be preached to all the nations' (*in omnes gentes primum oportet praedicari euangelium*). The change from the passive to the active voice is significant given Patrick's overall sense of his part in fulfilling what is commanded about preaching in the gospels: Jesus spoke about what has to have taken place before the eschaton, Patrick is setting out to help in accomplishing this result.

185. Sir. 29:30. On Patrick's use of this verse in combination with Mark 13:10; see O'Loughlin 2001b.

186. 2 Tim. 2:9.

187. Cf. John 13:37

188. Cf. Rom. 1:5.

189. Cf. Isa. 26:15.

190. Cf. 2 Cor. 12:15.

191. Cf. Phil. 2:8.

192. Cf. Rom. 1:14.

193. Cf. John 3:5.

194. Cf. 2 Cor. 8:6; and Heb. 11:40 and Rev. 15:8; it is unclear what 'brought to completion' (*consummarentur*) means here or in other passages in the *Confessio*, see the discussion in Chapter 5 above.

195. Jer. 16:19.

196. Rom. 1:2.

profit".[197] And in another place:[198] "'I have set you to be a light for the nations, that you may bring salvation to the uttermost parts of the earth.'"[199]

[39] And it is there [in Ireland] that I desire 'to wait for the promise'[200] of him who never deceives us and who repeatedly promises in the gospel: 'they will come from the east and from the west and from the south and from the north and recline at table with Abraham, Isaac and Jacob.'[201] So we believe that believers will come from the whole world.

[40] So it is right and proper that we should fish well and carefully – as the Lord warns and teaches us saying: 'Come after me and I shall make you fishers of men.'[202] And again[203] he says through the prophets: 'Behold! I send out fishermen and any hunters, says

197. Jer. 16:19.

198. Cf. John 19:37, which is the model for Patrick's use of Scripture here. In John two verses are quoted in a *catena* and it is this combination which is brought to fulfilment; here Patrick uses the same device and even echoes John's language: John has *Et iterum alia scriptura dicit*: ... , while Patrick has *Et iterum*: ...

199. Acts 13:47.

200. Acts 1:4.

201. Matt. 8:11; it should be noted that Patrick adds the two others corners of the world – south and north – to the gospel text; this is to be explained by his conflation from memory of Matthew's text with the parallel verse in Luke at 13:29 (see *Epistola* 18 where Patrick also quotes this verse from Matthew but without any influence from the Lucan text. The addition is not found in the Bieler edition, but is in the text in White: *sicut in euangelio pollicetur: Uenient ab oriente et occidente et ab austro et ab aquilone, et recumbent cum Abraham et Isaac et Iacob; sicut credimus* ... Here White follows the text of the Book of Armagh (fol. 24r) which, here, is the text to be preferred as this addition is not just the result of a scribe 'filling out' a quotation from memory; first in that the phrase 'from east to west' (or variants of it such as 'from the rising of the sun to its setting') are common in Scripture while 'from north to south' or from all four points, are not; and second, in the text of Matthew in the Book of Armagh (fol. 37ra) this addition is not found – if this addition were a peculiarity of the scribe's gospel text it should have affected the gospel itself as much as the text of the *Confessio*.

202. Matt. 4:19.

203. Cf. John 19:37.

God,'[204] and so forth. So truly it is our task to caste our nets[205] and catch 'a great multitude'[206] and crowd for God; and [to make sure] that there are clergy everywhere to baptise and preach to a people who are in want and in need. This is exactly what the Lord warns and teaches about in the gospel when he say: 'Go therefore,' now, 'and teach all the nations, baptising them in the name of the Father and of the Son and of the Holy Spirit, teaching them to observe all that I have commanded you; and behold, I am with you always even to the close of the age.'[207] And again[208]: 'Go into all the world and preach the gospel to the entire universe. He who believes and is baptised will be saved; but he who does not believe will be condemned.'[209] And again[210]: 'this gospel of the kingdom will be preached throughout the entire universe, as a testimony to all nations; and then the end will come.'[211] And likewise the Lord foretold this through the prophet when he says: 'And in the last days it shall be, says the Lord, that I will pour out my Spirit upon all flesh, and your sons and your daughters shall prophesy, and your young men shall see visions, and your old men shall dream dreams; and indeed on my manservants and my maidservants in those days I will pour out my Spirit; and they shall prophesy.'[212] And the prophet Hosea says: 'Those who were not my people I will call "my people," and her who was not beloved I will call "my beloved." And in the very place where it was said to them, "You are not my people," they will be called "sons of the living God."'[213]

[41] Such indeed is the case in Ireland where they never had knowledge of God[214] – and until now they celebrated only idols

---

204. Jer. 16:16.
205. Cf. Mark 1:16; John 21:11.
206. Luke 6:17 and cf. Luke 5:6.
207. Matt. 28:19–20; note his added emphasis of urgency: 'Go therefore now ... '
208. Cf. John 19:37.
209. Mark 16:15–6; I have rendered *uniuersus mundus* as 'entire universe' as this cosmological nuance is present in the original, and in the Latin, but is not captured by a phrase like 'whole world' or 'all creation'.
210. Cf. John 19:37.
211. Matt. 24:14; see previous note on the words 'entire universe'.
212. Acts 2:17–18; and cf. Joel 2:28–9.
213. Rom. 9:25–6; note that it is Paul who says this is Hosea; cf. Hos. 1:9–10; 2:1; 2:23. Cf. also *Confessio* 59 below.
214. Cf. Rom. 1:28.

and unclean things.[215] Yet recently, what a change: they have
become 'a prepared people'[216] of the Lord, and they are now called
'the sons of God'.[217] And the Irish leaders' sons and daughters are
seen to become the monks and virgins of Christ.[218]

[42] Indeed, on one occasion this happened. A blessed Irish
woman of noble birth, a most beautiful adult whom I had baptised, came back to us a few days later for this reason. She told us
how she had received a divine communication[219] from a messenger of God which advised her to become a virgin of Christ and
that she should move closer to God. Thanks be to God, six days
after that she avidly and commendably took up[220] that life which
is lived by all who are virgins of God. This, of course, is not to the
liking of their fathers and they have to suffer persecution and false
accusation from their parents.[221] Yet despite this their number
keeps increasing and we do not know the number of those born
there from our begetting – apart from widows and those who are
continent. But of all these women those held in slavery have to
work hardest: they are continually harassed and even have to
suffer being terrorised. But the Lord gives grace to many of his
maidservants, and the more they are forbidden to imitate[222] [the
Lord], the more they boldly do this.

215. This notion in Patrick reflects Paul's thinking in Rom. 1:19–24 (cf. 2 Kings
      17:12).
216. Cf. Luke 1:17; what is meant in this context by a '*perfecta plebs*' ('a prepared'
      or 'a completed people') is unclear; see the discussion in Chapter 5 above.
      The reading has also troubled both scribes and editors: White 1905 has
      quomodo nuper facta est plebs Domini ... and this reading was followed by
      Bieler; however, while that reading makes sense, the more difficult reading
      is to be preferred (which, in any case, has better authority in the manu-
      scripts) rather than simply trying to eliminate a difficulty with a plausible
      reading. By 1918 White had changed his mind on this problem and had
      opted for the reading *quomodo nuper perfecta est plebs Domini* ... .
217. Cf. 1 John 3:1 (and Rom. 8:14; 9:26).
218. The word 'virgin' (*uirgo*) means here something similar to our word 'nun'.
219. Cf. Acts 10:22 (and cf. Rom. 11:4).
220. Cf. Matt. 11:12.
221. Cf. Luke 21:16.
222. This is an echo of the Pauline notion of imitating Christ as being the guide
      to Christian behaviour; cf. the notes on *Confessio* 59 where there is a fuller
      comment and references.

[43] This, therefore, is the situation: even if I were willing to leave them and go to Britain – and I was all set[223] to go there, and wanted to go for it is my homeland and where my family is – and Gaul 'to visit the brethren'[224] and see the face of my Lord's saints – God knows how much I wanted to do this; I am 'bound in the Spirit,' who 'testifies to me'[225] that should I do this he would find me as guilty.[226] Moreover, I fear the loss of the work I have begun here, and so it is not I but Christ the Lord who has ordered me to come [here] and be with these people for the rest of my life. If the Lord wills it,[227] he will guard my way from every evil,[228] that I might not sin in his presence.[229]

[44] However, I hope I have done the right thing, for 'as long as I am in this body of death'[230] I do not trust myself because he is strong[231] who daily tries to drag me away from faith and from the genuine religious chastity which I have chosen for Christ my Lord until the end of my life. But the hostile flesh[232] is always drawing me towards death,[233] namely, towards doing those enticing things which are forbidden. While I know in part[234] those matters where I have had a less perfect life than other believers, I do acknowledge this to my Lord and I am not ashamed[235] in his sight[236] – 'for I do not lie.'[237] From the time I knew him, from youth,[238] the love of

223. Cf. Ps. 118:60.
224. Acts 7:23; 15:36.
225. Acts 20:22–3.
226. The notion is that he would be designated for the future as one who has committed a crime and is in the state of being guilty for this departure; there seems to be an echo of something like the mark that the Lord imposed on Cain which continually reminded those who saw him that he was a guilty man (cf. Gen. 4:15).
227. Cf. Jas. 4:15.
228. Cf. Ps. 118:101.
229. Cf. Luke 15:18, 21.
230. 2 Pet. 1:13; Rom. 7:24.
231. The 'strong one' is Satan; the identification is based on Matt. 12:27 and Mark 3:27.
232. Cf. Rom. 8:7.
233. Cf. Prov. 24:11.
234. Cf. 1 Cor. 13:9.
235. Cf. Rom. 1:16.
236. Cf. Eph. 1:4.
237. Gal. 1:20.
238. Cf. Ps. 70:5.

God and the fear of him have grown within me, so that, with the Lord's help, 'I have kept the faith'²³⁹ until now.²⁴⁰

[45] So if there is anyone who wants to laugh [at me] or insult [me] they can. But I will not hide, nor be silent about those 'signs and wonders'²⁴¹ which were shown to me by the Lord many years before they actually occurred: for he knows everything 'from all eternity'.²⁴²

[46] So I should give God thanks without ceasing²⁴³ for he often forgave my stupidity²⁴⁴ and negligence²⁴⁵ – on more than one occasion – in that he was not fiercely angry²⁴⁶ with me who had been appointed his helper.²⁴⁷ Yet, I was not quick in accepting what he had made clear to me and as 'the Spirit reminded me.'²⁴⁸ And the Lord 'was merciful' to me 'a thousand, thousand times'²⁴⁹ because he saw what was within me and that I was ready²⁵⁰ but that I did not know what I should do about my state [of life]. All the while many were forbidding my mission: behind my back among themselves they were telling stories and saying; 'Why does this man put himself in danger among enemies "who do not know God"²⁵¹?' I can truly testify that this was not from malice, but because it did not seem right to them that one as rustic as myself should do such a thing. Then, I was not quick to acknowledge the grace that was in me²⁵²; now, what I ought to have done before seem right to me.

[47] So now, without any affectation, I have told my brethren and

---

239. 2 Tim. 4:7.
240. Cf. Ps. 69:17.
241. Dan. 3:99; 6:27.
242. 2 Tim. 1:9.
243. Cf. Eph. 1:16; 1 Tim. 2:13.
244. Cf. Ps. 68:6.
245. Cf. Ps. 88:8.
246. 2 Kings 17:18.
247. Cf. 1 Cor. 3:9.
248. John 14:26.
249. Cf. Exod. 20:6.
250. Cf. Ps. 118:60.
251. 2 Thess. 1:8.
252. Cf. 1 Tim. 4:14.

fellow-servants[253] They believed me because 'I warned and I warn'[254] in order to make your faith more sure and robust.[255] Would indeed that you would imitate greater things and do more powerful things![256] This would be my glory,[257] for 'the wise son is the glory of the father.'[258]

[48] You all know, as does God, how I lived among you from my youth[259] 'in the faith of truth'[260] 'and with sincerity of heart'.[261] Furthermore, I have acted with good faith towards the nations [i.e. non-Christians] among whom I live, and will continue doing so in the future. 'God knows'[262] 'I have taken advantage of none'[263] of them; and for the sake of God[264] and his church I would not think of doing so, lest I should provoke persecution[265] of them and of us all, and lest the name of God be blasphemed through me – for it is written: 'Woe to the man through whom the Lord's name is blasphemed'.[266]

[49] 'Now even if I am unskilled in everything',[267] yet I have tried

---

253. This designation of others uses terms frequently found, and linked, in the New Testament, cf. Rev. 6:11.
254. 2 Cor. 13:2.
255. Cf. Job 4:3–4.
256. This is an echo of the Pauline theme of imitation, cf. the notes on *Confessio* 59 for a fuller note.
257. Cf. 1 Thess. 2:20.
258. Prov. 10:1; Lat. *'filius sapiens'*; this phrase was destined to play an important role in insular Christianity for several learned holy men were given the designation *'sapiens'*, for example the theologian Ailerán (died c. 665) was known as *Aileran Sapiens*; (cf. also Prov. 15:20; 17:6; Sir. 3:13).
259. Cf. Ps. 70:17.
260. 2 Thess. 2:13.
261. 1 Cor. 5:8.
262. 2 Cor. 12:2; see *Confessio* 24 and 27 above.
263. 2 Cor. 12:17; and cf. 2 Cor. 7:2.
264. Cf. 1 Pet. 2:13.
265. Cf. Acts 13:50.
266. This quotation is a combination of Matt. 18:7 and Rom. 2:24; however, Rom. 2:24 is the text that Patrick has in mind for it states that 'it is written that "The name of God is blasphemed among the Gentiles because of you"' which is Patrick's exact context; in Paul it is an echo of Isa. 52:5 and Ezek. 36:20.
267. 2 Cor. 11:6.

in some small way to guard myself for [the sake of] the Christian brethren and the virgins of Christ and 'the religious women'[268] who of their own accord used to give me little gifts. And when they threw any of their ornaments on the altar, I used to return these to them though they were often offended that I should do that. But I did it because of the hope of eternity[269] and so that I could guard myself carefully in everything.[270] Thus, infidels could not, for any reason, catch either me or my ministry of service. And furthermore, by this course of action I did not give unbelievers reason, in even the least matter, to speak against me or to take my character.[271]

[50] Maybe when I baptised all those thousands, I hoped to get even half a penny from one of them? 'Tell me and I will return it to you!'[272] Or when the Lord ordained clergy everywhere through me as his mediocre instrument, and I gave my ministry to them for free, did I even charge them the cost of my shoes? 'Tell it against me and I will' all the more 'return it to you!'[273]

[51] 'I spend myself'[274] for you that you might lay hold of me.[275] Indeed I have travelled everywhere for your sake: I have gone amid many dangers: I have gone to places beyond where anyone lived; and I have gone where no one else had ever travelled who would baptise, or who would ordain clergy, or bring the people to completion.[276] With God's help, I have carried out all these things lovingly, carefully, and most joyfully[277] for your salvation.

---

268. Cf. Acts 13:50.
269. Cf. Wisd. 3:4.
270. Cf. Eph. 5:15.
271. Cf. 1 Pet. 2:12.
272. 1 Sam. 12:3.
273. 1 Sam. 12:3 (Vetus Latina).
274. 2 Cor. 12:15.
275. Cf. Matt. 22:15; there is irony here on Patrick's part: the allusion is to those who wished to trap Jesus. Patrick wished himself to be trapped by them so that by this they might be entrapped by his message (cp. Horace: 'Captured Greece, her brutal capturer captured and brought the arts to rural Rome' (*Epistola* 2,1,156)).
276. Cf. *Confessio* 38 above; and the discussion of the passage in Chapter 5 above.
277. Cf. 2 Cor. 12:15.

[52] Sometimes I gave presents to kings – over and above the wages I gave their sons who travelled with me – yet they took me and my companions captive. On that day they avidly sought to kill me, but the time had not yet come.[278] Still they looted us, took everything of value, and bound me in iron. But on the fourteenth day the Lord freed me from their control, and all our belongings were returned to us for the sake of God[279] and 'the close friends'[280] we had seen earlier.

[53][281] You all know well how much I paid those who are judges in all the areas[282] I visited frequently. I suppose I must have paid out the price of fifteen among them, so that you might enjoy me and I might always enjoy you in God.[283] I am neither sorry about it, nor is it enough for me, so still 'I spend and I will spend all the more.'[284] The Lord is powerful and so he can grant me afterwards that 'I might spend' myself 'for your souls'.[285]

[54] Behold, 'I call God as the witness in my soul that I do not lie'[286]; nor would write in such a way that it would be 'an occasion of greed or false praise'[287]; nor do I do so out of a desire for honour from you. It is enough for me that honour which is not yet seen,[288] but which is believed in by the heart[289]: 'for he who promised is faithful'[290] and never lies.

---

278. Cf. John 7:6.
279. Cf. 1 Pet. 2:13.
280. Acts 10:24.
281. Note the discontinuities in the narrative: those criticising him seem to be clerics abroad over a personal sin, and at other times Christians or non-Christians in Ireland giving out about money and bribes. Sometimes it seems he has left Ireland, at other times that he is writing in Ireland, sometimes that his ideal reader does not know Ireland, sometimes, as here, that they know all the details of his work.
282. This phrase is used on several occasions in Scripture, e.g. Gen. 41:46.
283. Cf. Rom. 15:24.
284. Cf. 2 Cor. 12:15.
285. 2 Cor. 12:15.
286. 2 Cor. 1:23.
287. Cf. 1 Thess. 2:5.
288. Cf. 2 Cor. 4:18.
289. Cf. Rom. 10:10.
290. Heb. 10:23.

[55] Moreover, I see that already 'in this present age'²⁹¹ the Lord has highly exalted me. I was not the sort of person [you would expect] the Lord to give this grace to, nor did I deserve it, for I know with the greatest certainty that poverty and woe are more my line than pleasures and riches – after all, Christ the Lord was poor for our sake²⁹² – and so I too am one who is miserable and unfortunate. Even if I wanted riches, I do not have them 'and I am not judging myself'²⁹³ for not a day passes but I expect to be killed or way-laid or taken into slavery or assaulted in some other way. But for the sake of the promise of heaven 'I fear none of these things'.²⁹⁴ Indeed, I have cast myself into the hands of God,²⁹⁵ the almighty one who rules everywhere,²⁹⁶ as the prophet has said:²⁹⁷ 'Cast your burden on God, and he will sustain you.'²⁹⁸

[56] Behold now 'I commend my spirit' to my 'most faithful God'²⁹⁹ 'whose ambassador I am'³⁰⁰ in my unworthiness; but since 'God does not have favourites'³⁰¹ and chose me³⁰² for this task that I might be just one of the least of his servants.³⁰³

[57] Therefore, 'I shall give to him for all the things that he has given to me.'³⁰⁴ But what shall I say to him? What can I promise to give my Lord? I have nothing of value that is not his gift!³⁰⁵ But

---

291. Gal. 1:4.
292. Cf. 2 Cor. 8:9.
293. 1 Cor. 4:3.
294. Acts 20:24.
295. Cf. Ps. 31:5 and Luke 23:46.
296. 1 Chr. 29:12.
297. The designation of the psalmist (David) as a prophet is based on Acts 2:30.
298. Ps. 54:22.
299. Cf. Ps. 31:5; Luke 23:46; Acts 7:59; 1 Pet. 4:19.
300. Eph. 6:20.
301. Deut. 10:17 and cf. Gal. 2:6 (cf. also 2 Chr. 19:2; Rom. 2:11; Eph. 6:9; Col. 3:25).
302. John 15:16.
303. Matt. 25:40; note Patrick's method, a sequence of identifications with Christ and Paul is presented: what they went through, he too is going through – thus he validates his own position and apostolic identity.
304. Ps. 115:12.
305. Cf. Wisd. 9:17.

'he searches the hearts and the inmost parts'[306] and [knows] that it is enough that I exceedingly desire, and was ready indeed,[307] that he should grant to me 'to drink his cup'[308] just as he granted it to the others who love him.

[58] So may it never happen to me[309] that my God should separate me from his 'people which he has acquired'[310] in the outermost parts of the earth. I pray God that he give me perseverance and deign to grant that I should render him faithful witness until [the moment of] my passing [from this life to the life to come],[311] all for the sake of my God.

[59] And, if at any time I have 'imitated something that is good'[312]

306. Ps. 6:9 (and cf. Rev. 2:23); most modern translations use some phrase like 'the depths of the soul' for what I have translated as 'inmost parts', but the more graphic nature of the Latin translation should be kept in mind: *renes*, literally, the kidneys.

307. Cf. Ps. 118:60.

308. This usage of a phrase from the gospels is most complex. The incident of the disciples proving their devotion by being prepared to drink the same cup as Christ is found in Matt. (20:20–8) and Mark (10:35–41). It is the Marcan account that is most directly relevant for there the two disciples are named and one of them is John (the 'Beloved', cf. John 13:23 etc.). So as Patrick understands the incident it means something like this: John says he is ready to drink the Lord's cup, this is granted to him and the other disciple; he is the one who loves and is loved by the Lord. So by identifying himself with these disciples, Patrick displays his discipleship, and expects that the cup will be granted. This will be a demonstration of the love between him and the Lord, and will be a promise of his place in the Kingdom in heaven.

309. Cf. 1 Macc. 13:5.

310. Isa. 43:21.

311. Patrick views death as a *transitus* – a move from one sort of life to another – this was a common way of presenting death in both the Fathers and the early Middle Ages; it occurs in contemporary Catholic theology only with reference to the Assumption of Mary.

312. Cf. 3 John 11; this notion of imitating something good is clearly an echo of this particular text in the New Testament, but it should be remembered that the notion that holiness consists in imitating holiness is a larger theme in early Christian writings, and especially Paul and other writings attributed to him: cf. 1 Cor. 4:16; 11:1; Eph. 5:1; Phil. 3:17; 1 Thess. 1:6; 2:14; 2 Thess. 3:7; 3:9; Heb. 6:12; 13:7. As a theme is occurs several times in Patrick, cf. *Confessio* 34, 42 and 47 above.

for the sake of my God whom I love, then I ask him to grant me
that I may shed my blood[313] 'for his name's sake'[314] with those
proselytes and captives, even if this means that I should lack even
a tomb,[315] or that my corpse be horribly chopped up by dogs and
wild beasts, or that 'the birds of heaven devour it.'[316] I do hereby
declare that should this happen to me, that I should have gained
my soul as well as my body.[317] For should any of these things
happen, there is no doubt that on the day[318] we shall arise in the
brightness of the sun,[319] this is in the glory of Christ Jesus our
redeemer,[320] we shall be 'sons of the living God'[321] and 'fellow
heirs with Christ'[322] and 'conformed to his image'[323]; 'for from
him and through him and in him'[324] we shall reign.

[60] But this sun which we see, rising each day for us by God's
command, it shall never reign, nor shall its splendour

---

313. Cf. Heb. 12:4.

314. Links the idea of suffering for the name (Acts 5:41; 9:16) with that of
making converts for the sake of the Lord's name (Rom. 1:5).

315. Cf. Deut. 28:26; Ps. 78:2–3.

316. Luke 8:5 supplies the wording; but the notion is found in the Old
Testament: Jer. 7:33; Ezek. 29:5; and especially in 1 Kings 16:4, and to a
lesser degree in 14:11.

317. There is an echo of two phrases from the gospel here: first, of Matt. 10:28
which raises the possibility of the destruction of the body independently of the soul ('And do not fear those who kill the body but cannot kill
the soul; rather fear him who can destroy both soul and body in hell') –
Patrick knows that though the body would be destroyed, the soul would
not be harmed, and so he is a follower of Christ's words in that he has
no fear for his body, but has a fear for his soul; and second, of Matt.
16:26 ('For what will it profit a man, if he gains the whole world and for-
feits his life?') – Patrick presents himself as one who would heed this
verse's message: he is prepared to lose the whole world, and gain his
soul.

318. Cf. Ruth 3:13.

319. Cf. Isa. 30:26.

320. Cf. 1 Cor. 15:43; Phil. 3:20–1.

321. Rom. 9:26 (and 8:16); cf. Hos. 2:1; cf. also *Confessio* 40 above.

322. Rom. 8:17.

323. Cf. Rom. 8:29.

324. Rom. 11:36; this is one of the great doxology phrases and should be seen
primarily as a direct echo of the actual liturgy in which Patrick took part,
rather than of Paul who is himself echoing the liturgy in his use of the
phrase in Romans.

last.[325] Likewise all those miserable people who worship it shall end up in a foul punishment. We, on the other hand, are those who believe in Christ, and adore him who is the true sun.[326] He is the sun which does not perish, and so we too, 'who do his will,' shall not perish.[327] And, as Christ 'will abide forever'[328] so he [who believes in him] 'will abide forever', for Christ reigns with God the Father almighty, and with the Holy Spirit, before all ages, and now, and 'through all the ages to come.'[329] Amen.

[61] So here it is! I have, again and again, briefly set before you the words of my declaration. 'I bear witness' in truth and joyfulness of heart 'before God and his holy angels'[330] that the one and only purpose I had in going back to that people from whom I had earlier escaped was the gospel and the promises of God.[331]

[62] I now pray for anyone who believes in, and fears, God who may perchance come upon this writing which Patrick, the sinner and the unlearned one, wrote in Ireland. I wrote it so that no one might say that whatever little I did, or anything I made visible according to God's pleasure, was done through ignorance. Rather,

---

325. Cf. Matt. 5:45 which speaks of God causing the sun to rise on both the righteous and sinners; here Patrick begins with the sun and then describes the rewards of both groups.

326. Christ as 'the sun' or 'the true sun' is a complex theme in early Christian writing which has survived in one or two places in the Latin liturgy even down to modern times. The theme uses a great variety of scriptural passages to develop its mythological coherence such as Matt. 13:43; 17:2; and Rev. 22:5, but these, and other passages like them, should be seen as just elements in a complex development.

327. Cf. 1 John 2:17.

328. Cf. Ps. 88:37; 1 John 2:17.

329. Rev. 11:15.

330. 1 Tim. 5:21 (and 2 Tim. 4:1 and Ps. 118:111 from which he derives the phrase to alter the quotation). Patrick no doubt thinks that the moment when he will give this testimony is when the Son of Man comes in the glory of the Father with his holy angels to repay each according to their deeds (cf. Matt. 16:27). See Patrick's *Epistola* 20.

331. This is a Pauline theme, cf. Rom. 9:4 and Gal. 3:21.

you should judge the situation and let it be truly believed that it was 'the gift of God.'[332] And this is my declaration before I die.

332. Cf. Eph. 2:8.

❧❧

CHAPTER 2

The Epistola militibus Corotici by St Patrick

Patrick's address to the soldiers of Coroticus

[1] Patrick, a sinner and one truly unlearned, declare myself to be a bishop set up by God in Ireland. I most certainly hold that what I am,[1] I have received from God. And so I live as an alien among the barbarians and a wanderer from the love of God,[2] as God is my witness. Not that I wished to utter anything so harshly or so roughly: but the zeal of God[3] forces me, and the truth of Christ[4] raises me up[5] for the love of neighbours and sons[6] for whom I gave up homeland and parents, and, if I am worthy, even 'my life up to the grave.'[7] I have sworn[8] to my God to teach the nations,[9] even if I am held in contempt by some.

1. Cf. 1 Cor. 15:10.
2. Patrick makes a contrast here between himself and Cain 'the wanderer' (Gen. 4:12); cf. *Confessio* 12.
3. Cf. 1 Macc. 2:54.
4. Cf. 2 Cor. 11:10.
5. Cf. Rom 10:9.
6. Cf. Sir. 25:2; 2 Cor. 5:14.
7. Matt. 26:38, and cf. Rev. 12:11 for the context in which the phrase is used.
8. Several MSS read *uiuo* ('I live'), others *uoui* ('I have vowed') which seems a far better reading.
9. Cf. Matt. 28:19.

[2] These words, which I have composed and written with 'my own hand,'[10] are to be sent, given and proclaimed to the soldiers of Coroticus. In doing this I do not speak to my compatriots[11] nor to 'fellow citizens with the' Roman 'saints'[12]; but to those who by their evil deeds are servants of the demons. In a hostile manner these allies of the Irish and of the apostate Picts live in death, and are bloodthirsty for the blood of the innocent Christians I have 'begotten' in countless numbers for God, as well as having strengthened[13] them 'in Christ.'[14]

[3] The day after the anointed neophytes – still in their white baptismal garb and with the fragrance of the chrism on their foreheads still about them – were cut down and cruelly put to the sword by these men, I sent to them a holy priest – one I had taught since his infancy – accompanied by other clerics with a letter. In it I asked them to give back to us baptised prisoners they had taken along with some of the loot. They treated the whole matter as a big joke.[15]

10. Philem. 19; writing with one's own hand carries with it a notion of special authority such as that conveyed by Paul at the end of his letters: 1 Cor. 16:21; Gal. 6:11; Col. 4:18; 2 Thess. 3:17; Philem. 19.

11. Three different words are used here: 'compatriots', 'citizens' and 'servants'; where Patrick uses *ciues* (literally 'citizens' or 'those who dwell in the same city with') the basic idea he wished this word to convey is a notion of alliance with others. This notion of being a fellow citizen with the servants of God or the devil is an important motif in the development of Latin theology, as in Augustine's *De ciuitate Dei*, and has Eph. 2:19 as its basic text.

12. Eph. 2:19; Patrick's text reads, somewhat awkwardly: *neque ciuibus sanctorum romanorum*; this is clearly an echo of Eph. 2:19: *estis ciues sanctorum et domestici Dei*.

13. Patrick writes '*atque in Christo confirmaui*' which seems to refer to a separate ritual from baptism (the action of being reborn in God); what is meant by this and similar phrases in the *Confessio* is unclear: see the discussion in Chapter 5 above.

14. Paul uses the phrase 'I have begotten in Christ' for his converts in 1 Cor. 4:15 – and that Pauline phrase is clearly echoed here; Paul also uses the phrase 'I have begotten' to express his relationship with Onesimus: cf. Philem. 10.

15. This should not be seen as an example of Patrick's political naiveté. The context is the parable of the evil tenants of the vineyard in Matt. 21:33–46, where after several warnings the lord of the vineyard sends his son; it is when this son is not respected as the lord expects, but is killed, that the moment of judgement comes for these wicked tenants. Patrick insists that it was not just an ordinary priest he sent to them, but one who was dear to him

[4] So now I do not know who to grieve for more[16]: those who were killed, those captured, or those whom the Devil has deeply ensnared in his trap.[17] They will be enslaved equally with him in the everlasting punishment of Gehenna.[18] For it is indeed true that 'he who commits sin is a slave of sin'[19] and shall be known as 'a son of the devil.'[20]

[5] So let everyone who fears God know[21] that [the soldiers of Coroticus] are strangers to me and to Christ, my God, 'for whom I am an ambassador.'[22] The father-killer and the brother-killer are raging wolves[23] 'eating up' the Lord's 'people like bread.'[24] As it is said: 'The wicked have destroyed your land, O Lord.'[25] For [the Lord] has wonderfully and mercifully planted [his law] in Ireland in these final times[26]; and, with the God's help, it has grown there.[27]

[6] I do not go beyond my authority for I have a share with those 'whom he called and predestined'[28] to preach the gospel with no

whom he had instructed since he was an infant; with this messenger rejected the moment has come for the final judgement to be delivered against these evil men.

16. The image is of Patrick grieving before the judgement is carried out and is reminiscent of Christ weeping for Jerusalem (cf. Matt. 23:37).
17. Cf. Acts 13:10.
18. Jas. 3:6 ('Gehenna' is used only here in the Latin Bible, but the image is a composite one; cf. O'Loughlin 1996b).
19. John 8:34.
20. Acts 13:10 (and cf. John 8:44). Note that Patrick sees himself as replacing Paul in Acts 13:8–12: Paul preaches, Paul is opposed, Paul judges, Paul condemns, and then punishment immediately follows.
21. Cf. Acts 13:16; Patrick appropriates to himself the whole speech (Acts 13:16–47) for he has been commanded to be a light to the nations and bring salvation to the ends of the earth (13:47 [cf. Isa. 49:6]). The theme continues in *Epistola* 6.
22. Eph. 6:20; note his view of ministry, this is not just an image of representative, but a full plenipotentiary minister.
23. Cf. Acts 20:29 (and cf. Matt. 7:15; 10:16).
24. Ps. 13:4 and cf. Ps 52:5
25. Ps. 118:126.
26. Cf. Acts 2:17.
27. There is a distinction here between planting and taking root; this is based on the parable of the sower (cf. Matt. 13).
28. Rom. 8:30.

small measure of persecutions[29] 'unto the very end of the earth.'[30]
So despite the fact that the Enemy[31] begrudges this through the
tyranny of Coroticus who fears neither God nor his chosen
priests, still it is to these priests he has granted the highest, the
divine, and the sublime power: 'those whom they shall bind on
earth shall be bound in heaven.'[32]

[7] So I earnestly entreat [all] 'you holy and humble of heart.'[33] It
is not lawful to seek favour from men such as these' nor 'to eat
food' or drink 'with them'[34]; nor to accept their alms until they
make satisfaction to God with painful penance and the shedding
of tears[35]; and free the baptised 'servants of God'[36] and the hand-
maids of Christ – for whom he was crucified and died.

[8] 'The Lord rejects the gifts of the wicked. [...] He who offers a
sacrifice from the goods of the poor is as one who sacrifices a son
in the sight of his father.'[37] 'The riches' he says 'which he has
unjustly gathered will be vomited from his belly, the angel of
death will hand him over to be crushed by the anger of dragons,
he will be killed with the viper's tongue, and an unquenchable fire
will consume him.'[38] Hence 'Woe to him who gathers for himself
from the things that are not his.'[39] Or [as it says elsewhere] 'What
does it profit a man if he gains the whole universe and suffers the
loss of his soul.'[40]

[9] But it would take too long to describe individual crimes and

29. Cf. Mark 10:29–30.
30. Acts 13:47.
31. The enemy is the devil (cf. Acts 13:10 and 1 Pet. 5:8).
32. Matt. 16:19. Note the idea of binding the strong man (Matt. 12:29), here
    identified with the devil, and Patrick's image of the priest as the judge.
33. Dan. 3:87.
34. 1 Cor. 5:11.
35. Cf. Ps. 6:6. Patrick refers to the practice of 'tearful penance'; cf. O'Loughlin
    and Conrad-O'Briain 1993, which examines fourth- and fifth-century theol-
    ogy.
36. 1 Pet. 2:16.
37. Sir. 34:23–4.
38. Job 20:15, 16, 26.
39. Hab. 2:6.
40. Matt. 16:26.

set out the testimonies from the whole law which deals with such greed.[41] [So here are the basics:]

- – avarice is a deadly crime[42];
- – 'You shall not covet your neighbour's goods'[43];
- – 'You shall not kill'[44];
- – A murderer cannot be with Christ [45];
- – 'He who hates his brother is a murderer'[46]; or
- – 'he who does not love his brother remains in death.'[47]

How much more guilty is the man who stains his hands with the blood of 'the sons of God'[48] whom [God] had acquired recently in the very ends of the earth[49] through the preaching of us who are so insignificant.

[10] Was it without God, or 'according to the flesh'[50] that I came to Ireland? Who forced me to come? 'I am one bound in the Spirit'[51] so that I cannot see any of my relatives.[52] Is it from within me that the holy mercy arises which I show towards this people – a people who once took me prisoner and destroyed the servants, male and female, of my father's estate?[53] I was a free man 'according to the flesh,'[54] my father a decurion, and I sold my

---

41. The notion of 'the testimonies of the whole law' is a complex one in patristic theology; for an introduction to the theme, cf. Sundberg 1959.
42. This is the only item on his list of basic moral rules that is not taken directly from Scripture, but it clearly echoes statements about greed such as Luke 12:15.
43. Exod. 20:17. This gathering of crimes is found in Rom. 13:9 and is based on the decalogue.
44. Exod. 20:13.
45. Cf. 1 Pet. 4:15.
46. 1 John 3:15.
47. 1 John 3:14.
48. Cf. Gal. 3:26.
49. Cf. Isa. 41:9 (and note it invokes the idea found elsewhere in Patrick's writings that he works at 'the ends of the earth').
50. 1 Cor. 1:17.
51. Acts 20:22.
52. Cf. Gen. 12:1.
53. 'Servants' (*seruos et ancillas*) in this context means slaves owned by his father.
54. 1 Cor. 1:17.

status for the benefit of others.[55] I am neither ashamed of this nor sorry, but thus I have arrived at this point: I am a servant in Christ to a foreign people for the ineffable glory 'of the eternal life which is in Christ Jesus our Lord,'[56] [11] even though my own people do not know me, for 'a prophet has no honour in his own country'[57]

Perhaps we are not from 'the one fold'[58] nor have we 'one God and Father,'[59] as he says: 'he that is not with me is against me; and he who does not gather with me, scatters.'[60] It is not right that 'one destroys, another builds.'[61] 'I am not seeking my own way,'[62] for it is not from me but from God's grace 'who put this care in my heart'[63] that I should be one of the hunters and fishers[64] whom long ago he foretold would come 'in the last days.'[65]

[12] They despise me, oh how they look down on me! What am I to do, O Lord?[66] Behold around me are your sheep torn to pieces and afflicted by those robbers[67] under the command of the bad-minded Coroticus. Far from the love of God is the man who hands over Christians into the hands of the Irish and the Picts. 'Fierce wolves' have devoured the flock[68] of the Lord which with

---

55. Patrick writes 'for the benefit of others' which invokes the Pauline notion of utility, cf. Rom. 3:1; and 1 Cor. 7:35; 12:7.
56. Rom 6:23; in this section Patrick seems to have a parallel between himself and Paul in mind, cf. Acts 21:39.
57. John 4:44.
58. John 10:16.
59. Eph. 4:6.
60. Matt. 12:30.
61. Sir. 34:28.
62. Cf. 1 Cor. 13:5.
63. 2 Cor. 8:16.
64. Cf. Jer. 16:16.
65. Acts 2:17.
66. Throughout this section of the letter Patrick draws on the sheep/flock imagery of the prophets (Ezek. 34 being the *locus classicus* of this imagery) and the gospels (especially John 10). This opening remark ('I am despised, so what am I to do?') seems to imply that he is answering a criticism that he was a bad shepherd who left his flock untended and so left them open to attack (cf. Jer. 23:1; Ezek. 34:2; John 10:12).
67. There are echoes of John 10:8–12 in this sentence.
68. Cf. Acts 20:29 (and cf. Matt. 7:15).

the greatest love and care[69] was truly increasing beautifully in Ireland. Indeed, I could not count how many of the sons and daughters of the rulers of the Irish had become monks and virgins of Christ. On account of this 'do not be pleased with the wrong done by the unjust, knowing that even unto the depths of hell it shall not please the wicked.'[70]

[13] Which of the saints would not be horrified at the prospect of fun, parties or enjoyment with the likes of these men. They have filled their homes with plunder taken from dead Christians and they live by this. Wretched men they do not know the poisonous lethal food that they share with their children and friends. They are like Eve who did not understand that in reality she gave death 'to her husband.'[71] All who do evil are like this, they work towards the everlasting penalty of death.[72]

[14] This is the practice of the Roman Christians of Gaul. They send suitable holy men to the Franks and other peoples[73] with great piles of money to buy back baptised captives. You, however, kill them and sell them to a foreign 'nation which does not know God.'[74] You are like someone who hands over 'the members of Christ' to a whore-house.[75] Do you have any 'hope in

69. This echoes John 21:15; the use of the image of being one charged with the love and care of the sheep is additional support for the supposition that Patrick here is defending himself against the charge of being a bad pastor.

70. Sir. 9:17; this verse cannot now be found in translations of the scriptures as it belongs to the so-called 'Expanded Text' which stands behind the Vetus Latina/Vulgate. It can only be conveniently found in editions of the Vulgate or old Catholic translations such as the Douay. For an account of these textual problems the fullest guide is Kearns 1969.

71. Gen. 3:6.

72. Cf. 2 Cor. 7:10.

73. The word *gentes* is used by a Patrick in the technical sense found in the scriptures as denoting the alternative to the People of God, cf. Christensen 1992; the apostles were to preach to and baptise these 'peoples' (Matt. 28:19) – but it is not clear from the passage whether Patrick thinks that the Franks and the other nations are still 'pagan' peoples or baptised peoples.

74. 1 Thess. 4:5; 'foreign nation' in this sentence clearly implies a non-Christian people.

75. The image is based on Paul (1 Cor. 6:15: 'Shall I therefore take the members of Christ and make them members of a prostitute? [*meretrix*]') whose words 'members of Christ' are quoted; however, Patrick does not see the members

God'?[76] Who can approve of you? Who can address you with any words of praise? God will judge – as it is written: 'Not only those who do evil, but those also who approve of it, will be damned.'[77]

[15] I do not know 'what' more 'to say or how to speak'[78] about these dead 'sons of God'[79] who the sword struck so harshly. Indeed it is written: 'Weep with those who weep'[80]; and in another place: 'If one member suffers, all the members suffer with it.'[81] This is the reason why the church suffers and mourns for its sons and daughters[82] who have not yet been put to the sword, but who were carried off and brought to distant lands where sin abounds openly,[83] grievously, and without shame. There freeborn men are offered for sale and Christians are made into slaves again,[84] indeed slaves of the worst and most unworthy of men: the apostate Picts.

of Christ being handed over to a person, but as being handed into a place: *in lupanar*. This word for a brothel carries with it some very strong images. First, it comes from a figurative word of a prostitute, *lupa*, which literally means 'a she-wolf' and so the image of the parts of Christ's body being devoured in an evil place is conjured up. Second, this word is used in the scriptures in Latin to describe the places where the Israelites pursued foreign gods (Num. 25:8; Ezek. 16:24, 31, 39) and as a result of their dealing with these places they had to face punishment. Thus Coroticus's behaviour is in keeping with his status as an apostate.

76. Acts 24:15.
77. Rom. 1:32.
78. John 12:49.
79. This phrase is used on four occasions in the New Testament (Matt. 5:9; Luke 20:36; Rom. 8:14, 19; Gal. 3:26) but since Paul seems to have the argument from Romans in his mind, it probably reflects Paul's usage there where the sons of God are those who have been delivered from slavery by Christ but who have to put up with sufferings in the present life as they await the full revelation of glory at the End.
80. Rom. 12:15.
81. 1 Cor. 12:26.
82. Cf. Matt. 2:18.
83. Cf. Rom. 5:20.
84. Patrick used the word *redacti sunt* [literally: they are reduced]; this echoes the Pauline theme in Rom. 8: the Christians are those delivered from slavery, and they must not fall back in fear and slavery (Rom. 8:15); so Patrick is not only concerned that they are physically the prisoners of the Picts and made into slaves, but being with these sinful men, they might fall back into a former spiritual slavery.

[16] So with sadness and grief I cry out: O 'most beloved' and radiant brothers and 'sons' – you are more than I can count – to whom I 'have given birth in Christ'[85] what shall I do with you? I who am not worthy to come to the assistance of God or men. 'The wickedness of the unjust has prevailed over us.'[86] We have become like strangers.[87] Perhaps they do not believe that we have received 'one baptism' and have 'one God and Father'?[88] That we were born in Ireland is an unworthy thing to them. As [Scripture] says: 'Do you not have one God? Why do each of you abandon your neighbour?'[89]

[17] And so 'my dearest friends,'[90] I grieve, grieve deeply, for you, but at the same time I rejoice within myself: 'I did not labour in vain'[91] and my journeying has not been useless. For while such an indescribably awful crime has occurred; still, thanks be to God,[92] it is as faithful baptised people that you have left this world to go to Paradise.[93] I can see you, you have not begun your migration to where 'there is no night, nor sorrow, and where death shall be no more'[94] and 'You shall rejoice leaping like calves let loose from their stalls. And you shall tread down the wicked, for they will be ashes under the soles of your feet.'[95]

[18] And then you will reign with the apostles, prophets and martyrs and take possession of an eternal kingdom. Of this he himself testifies when he says: 'They will come from east and west and sit at table with Abraham, Isaac and Jacob in the kingdom of the

85. Cf. 1 Cor. 4:14–15.
86. Cf. Ps. 64:4.
87. Cf. Ps. 68:9.
88. Cf. Eph. 4:5–6.
89. Mal. 2:10.
90. 1 Cor. 10:14.
91. Phil. 2:16.
92. This phrase is found on many occasions in the liturgy and in the writings of Paul, e.g. Rom. 6:17, and was probably used by Patrick as a 'stock phrase' suitable for almost any occasion.
93. Cf. Luke 23:43; 2 Cor. 12:4; Rev. 2:7. This sentence became one of the 'sayings' of Patrick that were remembered by his communities; see the 'Sayings', n. 2.
94. This is a conflation of Rev. 22:5 and 21:4.
95. Mal. 4:2–3.

heavens.'[96] 'Outside are the dogs and sorcerers and murderers and'[97] 'liars and perjurers, their lot shall be in the lake of everlasting fire.'[98] It is not without good reason that the apostle says: 'If the just man is barely saved, where will the sinner and the impious transgressor of the law appear?'[99]

[19] What then is the case with Coroticus and his criminal band? Where will these rebels against Christ appear? They are the ones who distribute baptised young women as prizes and all for the sake of a wretched temporal kingdom which will vanish[100] in a moment[101] like a cloud,[102] or indeed 'like smoke scattered by the wind.'[103] 'So the' lying 'sinner will perish from before the face of the Lord, but the just will feast'[104] in great harmony with Christ. 'They will judge the nations and rule'[105] over wicked kings for ever and ever.[106] Amen.

[20] 'I testify before God and his angels'[107] that it will come about just as he has indicated by one as unlearned as myself. These are not my words but words which never lie: those of God and his apostles and prophets. I am but the one who has announced them in Latin.[108] 'He that believes will be saved, he

96. Matt. 8:11; compare Patrick's use of this image in *Confessio* 39.
97. Rev. 22:15; Patrick intends the whole verse to be understood: 'Outside are the dogs and sorcerers and fornicators and murderers and idolaters, and every one who loves and practises falsehood.'
98. Rev. 21:8; 'But as for the cowardly, the faithless, the polluted, as for murderers, fornicators, sorcerers, idolaters, and all liars, their lot shall be in the lake that burns with fire and sulphur, which is the second death.' This conflation is a product of memory through similar items in a list triggering a combination of both lists. See also Mal. 3:5 and 1 Tim. 1:10.
99. 1 Pet. 4:18 (and cf. Prov. 11:31).
100. Patrick's argument here is based on the idea of the distance between earthy riches and the eternal kingdom as found in texts such as Luke 12:33–4.
101. Cf. 1 Cor. 15:52.
102. Cf. Isa. 44:22.
103. Cf. Wisd. 5:15.
104. Ps. 68:2–3.
105. Wisd. 3:8.
106. Cf. Rev. 20:10; 22:5.
107. 2 Tim. 4:1; 1 Tim. 5:21. See *Confessio* 61.
108. Patrick uses the forensic tone again: you now stand warned!

who does not believe will be condemned.'[109] 'God has spoken.'[110]

[21] I earnestly request that any servant of God who is capable of bringing these tidings to public notice should do so: let such a messenger neither hide nor detract from them but read them aloud so that every people and Coroticus himself should hear them. If this happens then God may inspire them, and they might return to him.[111] For though it be very late, it may be they will repent of their impious actions – being the murderers of the Lord's brothers – and release the baptised captives they have taken. Thus they would merit to live[112] in God and be healed for this life and eternity.[113]

Peace in the Father and the Son and the Holy Spirit. Amen.[114]

---

109. Mark 16:15–16.
110. This is a phrase used on many occasions in the scriptures, but the two uses in the Psalms (59:8 and 107:8) are especially interesting: 'God has spoken through his saint.'
111. Cf. 2 Tim. 2:25–6.
112. There is an echo here, in that a murderer is allowed to live, of Acts 28:4.
113. These links being made between murderers within the Christian community and eternal life probably depend on 1 John 3:15 where the author says 'and you know that murderers do not have eternal life abiding in them.'
114. In the Book of Armagh there is a colophon giving Patrick's date of death as March 17 – this date, also found in seventh-century liturgical calendars, is one of our best attested 'facts' about Patrick's life.

❦

CHAPTER 3

The 'Sayings' of St Patrick

[1] On my journeys through the regions of Gaul, through Italy, and even among the islands of the Tyrrhenian Sea, I had as my leader the fear of God.[1]

[2] You have rested from this world to go to paradise.[2] Thanks be to God.[3]

[3] The church of the Irish, which is indeed that of the Romans; if you would be Christians, then be as the Romans, and let that the song of praise be sung among yourselves at every hour of prayer: Lord have mercy,[4] Christ have mercy.

1. Cf. Rom. 3:19 (and Ps. 36:2).
2. This is certainly a saying that goes back to Patrick himself for it is taken from *Epistola* 17. Cf. Luke 23:43; 2 Cor. 12:4; Rev. 2:7.
3. This phrase is found on many occasions in the liturgy and in the writings of Paul, e.g. Rom. 6:17. Bieler 1979, p. 124 considered this 'Thanks be to God' to be a separate saying; however, this both defies the logic of the content of both phrases, and ignores the fact that Patrick wrote 'thanks be to God' just before 'You have rested ...' in the *Epistola*. What the tradition has done is to keep an entire expression of Patrick and reverse the order so that it makes sense as sentiment taken on its own apart from its written context in the *Epistola*.
4. These phrases are in Greek in the *dicta*, indicating their origin in the liturgy, the Kyrie; this form is also found in the New Testament on several occasions, e.g. Matt. 17:15. The Kyrie is first definitely attested in litanies from fourth-century Jerusalem and Antioch, and probably entered the western

Every church that follows me, let it sing: Lord have mercy, Christ have mercy, Thanks be to God.

Eucharistic liturgy during the time of Pope Gelasius (492–496). This dating has been used by many scholars, following Kenney 1929, p. 334, as proof that this formula could not belong to the historical Patrick. However, while the pontificate of Gelasius is the first evidence in a western *Eucharistic* context, the prayer form properly belongs to the litanical forms of liturgy and is found in nearly all the historic liturgies. There is therefore nothing impossible in it being in used in litanies by Patrick in the later fifth century, and indeed it is its more general use in litanies that led to its incorporation into the Eucharistic liturgy (cf. Jungmann 1951, vol. 1, pp. 333–46; and Grisbrooke 2002).

CHAPTER 4

The Hymn to St Patrick

Attributed to St Secundinus[1]

1. Hear ye all[2] who love Christ about the holy merits
of that blessed man in Christ: Bishop Patrick;
hear how in goodness and actions he was like the angels,
and who on account of his perfection of life is made equal to the
   apostles.

2. In everything he kept the blessed commands of Christ,[3]
and his works shine out brightly among humans
and these people follow his holy and wondrous example,
so that they might glorify the Lord and Father in the heavens.[4]

3. Steadfast he was in the fear of God and unshakable in faith,[5]
and upon these [foundations], as on Peter, his church was built,[6]
the lot of his apostolate came from God,[7]
and the gates of hell shall not prevail against it.[8]

1. This translation is based on the Latin text found in Bieler 1953a.
2. Cf. Ps. 48:2 (and Deut. 32:1); for a discussion of the opening line, see
   Orchard 1993, pp. 154–6.
3. Luke 1:6.
4. Matt. 5:16.
5. Cf. Tobit 2:14 and 2 Cor. 7:1: this line employs two common scriptural phrases in combination.
6. Matt. 16:18 with an additional strand of allusion to Luke 22:32.
7. Acts 1:17, and cf. Gal. 1:1.
8. Matt. 16:18; on how this image was understood in the seventh century, cf.
   O'Loughlin 1996b.

4. The Lord chose him[9] to teach the barbarous nations,[10]
and to fish there with the nets of doctrine,[11]
and to draw the believers from the world towards grace,
so that they could follow the Lord to a celestial seat.[12]

5. He sold the chosen evangelical talents of Christ,[13]
and he requires back with interest[14] the Irish who are among the
nations,[15]
this is the price of the work of his laborious voyage,
so that he can possess with Christ the joy of the kingdom of heaven.[16]

6. Faithful minister of God[17] and outstanding messenger,[18]
he presented to the good people the shape and example of the
apostles;[19]
he preached by words and deeds to the people of God,
so that he whom his words would not convert might be moved by
a good deed.[20]

7. He has glory and honour with Christ forever,[21]
he is venerated by all as an angel of God,[22]
he whom God sent, like Paul as an apostle to the nations,[23]
that he might offer human beings guidance[24] to the kingdom of God.

9. Luke 6:13 (and cf. Deut. 7:6 and Sir. 45:4).
10. Matt. 28:19; and cf. Acts 9:15.
11. Cf. Jer. 16:16; this image is drawn from Patrick's *Confessio* 40 and was then taken up, from this hymn, by Muirchú, *Vita*, 6.
12. This line combines two images: first, that found in Matt. 19:28; second, that found in Eph. 1:20; 2:6; Col. 3:1.
13. Matt. 25:14–30 is the source of the overall image.
14. Matt. 25:27.
15. Cf. Rom. 2:24; 1 Cor. 5:1; Gal. 2:8; 1 Pet. 2:12.
16. Cf. Matt. 25:21, 23, 34.
17. Col. 4:7; and cf. Col. 1:7; Eph. 6:21.
18. Cf. Hag. 1:13.
19. Titus 2:7.
20. Cf. Heb. 10:24.
21. Cf. 1 Tim. 1:17; the phrase 'glory and honour' is used on eleven occasions in the New Testament.
22. Cf. Gal. 4:14.
23. Cf. Acts 26:17; Rom. 11:13.
24. Cf. Matt. 15:14; there is a verbal play on the biblical text: one blind man gives guidance (*ducatum praestet*) to another and both fall; Patrick, by implicit contrast, offers guidance (*ducatum praeberet*) that leads to the opposite of falling.

8. Humble in spirit[25] and body from the fear of God,
the Lord rests on him[26] on account of his good deeds,
he carries in his flesh the righteous marks of Christ,[27]
while bearing the cross[28] in which alone he glories.[29]

9. Diligently he feeds[30] the believers with heavenly banquets,
and lest those who are seen with Christ should drop off from the
    way,[31]
he hands out to them, as one would loaves, the evangelical
    words,[32]
in his hands they are multiplied[33] like manna.[34]

10. Out of the love of God he guards his chaste flesh,
that flesh which he prepares to be a temple of the Holy Spirit[35]
by whom he is constantly possessed with pure actions,
which he offers to the Lord as an acceptable and living sacrifice.[36]

11. He is the light of the world,[37] he is the great lit-up one of the
    gospel,[38]
lifted high on a lamp stand[39] and shining out to the whole
    world,[40]

25. Isa. 57:15.
26. Cf. 1 Pet. 4:14.
27. The verse refers to the 'stigmata Christi' and applies to Patrick what Paul says
    of himself in Gal. 6:17.
28. Cf. Matt. 16:24.
29. Cf. Gal. 6:14
30. Cf. John 21:15.
31. Cf. Matt. 15:32.
32. Cf. Matt. 4:4.
33. Cf. Matt. 14.
34. Cf. Exod. 16:31, and cf. John 6:31, 49.
35. 1 Cor 6:19.
36. Rom 12:1.
37. This verse is based on the succession of images in Matt. 5:14–16, but its lan-
    guage also shows the influence of the parallel passage in Luke 8:16; in Matt.
    5:14 Christ says to the disciples 'You are the light of the world' (Vos estis lux
    mundi) and then Patrick is said to be this.
38. Matt. 5:15; Christ says 'Nor does one light a lamp' (neque accendunt lucer-
    nam), Patrick is just this lit-up one (accensum) mentioned in the gospel.
39. Matt. 5:15.
40. Cf. Matt. 5:16.

the king's secure city[41] situated on a mountain top,[42]
there the Lord possesses a great many things.

12. He is the one who is called greatest in the kingdom of the
     heavens,[43]
for he fills out with good deeds those things which he teaches in
     sacred words,
from his good example emanates the very shape of fidelity,
and he trusts in God[44] in his pure heart.[45]

13. Boldly he proclaims the name of the Lord to the nations,[46]
giving them the eternal grace of the washing of salvation,[47]
for whose sins he prays daily to God,
and he offers sacrifices for them, offerings such as God might find
     worthy.

14. He spurns all the glory of the world for the sake of the divine
     law,
he thinks of all that as the sweepings of the table,
nor is he moved by this world's violent lightning,
but in all his troubles he rejoices because he suffers for Christ.

15. A good pastor and a faithful shepherd of the gospel's flock,[48]
whom God has chosen to guard the people of God,
and to feed[49] his people with divine truths,
since he has followed Christ's example and offered his soul for
     them.[50]

16. On account of his merits, the Saviour has promoted him to be
     a pontiff,

41. Cf. Matt. 5:35.
42. Cf. Matt. 5:14.
43. Matt. 5:19.
44. 1 John 3:21.
45. Matt. 5:8.
46. Cf. Acts 26:20.
47. Cf. Titus 3:5.
48. John 10:11.
49. Cf. John 21:15.
50. Cf. Phil. 2:30.

so that he might train clerics to be part of the heavenly host,[51]
he distributes to them their heavenly portions of food[52] and their
    vestments,
which are covered with sacred and divine utterances.[53]

17. He is the messenger of the King inviting the believers to the
    wedding feast,[54]
he is the one decorated in the dress of the wedding garment,[55]
he is he one who pours out the celestial wine in celestial vessels,
offering as drink the spiritual cup to the people of God.

18. He has found the holy treasure in the sacred book,[56]
he has seen the divinity in the flesh of the Saviour,
this treasure he had bought with his holy and perfect merits,[57]
and because his soul sees God, he is called 'Israel'.[58]

19. He is the faithful witness[59] of the Lord in the catholic law,
whose words are sprinkled on divine oracles
lest human flesh rot away and be eaten by worms,
rather than be salted with a celestial flavour for the sacrifice.[60]

20. He is the true and noble carer of the gospel's field,[61]

51. Cf. Luke 2:13.
52. Cf. Ps. 103:27; 144:15.
53. This is a complex image based on the garments of Aaron, the Old Testament
    antitype of the Christian pontiff, on whose splendid heavenly robes (cf.
    Exod. 28 and 39) were inscribed images (cf. Wisd. 18:24), and this theme
    was developed in other documents which would now be labelled
    'apocrypha' – I am indebted to Margaret Barker for help in clarifying the
    meaning of these lines.
54. Matt. 22:3; and cf. Rev. 19:1–7.
55. Matt. 22:11–12.
56. Cf. Matt. 13:44.
57. Cf. Matt. 13:44.
58. Why Patrick should be given the name 'Israel' is based on the etymology of
    the name 'Israel' given by Jerome in his work *On the Hebrew Names*; there
    he says that 'Israel means either "to see God" or "the man or mind seeing
    God"' (*Liber interpretationis hebraicorum nominum* 13, 21).
59. Cf. Rev. 1:5; 2:13; 3:14.
60. Cf. Mark 9:48–50.
61. Matt. 13:24–30.

whose seeds are seen to be the gospels of Christ,[62]
which he sows in the heard of the prudent with his divine mouth,
whose hearts and minds he ploughs with the Holy Spirit.

21. Christ himself chose him to be his vicar on earth,
he who frees captives from a double slavery,[63]
he who had redeemed many human beings from servitude,
and delivers innumerable people from the dominion of Satan.

22. He sings the psalms of God along with the canticles from the
      Apocalypse,[64]
which he teaches in order to build up the people of God,
he believes the law which dwells in the Trinity of sacred name,
and he teaches one substance of three persons.

23. He has girded himself with the Lord's belt,[65] by day and by
      night
he prays to the Lord God without ceasing[66];
the prize of his great labour is ready to come to him,
when he will reign over Israel with the apostles.[67]

---

62. Cf. Matt. 13:38.
63. The meaning of this 'double slavery' was already obscure to Muirchú, see
    Vita 1,10.
64. The phrase *Ymnos cum Apocalipsi salmosque* refers to the Book of Psalms
    and the canticles from the Book of Revelation which were used in the liturgy
    as hymns; one of these, the song of the marriage of the Lamb (Rev. 19:1–7),
    may be part of the mosaic of allusions in verse 17. However, we should be
    cautious in any claim to understand this line for it was obscure to Muirchú
    (*Vita* 3,1) who shared the culture of the hymn's creator to a far greater
    extent than we do.
65. Cf. Sir. 45:9 and Rev. 1:13.
66. Cf. 2 Tim. 1:3.
67. Cf. Matt. 19:28.

❦

CHAPTER 5

The Vita Patricii
by Muirchú[1]

Dedication[2]

My lord Aed,[3] 'many have made an attempt to put order on this historical account according to what their fathers and those who were story-tellers have handed down since the beginning.'[4] However, because of the great difficulty of this work of narration, the diversity of opinions, and the many suspicions of many

---

1. The text of the *Vita* is notorious for the problems it causes editors. The text given here substantially follows Bieler 1979. While this is not without its problems, it provides a good working text for anyone whose primary interest is in the intellectual/religious ambience of the *Vita*, rather than as a witness to late-seventh and eighth-century Irish political history.
2. In the edition and many translations this is referred to as 'the preface', however, at the beginning of the next section we have the statement that 'here begins the prologue.' It is better to see this as the dedication and apology for writing.
3. Aed of Sleaty (a few miles from Carlow town) was already one of the bishops supporting Armagh's claim to be the first church in Ireland. This may have been the occasion for his commissioning of the *Vita*, cf. Hughes 1966, pp. 86, 113–5.
4. Luke 1:1–2; Muirchú is showing that his account of Patrick is a sacred narration and analogous to the story Luke tells in his gospel. The word *narratio* is used on several occasions in this preface and the word 'narrative' springs immediately to mind. I am avoiding that word as when we consider the overall quality of Muirchú's writing it is not fanciful to see in his use of

people, they never arrived at the one and certain path of history. And so, if I am not mistaken, like boys being brought into the arena, as our proverb has it, I have set out on the dangerous and deep ocean[5] of sacred narration in what is, given my abilities, a little child's rowing boat.[6] This ocean has towering waves and sharp reefs and no one has sailed it before me except my father, Cogitosus. But lest you imagine that I am trying to make a mountain out of a molehill, I shall only try to expound a selection from the many deeds of Patrick. I shall do it with little expertise from authors whose worth is less than certain, with a frail memory, weak intellect,[7] and in a wretched style.[8] That I do it at all is only in respectful obedience to your command,[9] and with the most pious affection for your holy charity and your authority.

Prologue

In the name of the king of heaven, the saviour of this universe, here begins the prologue of the life of St Patrick the confessor.

Time, place and person are required. Now 436 years are reckoned from the death of our Lord Jesus Christ to the death of Patrick.[10]

In a book belonging to Ultán, bishop of Connor,[11] I have found four names for Patrick:

[1] Holy Magonus (which means 'famous'); [2] Sochet ... ... [3]

> *narratio* the technical sense given to that word by Augustine in *De doctrina christiana* where it means the careful retelling of the facts so that if there are providential interventions by God in human history these may be clearly seen. On the importance of this concept in insular intellectual life in the late seventh century, cf. O'Loughlin 1997b.
>
> 5. Cf. Isidore of Seville, *Etymologiae*, 13,18,5.
> 6. Cf. Isidore of Seville, *Etymologiae*, 19,2,1; similar images are used by others writing saint's lives, such as the author of the *Life of St Samson of Dol* and Cogitosus in his *Life of St Brigit*. But there may also be a pun here for *Muir cu* means literally 'sea hound'.
> 7. Cf. Vincent of Lérins, *Commonitorium*, 1,6.
> 8. This is the *topos* of humility.
> 9. Another humility motif, cf. Vincent of Lérins's opening remarks in his *Commonitorium*.
> 10. This section is garbled in the manuscripts, cf. O'Loughlin 1996c where this passage is studied in detail.
> 11. See Chapter 6, where this book by Ultán is discussed

Patrick his own name; [4] Cothirthiacus, because he served four houses of wise men.[12] One of these wise men, Miliucc moccu Bóin, bought Patrick and he remained in his service for seven years. Patrick, son of Calpornius, had four names: Sochet when he was born; Cothirthiacus while a slave; Magonus when he was a student; and Patrick when he was ordained.

[His life will be treated in Book 1 under these] Headings[13]

1. Patrick's origins and first captivity.
2. His voyage with the pagans, their anger in a deserted country, and how God granted him and the pagans food.
3. His second captivity when he was held prisoner for sixty days.
4. The reception he received from his parents as soon as they recognised him.
5. About his age when he set out for the apostolic see and his desire to learn wisdom.
6. How he encountered St Germanus among the Gauls and so did not go any further.
7. About the time the angel visited Patrick and asked him to come here.
8. About Patrick's return from Gaul, and the ordination of Palladius who then died.
9. About his ordination by St Amatorex after Palladius's death.
10. About the king at Tara at the time when Patrick brought baptism.
11. Patrick's first journey on this island to redeem himself from Miliucc, before he redeemed others from the devil.
12. About Miliucc's death and what Patrick said about his off-spring.

---

12. The word used by Muirchú is *magus* and this is often rendered as 'druid'; however, since all Muirchú's names for pagan officials are derived from the scriptures, I shall render this word as 'wise man', but noting that it has an additional connotation which is something like 'magician' or 'soothsayer'; cf. O'Loughlin 2002b; and O'Loughlin 2003.
13. This list is the work of a later writer (cf. Thompson 1980, p. 13); the purpose of such lists in books from the early Middle Ages is not simply that of a modern list of chapters, but was intended to form a summary of the work. They form, in effect, an abbreviated *vita* within the *Vita* – and show us, incidentally, how the work was read by later generations.

13. St Patrick's teaching when the decision was taken about the celebration of the first Easter in Ireland.

14. About how the first Easter sacrifice took place in Ireland.

15. About the pagan feast at Tara on the same night when Patrick adored the Paschal Lamb.

16. How King Loíguire travelled from Tara to meet Patrick on Easter night.

17. How Patrick was called to the king, of the faith of Ercc son of Daig, and the death of a wise man that night.

18. On the anger of the king and his retinue at Patrick, on God's plague upon them, and how Patrick was transformed in the presence of the pagans.

19. Patrick's arrival at Tara on Easter day and the faith of Dubthach moccu Lugir.

20. On the context of Patrick and the wise man that day and his wonderful displays of divine power.

21. On King Loíguire's conversion and Patrick's prophesy about his kingdom after him.

22. On the teaching, baptism, and signs of St Patrick following Christ's example.

Book 1[14]

[1] Patrick, called Sochet, was a Briton. His father was Calpornius, a deacon, and his father (as Patrick himself tells us) was Potitus, a presbyter, and they lived in Bannavem Taburniae that is not far from our own sea (I am reliably informed this is what is now called Ventia).[15] His mother's name was Concessa.

14. In some of the manuscripts the book is divided into two books; in others it is without any explicit divisions. However, it is clear from the work's content that Muirchú intended his work to be in three books: book 1 dealing with Patrick's background and training, and culminating in the events of Easter Night at Tara; book 2 dealing with Patrick as a man of holiness and holy power in his dealings with human beings; and book 3 dealing with Patrick's dealings with supernatural beings and the events at the end of Patrick's life and afterwards. The existence of this threefold division in the earliest copies of the *Vita* is confirmed by confusions in the two lists of headings: the first list covers only book 1 and what I identify as book 2, and the second surviving list covers book 3, and some chapters have been misplaced.

15. The location of Patrick's home that as exercised so many scholars over the last century was already a matter of dispute in Muirchú's day.

Patrick was sixteen when, with others, he was captured and brought to this barbarian island and detained by a cruel pagan king.[16] And for six years, in the manner of the Hebrews,[17] 'with fear' of God and 'trembling' as the psalmist says,[18] with vigils and many prayers – a hundred by day and the same number by night,[19] he freely 'rendered to Caesar the things of Caesar, and to God the things of God.'[20] Up to that time he was ignorant of the true God, but, since the Spirit was now fervent in him, he began to fear God and to love the almighty Lord. Then, after many sorrows, after hunger, thirst, cold, exposure,[21] after pasturing flocks, after many visits of Victoricus (the angel sent to him by God), after many great well-known miracles, after many revelations from God[22] (I shall mention just two examples: 'It is good that you fast for soon you will be going home,' and 'Behold, your ship is ready' – but it was not near him but two hundred miles away where he had never been!) Patrick fled that pagan tyrant 'and his practices'[23] and accepted the sacred companionship of the eternal and heavenly God. So, by divine command, he sailed to Britain with pagan barbarian strangers who worshipped false gods. He was twenty-three years of age.

[2] After sailing, like Jonah,[24] for three days and nights; Patrick had to march, like Moses, for twenty-eight days and nights through a desert[25] forced on by the pagans who, like the Jews, murmured about being almost dead from hunger and thirst.[26] Their leader teased him by asking him to call on his god to save

---

16. Throughout the work, Muirchú distinguishes between barbarians (*barbari*) i.e. non-Romans, and pagans (*gentiles*) i.e. non-Christians.

17. Cf. Exod. 21:2 and Deut. 15:12.

18. Ps. 54:6; and cf. Eph. 6:5.

19. *Confessio* 16; O'Leary 1996, p. 291, has argued that this expression of a hundred prayers by day and a hundred by night might be derived from the [so-called] Ps-Abdias's *Historia apostolica*; but this hypothesis is an unnecessary complication as its obvious source is Patrick's own assertion.

20. Matt. 22:21.

21. Cf. 2 Cor. 11:27 (and compare Paul's account of his trials 2 Cor. 11:24–8).

22. Cf. Rom. 11:4; Muirchú is following Patrick's usage, see *Confessio* 17.

23. Col. 3:9.

24. Cf. Jonah 2:1.

25. Allusion to the events of the Exodus in Exodus and Numbers.

26. Cf. Exod. 15:24.

them from perishing.[27] So seeing their need and having pity on them,[28] sharing their suffering, crowned with merit, glorified by God,[29] Patrick supplied them by God's help with an abundance of food from a herd of pigs. These were sent to him by God just as he once sent a flock of quails [to the Israelites].[30] They also, like John [the Baptist] found wild honey, but as the worst of pagans they did not deserve locusts, but only pigs.[31] St Patrick did not touch this food as it had been sacrificially offered,[32] and he suffered no ill effects nor any sense of hunger or thirst.[33] And that same night while he was sleeping Satan attacked him violently – it was as if he were burying Patrick under great stones crushing his limbs. But Patrick called loudly on Elijah twice[34] and immediately the sun rose over him; its splendour scattered the gloomy darkness,[35] and Patrick's powers returned to him.

[3] Many years later Patrick was again captured by strangers. On the first night of this captivity the Lord gave him a revelation[36] saying: 'You will be with your enemies for two months.' And it happened in just that way for the Lord freed him from their hands[37] on the sixtieth day. Moreover he provided Patrick and his followers with food, water and fire for ten days until he encountered other people.

[4] After a few years Patrick was at last back home resting with his parents and relatives. He was received as a son, and they begged him that after his trials and tribulations he never go away again. But he would not agree to this, and while he was at home many visions were given to him.

---

27. The imagery here is related to Jonah 1:14–6.
28. Cf. Matt. 9:36.
29. Cf. Matt. 9:8 and Gal. 1:24.
30. Cf. Exod. 16:13; Num. 11:31; Ps. 104:40.
31. Cf. Matt. 3:4.
32. Cf. 1 Cor. 10:28–9.
33. Cf. Dan. 1:5–16.
34. Cf. Mark 15:35.
35. Cf. Joel 2:2 and Zeph. 1:15; and Acts 13:11 as antitype.
36. Cf. Rom. 11:4.
37. Cf. Gen. 37:21.

[5] He was then nearly thirty, and, as the apostle says, in 'mature manhood, to the measure of the stature of the fullness' of the age 'of Christ.'[38] Then Patrick went off to visit the apostolic see, the head of all the churches of the whole world. He wanted to learn and understand the divine wisdom, and participate in the holy mysteries to which God was calling him, for he wanted to bring divine grace to foreign nations[39] by converting them to the Christian faith.

[6] So Patrick left Britain for Gaul with his heart set on crossing the Alps to reach his final goal: Rome. On this journey he discovered a great gift in the most holy bishop Germanus of the city of Auxerre. He remained with him for a long time – like Paul at the feet of Gameliel[40] – as a perfect student, patient and obedient. Patrick devoted himself whole-heartedly to wisdom, learning and chastity – all that is useful for mind and soul. He kept himself, with great fear and love of God, in goodness and simplicity of heart, a virgin in spirit and body.

[7] After a long time there (some say thirty, others forty, years) his faithful old friend Victoricus (who predicted, when he was a slave in Ireland, what would happen to him) began to visit him frequently to say that it was now time for him to fish with the evangelical net[41] among the wild and barbarian nations whom God had sent him to teach.[42] There he was told in a vision: 'The sons and daughters of the Wood of Foclut are calling you' etc.

[8] So when an opportune time came he began, with divine help, his journey towards the work for which he was long prepared, that of the gospel.[43] Germanus sent a presbyter Segitius with him so

---

38. Eph. 4:13; and cf. Luke 3:23.

39. This section more echoes the mentions of 'the nations' in the Synoptic Apocalypse (e.g. Matt. 24:14) than the commands to evangelise (e.g. Matt. 28:19).

40. Cf. Acts 22:3.

41. The origin of this image is Jer. 16:16; however, Muirchú has an intermediate source which is verse 4 of the hymn *Audite omnes amantes* which, in turn, draws the image from Patrick's *Confessio* 40.

42. Cf. Matt. 4:18; 13:47.

43. Cf. Rom. 1:1.

that he would have a fellow witness for he had not yet been ordained to the episcopal grade by the holy lord Germanus.[44] They were certain that Palladius, archdeacon of Pope Celestine, bishop of the city of Rome (the forty-second[45] successor from Saint Peter the Apostle in holding the apostolic see) had been ordained and sent to convert that island which is situated in the cold and wintry regions. But how could [Palladius] do this when 'no one can receive anything except what has been given from heaven'?[46] Those wild and vicious people would not easily accept his teaching, and Palladius did not want to spend long in a land not his own. So he decided to return to Pope Celestine. Having crossed the sea from Ireland to Britain, he died there while making his way back to Rome.

[9] At Ebmoria Patrick and his companions heard of the death, in Britain, of Palladius from the latter's disciples, Augustine and Benedict. So they detoured to meet a wonderful man called Amathorex who lived nearby. There Patrick, 'knowing all that was to happen to him,'[47] accepted the episcopal grade from the holy bishop Amathorax. There also, and on the same day that Patrick was ordained, his companions Auxilius and Iserninus received the lesser grades. While they were accepting the blessings and doing everything perfectly according to custom, they sang the verses of the psalmist: 'You are a priest forever according to the order of Melchizedek'[48] – something so specifically appropriate for Patrick!

Then in the name of the holy Trinity, our venerable traveller went on board a ship that was ready and waiting for him. Arriving in Britain he travelled across it as quickly as possible – no one seeks the Lord with idleness[49] – and then with a favourable wind he crossed over our sea.

44. The technical language for bishops, priests, deacons, and other ministries corresponds precisely to late seventh-century canonical usage as found in such works as the *Collectio canonum hibernensis*. The translation attempts to echo that language.
45. See Bieler 1979, p. 198.
46. John 3:27.
47. John 18:4.
48. Ps. 109:4 (and cf. the New Testament uses of this verse: Heb. 5:6; 6:20; 7:11; 7:17).
49. Muirchú presumes this is a known proverb, but I have been unable to find other instances of it; it is possible that it is inspired by Matt. 25:26.

[10] At that time there was a mighty and fierce pagan king in those parts.[50] This was the Emperor of the Barbarians, who reigned at Tara that was then the capital of the kingdom of the Irish. This king was Loíguire, son of Níall, whose family rule almost the whole island. He had with him seers and wise men and augurs and spell-casters[51] and those skilled in every one of the evil arts. They were able to know and predict everything – according to the pagan idolatrous custom – before it occurred. Two of these were preferred by the king above the rest: Lothroch (also called Lochru) and Lucet Máel (also called Ronal). With their magical skill this pair often declared that they could see another way of life about to come to Ireland from outside. It would be like a kingdom, it would come from far way across the seas, and it would bring an unknown and gentle teaching[52] with it. This teaching would be given out by a handful, yet be received by many, and held in honour by all. It would overthrow kingdoms, kill the kings who resisted it, seduce the crowds, destroy all their gods, cast out their own skills and works, and this coming kingdom will last forever. They also pointed to the man who would bring this new way of life and persuade people [to accept it]. They prophesied in words that made up a kind of poem which was often recited in those days, and especially in the two or three years just before Patrick's coming. Because of their 'language's peculiar idiom'[53] the poem's meaning is not very clear, but here it is:

> One with shaven head will come here with his curled-headed
>   stick
> He will sing foul things from his home with perforated head
> From his table in the front part of his house his whole family
>   will reply to him: 'Let it be! Let it be!'[54]

50. This chapter is a 'flashback' (i.e. it departs from the forward temporal sequence of the account of the saint) and it is placed here to set the scene for something that will happen later when Patrick meets Loíguire.
51. Cf. 2 Chr. 33:6.
52. For this emendation, see O'Loughlin 2002b, p. 132.
53. This phrase is taken from Jerome's *Prologue to the Book of Job* (these were a standard part of the biblical apparatus in scriptural codices in Muirchú's time).
54. This phrase (*Fiat, fiat*) is found in this form is Judith (10:9; 13:26; 15:12) and, more importantly, in the more used Latin version (that based on the Septuagint) of the Psalms (40:14; 71:19; 88:53; 105:48); it renders the phrase 'Amen, Amen.'

We can say this far more clearly in our own language: when all these things happen,[55] our kingdom – which is pagan – shall not stand.'[56] With the advent of Patrick came the destruction of the cult of the idols,[57] and he filled everything with the universal faith of Christ. We have said enough about these things,[58] now back to our story.

[11] His voyage over, the holy man, heavy with marvels and spiritual riches from beyond the seas, found a suitable landing place in the region of the Cúala – a famous harbour called Inber Dee.[59] There Patrick thought that the best thing to do was to first redeem himself from slavery. So he was eager to go to the northern regions and find the pagan Miliucc who had held him captive. He brought with him twice the price of his servitude, namely the heavenly and the earthly,[60] that he might free the man he once served as a slave. So before he reached the island that is today named after him, Patrick turned the prow of his ship, and leaving Brega and the regions of the Conaille and Ulaid to one side, travelled to the inlet of Bréne. They eventually landed at Inber Slane. He and his companions hid their little boat there and went a little inland to rest. But the swineherd of Díchu, (although a pagan, this man was naturally good), and, by the way, the barn in which he lived is now called after Patrick, found them while they were resting, and thinking them to be 'thieves or robbers'[61] he

55. Cf. Matt. 24:33.

56. Muirchú, whose native language was Irish and for whom Latin was a learned language, engages in a literary conceit here in telling his audience that *their* language is a foreign one, and *our* language (in this case Latin) can express this more clearly. To wish to identify himself with Latin to this extent may indicate that he sees this as the Christian language or the language of light and sophistication.

57. Cf. Wisd. 18:6.

58. Cf. 3 John 10.

59. The geographical locations of the various places mentioned in the *Vita* are matters of controversy among historians; it would take us too far from our purpose here to attempt identifications.

60. This is Muirchú's attempt to explain *Audite omnes*, verse 21.

61. John 10:1; in the gospel, John 10:1–5, anyone who does not come into the sheepfold by the gate is considered a thief and a robber; it is the shepherd who comes in by the gate and the gatekeeper opens the gate for him. Muirchú wants his audience to appreciate the irony that the good pagan tells

went to tell his master. Unawares, the swineherd led Díchu upon them. Díchu's intention was to kill them, but the moment he saw St Patrick's face the Lord changed his thoughts to the good. So Patrick preached the faith to him, and there and then he believed Patrick. Thus Díchu was the first of all the people [to be converted]. The saint rested with Díchu for some days. But the saint wished to depart quickly to visit Miliucc and bring him his price, for thus he might convert him to the faith of Christ. He left his boat with Díchu and began to make his way by land through the region of the Cruithni until he reached Slíab Mís, the mountain on which he worked as a captive many years earlier and where he had seen the angel Victoricus leave his swift footprint on a stone when, in Patrick's sight, he was ascending into heaven.[62]

[12] But Miliucc heard that his slave was coming to see him to make him, by force as it were, change his ways. He did not want this at the end of his life as he did not want to become a subject to his former servant, nor that the servant should now rule over him. At the devil's prompting he decided to destroy himself by fire. So he gathered all his possessions in the house where he was once a king, and set fire to them and himself. St Patrick standing on the right hand side of Slíab Mís – where now for the first time since his return he saw where as a slave he had received such grace – saw the fire lit by the chief with his own eyes. (A cross marks the spot where St Patrick stood to this very day.) Standing there he was speechless, and for two to three hours he wept, sighed and mourned without saying one word.[63] Then he said: "'I do not know, God knows"[64] this human ruler chose to commit himself to

the truth that they are there (the representatives of the true shepherd), but as a pagan he does not recognise their real identity and so mistakes them for the opposite group mentioned in the gospel.

62. This sentence is modelled on Acts 1 (especially 1:9); the notion of the angel leaving a visible footprint in the place of his ascension is parallel to a belief that the footprints of Jesus were visible on Mount Olivet. This story is told in Adomnán's *De locis sanctis* 1,23 – a work roughly contemporary with Muirchú; the presence of this image here suggests that the *De locis sanctis* was written before the *Vita Patricii*.

63. There is an echo here of Christ weeping over Jerusalem (Luke 19:41): the city that would not receive his message and suffered destruction.

64. 2 Cor. 12:2.

the flames lest he should believe in, and serve, the eternal God at the end of his life. "I do not know, God knows"[65] none of this king's sons "shall sit upon his throne"[66] "from generation to generation."[67] And indeed his descendants shall be subject to others forever.' This said, he prayed and armed himself with the sign of the cross,[68] and quickly turned about and went back to the region of the Ulaid along the same route he came. On his return to Mag Inis he remained with Díchu for many days. While there he travelled about the whole region and chose it as a place he loved; and faith began to grow there.

[13] It was coming close to the time of the Passover.[69] This was the first Passover to be celebrated to [the glory] of God in this Egypt which is our island, resembling as it were the Passover, of which we read in Genesis, in the Land of Goshen.[70] Patrick and his companions discussed with the pagans amongst whom God had sent them where they should celebrate this first Passover. After many suggestions were put to them, St Patrick, by divine inspiration, finally decided that this great solemnity of the Lord – since it was the head of all the solemnities – should be celebrated in the great plain of Brega for there was the greatest kingdom of these pagan peoples,[71] the head of all their paganism[72] and idolatry. There, as the Psalmist says, he 'crushed the head of the dragon.'[73] There an unstoppable spike would be driven into the

65. 2 Cor. 12:2.
66. Miliucc's throne is contrasted with 'the throne of David' (e.g. 2 Sam. 7:13-6; 2 Chr. 7:18; Ps. 88:4, 29, 36), which is established for ever.
67. This is a biblical phrase, e.g. Exod. 17:16, or Ps. 78:13.
68. On the significance of this gesture, see Haselock 2002.
69. The word used is *Pascha* which could be translated as 'Easter'; however, in Latin the same word is used for the Christian feast as is used for the Passover in both Old and New Testaments and therefore it calls up a wealth of biblical imagery (as is the case here in Muirchú) which 'Easter' does not. Therefore, since the normal biblical translation of *Pascha* is 'Passover' this is the word adopted here.
70. In Gen. 45:10—50:8 we are told that the Israelites settled in 'the land of Goshen' in Egypt, but nowhere in Genesis is there mention of the Passover. The first Passover is described in Exod. 12, but it could be inferred from Exod. 9:26 that the Israelites were still there at the time.
71. Literally: of these nations.
72. Literally: of their 'gentile-ness'.
73. Ps.73:14.

head of all idolatry[74] with the hammer of a work joined to strong
faith[75] by the spiritual hands of St Patrick and his companions.
'And so it happened.'[76]

[14] So they put to sea leaving that good man Díchu in full faith[77]
and peace, and went to Mag Inis. Now in the fullness of their
ministry, the coast was on their right hand, as was fitting, unlike
earlier when it was on their left. After a good and swift trip they
landed at Inber Colpdi. Leaving their boat they walked to the great
plain and by evening they had reached the burial mounds of Fíacc.
These, so the old story goes as it was told by Ferchertne (one of the
nine wise-man prophets of Brega), were dug by the men, that is
the servants, of Fíacc. And there Patrick and his companions made
camp and offered, with the every devotion of spirit, 'to the most
high God'[78] the Passover 'sacrifice of praise,' and so fulfilled 'the
word of the prophet.'[79]

[15] Now that year another solemnity, this one of idolatry when the
pagans gathered with many spells, feats of magic, and idolatrous
superstitions, was being held at the very same time.[80] Hence the
king, his satraps, leaders, princes, and the nobles of the people had
gathered there.[81] King Loíguire had also called to Tara all the wise
men, those who can predict the future, and those who were trained

---

74. The imagery is from Judg. 4:17–22; see O'Loughlin 2003, p. 132.
75. Cf. 1 Pet. 5:9.
76. Acts 27:44.
77. Cf. Acts 6:5.
78. Cf. Sir. 7:11.
79. Muirchú seems to have in mind Tobit 8:19. This verse, present in the
    Vulgate, is no longer found in modern editions/versions, and reads: 'May
    their hearts, O Lord, always swell with thanksgiving and their lives, which
    you have preserved, be a sacrifice of praise to you until all of the peoples
    acknowledge that you alone are God in all the earth.' However, it could be a
    simpler allusion to Ps. 49:14. The actual phrase used by Muirchú about 'the
    word of the prophet' is taken from Luke 3:4.
80. This whole chapter of the *Vita* is based on Dan. 3:1–24, 91–7; for a detailed
    examination of how Scripture is used here, see O'Loughlin 2003, pp. 128–9.
81. The word 'satraps' is used in the Vulgate as the term for officials in several
    pagan courts (e.g. Judg. 3:3), but the imagery here is that of the gathering of
    all the officials and powerful in the land that was called by Nebuchadnezzar,
    king of Babylon, for the great event of idolatry which is found in Dan. 3:2–3.

or could teach every skill and art.[82] Loíguire at Tara was like Nebuchadnezzar at Babylon who had done likewise.[83] And on the very
night St Patrick was celebrating the Passover, they were partaking of
the worship of their great pagan festival. Now there was a custom
among the pagans – made clear to all by edict[84] – that it would be
death for anyone, wherever they were, to light a fire on that night
before the fire was lit in the house of the king (i.e. the palace of
Tara). So when St Patrick celebrating the Passover lit the great
bright and blessed divine fire it shone out clearly and was seen by
nearly everyone living in the plain of Tara.[85] And those who saw it
viewed it with great wonder. All the elders and nobles of the nation
were called into the king's presence and he spoke to them:[86] 'Who is
this man who has dared to commit such a crime in my kingdom? Let
him perish by death!' And the answer from those around him was
that they did not know. Then the wise men answered: '"O king, live
forever!"[87] This fire, which we see lit this night before the fire of your
own house, must be quenched this night. Indeed, if it is not put out
tonight, it will never be extinguished! You should know that it will
keep rising up and will supplant all the fires of our own religion. The
one who lit it, and the kingdom he is bringing upon us[88] this night,
will overcome us all – both you and us – by leading away everyone
in your kingdom. All the kingdoms[89] will fall down before it,[90] and

---

82. Cf. Dan. 2:2.
83. Cf. Dan. 3:2–3. The image of Nebuchadnezzar as the type of the pagan king
    stands behind this reference. The image is built up from the stories in 2
    Kings, Jeremiah and Daniel 2 where he receives a dream of what will hap-
    pen to him at the end of his days, and many other references. This image was
    compounded by liturgical references to him such as the collect
    Nabochodonosor Rex in Easter ceremonies.
84. Cf. Dan. 6:7–9.
85. For the background to Muirchú's understanding of the Paschal Fire, cf.
    MacGregor 1992, pts 2 and 3.
86. The imagery is that of Herod with the wise men, cf. Matt. 2:4–6.
87. Dan. 6:6 (and cf. Dan. 5:10; 2:4).
88. Cf. Luke 11:22–5.
89. Cf. Matt. 4:8.
90. Cf. Dan. 3:7. The point is complex, for Daniel, a wise man, tells how all the
    peoples fell down before the idol at Nebuchadnezzar's feast; here at the idol-
    atrous feast a pagan wise man tells the king how the people will fall down at
    the feast of the true God. Cf. also Ps. 71:11. This episode has been examined
    in detail by McCone 1990, pp. 86–99.

it will fill the whole country and it 'shall reign forever and ever.'[91]

[16] Just as with Herod, 'when the king heard this he was' very 'troubled, and with him the whole city' of Tara.[92] So he said this in reply: 'This will not happen! But let us go there to see what is going on,[93] and then we can capture or kill the people who are committing this crime in our kingdom.' So, following a practice they had received from their gods, the king ordered three times nine chariots made ready, and he took with him Lucet Máel and Lochru since they were his greatest wise men and more excellent than all the rest in a conflict.

It was at the end of the night that Loíguire left (and as was appropriate to the occasion the heads of both men and horses were turned to the left[94]) Tara for the burial ground of the men of Fíacc. Travelling along the wise men with the king said: 'O king, you should not yourself go into the place where the fire is burning in case this would later cause you to adore the man who lit it. Instead, you should remain outside and let the man be called to you so that he can adore you, and you be in charge of him. Then in your sight we can dispute with this man, and you can judge between us.' The king replied that 'This is a wise policy and I shall follow it.' When they arrived they dismounted from their chariots and horses,[95] but they did not go within the circle of the place of the fire, rather they sat down nearby.

[17] So Patrick was called to come out into the king's presence outside the place of light. Meanwhile, the wise men said to the group: 'Let us not get up when he comes, for anyone who gets up at his coming will later believe him and adore[96] him.' Patrick,

---

91. Rev. 11:15.
92. Matt. 2:3.
93. Cf. Ruth 3:18.
94. The significance of this detail, and other references to 'left' and 'right', is not understood.
95. Cf. Ps. 19:8.
96. The Latin word *adorare* is used; the later verbal distinctions of *adorare/latria* (worship due alone to God) and *uenerare/dulia* (respect, veneration due to the holy) was not yet universal, and it would be anachronistic to 'correct' the text in translation (e.g. by the use of 'venerate') to a later standard of verbal orthodoxy. Such 'corrections' are already found in medieval authors who used Muirchú.

seeing all the horses and chariots as soon as he got up, went towards them. The appropriate verse of the psalmist was on his lips and in his hearts:[97] 'Some take pride in chariots, and some in horses, but we shall walk in the name of [the Lord] our God.'[98]

When Patrick came out they did not rise. But one man, with the Lord's help, was unwilling to obey the wise men's dictates. He was Ercc, son of Daig, whose relics are now adored in the city called Slane. When he arose, Patrick blessed him, and he believed in the eternal God. Then the duel of words began. The wise man Lochru wanted to provoke the saint, so within earshot of him he started to insult the Catholic faith with vile and filthy words. At that moment Patrick caught him with his eye (and like what Peter said about Simon) and let out a mighty, powerful and confident cry to the Lord: 'O Lord who can do all things, and in whose power all things are held in existence, and who has sent me here, grant that this unholy man who blasphemes your name may now be lifted up and cast outside, and die speedily.'[99] This said, the wise man was lifted up into the shy, and then he fell back down to earth splitting his skull on a rock. Thus he died in their presence and the pagans feared.[100]

---

97. On this theme of lips and heart, cf. Isa. 29:13 as used in Matt. 15:8 and Mark 7:6; and cf. also Sir. 12:15.

98. Ps. 19:8.

99. Bieler in his edition suggests that this may be a reference to either, or both, of the apocryphal texts known as the Passion of the Apostles Saints Peter and Paul (*Passio sanctorum apostolorum Petri et Pauli*), ch. 56; and the *Acts of Peter with Simon*, ch. 32. Although he mentioned two apocryphal works, Bieler was clearly of the opinion that it was this second work, the *Acts of Peter with Simon* that was the source here, cf, Bieler 1975, p. 651. More recently, O'Leary 1996, pp. 294–5 has argued that it more closely resembles another version of the *Acts of Peter and Paul*: the *Passio apostolorum Petri et Pauli*. The work was used in Ireland at a very early period (cf. McNamara 1975, pp. 99–101 for comment; and Herbert and McNamara 1989, pp. 99–105 for text). In it there is a contest similar in form to that found in Muirchú: Peter the apostle disputes with Simon the Wise Man (*Magus*) in the presence of the pagan ruler, the Emperor Nero, as to the truth of Christianity; and the result is the death of Simon. However, there is no verbal similarity between these texts, and the death of Simon, while caused by Peter, is not directly a curse; so it could be maintained that the reference by Muirchú to Peter and Simon is only a general reference to the incident in Acts 8.

100. Cf. Isa. 41:5.

[18] So angered were the king and his group by Patrick's actions that they wanted to kill him. The king shouted: 'He is going to destroy us: Grab him!' When St Patrick saw that the blasphemous pagans were about the strike, he stood up and cried out: 'Let God rise up, let his enemies be scattered; let those who hate him flee before him.'[101] At once, darkness descended on them so that those blasphemers fought and clashed with one another in a horrible commotion.[102] The earth shook,[103] the axles of their chariots were crunched together, while horses and chariots were driven headlong over the plain, and only a handful, half-alive,[104] reached Mount Monduirn. In this curse by Patrick seven times seven men perished in the presence of their king; and all at the fruit of the king's own words. The curse continued until there were just four people left: the king himself, his wife, and two Irishmen. They stood there trembling with fear. Then the queen went and spoke to Patrick: 'O righteous and powerful one, do not destroy the king for he is coming to kneel and adore your Lord.'

Terror-driven, the king came into the holy presence and made a display of adoration with his knees, but not with his will. Just after they had departed, the king called St Patrick over to him. His words were deceptive for he wanted to kill Patrick no matter what. But Patrick knowing the thoughts[105] of this most evil king[106] blessed his company of eight men and a boy in the name of Jesus Christ and began to go towards the king. The king was counting them as they approached, when in an instant he could no longer see them. All that the pagans could see was eight deer and a fawn going as if to the desert. So in the early light the king, and the others who had escaped Patrick's curse, turned back towards Tara. He was downcast, fearful, and conscious of his ignominy.

---

101. Ps. 67:2.
102. Cf. Heb. 11:34.
103. This imagery of commotion, darkness (cf. the conflict of Paul with Barjesus in Acts 13:6–12), and earthquake (cf. Matt. 27:54 and Acts 16:26) as a result of a divine intervention is found in several places in the scriptures.
104. Cf. Luke 10:30; and Patrick's *Confessio* 19.
105. Cf. Matt. 12:25; 16:8.
106. There are verbal echoes of the description in 2 Kings 21 of Manasseh who was proverbially *the* evil king.

[19] The next day, which [for us] was the Day of the Passover [Easter Day], was for the pagans the day of their greatest festival; and many kings, princes, and wise men had gathered with Loíguire for a feast.[107] While they were eating and drinking in the palace of Tara,[108] some speaking about what had happened, others turning it over in their minds, Patrick with only five companions appeared among them having come in through 'closed doors' in the way we read about Christ.[109] He went there to proclaim and demonstrate the holy faith in Tara in the presence of all nations.[110] As he entered the dining hall of Tara only one out of the whole group stood to salute his arrival. This was Dubthach maccu Lugir, the greatest of the poets. (With him there was another poet called Fíacc who was then no more than a boy. But Fíacc later became a famous bishop, and today his relics are adored in Sleaty.)[111] When Dubthach stood to honour St Patrick, the saint blessed him and he was the first who believed in God on that day,[112] 'and it was reckoned to him as righteousness.'[113] Seeing Patrick, the pagans asked him to eat with them so that they could test him later. And he, 'knowing all that was going to happen'[114] accepted their invitation.

107. The phrase 'kings and princes' is found on several occasions in the scriptures e.g. Jer. 44:17, Dan. 9:6, Neh. 9:32; and often there is the sense that they were gathered to witness a divine action: e.g. Isa. 19:11; 49:7, or Ps. 76:12. This seems to be the motive here: they are assembled for their purposes, yet God uses this for his own, and their gathering provides a suitable audience for his mighty deeds through Patrick.
108. The imagery is drawn from the description of King Belshazzar's feast in Dan. 5.
109. Cf. John 20:19–29.
110. Muirchú combines the notion of testifying to all peoples (Matt. 24:14 and *Confessio* 3) with that of bearing witness before hostile authorities (Luke 21:12).
111. This reference shows that there was already a cult in Sleaty – the *Vita* was written at the command of Aed who was bishop there – with a connection with Patrick, or a cult that could be connected with the principal Irish cult, i.e. of Patrick, that the *Vita* was promoting.
112. This notion of believing on the day of hearing the word is modelled on the accounts of large numbers being converted in Acts 2:41 on the first day of preaching (Pentecost).
113. Gen. 15:6; and cf. Ps. 105:31; 1 Macc. 2:52; Rom. 4:3, 9, 22; Gal. 3:6; Jas. 2:23.
114. John 18:4.

[20] 'While they were' all 'eating,'[115] one of the wise men, called Lucet Máel, despite having taken part in the nocturnal conflict when his colleague perished, still wanted to challenge Patrick. His first move was to slip something into Patrick's cup from a flask he had with him.[116] Those around him watched to see what Patrick would do. When St Patrick recognised what kind of test this was he blessed his cup. Its contents now became like ice. Then he turned it upside down and only the drop added by the wise man fell out. Blessing it again the contents returned to their natural liquid form, 'and they were all amazed.'[117]

After the cup test the wise man said: 'Let us perform signs in this great field.'[118] So Patrick asked him which kind they should perform. The wise man said: 'Let us call down snow upon the earth.' But Patrick said: 'I do not wish to do anything which is contrary to the will of God.'[119] So the wise man said: 'I will bring it upon the earth for all to see.' Then sending forth magical spells he covered the whole field with snow. It reached the height of a man's belt in depth, and all saw it 'and were amazed'.[120] Then the saint said: 'Behold we have all seen this, now get rid of it!' The wise man

115. Matt. 26:26.

116. This constitutes a particular kind of text for Muirchú: the saint in accordance with Mark 16:18 cannot be injured by any deadly thing in his drink; and note the incident of Paul with the viper in Acts 28:1–6. Hence I depart from Bieler's text, but go with two of the manuscripts, in reading 'After the cup test (*poculum*)' rather than 'after a little while (*paululum*)'. Note that Muirchú sees it as a *kind* of test (*hoc probationis genus*).

117. Mark 1:27.

118. Muirchú's notion of a miracle (*signum*) becomes clear here. He combines the New Testament notion of a miracle as that which produces 'amazement' (*stupor*), e.g. at Luke 5:26, in the Synoptics with that found in John, e.g. John 2:18 where the miracle is a 'sign' (*signum*); in both cases it is the recognition of the event that reveals the person who instigates it. The miraculous is testimony to the power that is present; this can be seen in the number of occasions when there is a connection between seeing 'signs and wonders' (*signa et prodigia*) and belief in some way or other (Matt. 24:24; Mark 13:22; John 4:48; Acts 4:30; 5:12; 14:3; 15:12; Rom. 15:19; 2 Cor. 12:12; 2 Thess. 2:9; Heb. 2:4).

119. This might seem to be an unusual humility given what Patrick had already done. However, allowing that it may be a dramatic refusal to encourage the wise man to do what he cannot undo – and so showing *a fortiori* the relative power of Patrick, it should be noted that sending snow has specific links in the tradition with the will of God; cf. Job 37:6; 38:22; Sir. 43:14.

120. Mark 1:27.

replied: 'I am unable to get rid of it until the same time tomorrow.' So the saint declared: 'You are capable of doing ill, but not of doing good. This is not the case with me.' Then as he cast his blessing around the field the snow disappeared. Without rain or mist or wind it went in a moment. 'The crowd' applauded and 'were amazed',[121] and 'it touched their hearts'.[122] A little later the wise man, by invoking the demons, was able to produce another sign. This time he called down the deepest darkness over the land so that all the people grumbled.[123] Then the saint said: 'Get rid of the darkness!' As before, the wise man could not do this. So the saint prayed, blessed it, and at once the darkness was driven out, the sun shone, and the people cried out and 'gave thanks'.[124]

After all these clashes between Patrick and the wise man had taken place before him, the king said to both of them: 'Throw your books into water, and we shall worship the man whose books escape undamaged.' Patrick answered: 'I will do this,' but the wise man said: 'I refuse to submit to the judgement of water with this man, for he holds water to be a god.'[125] Presumably the wise man had heard that baptism was given through water by Patrick. So the king then replied: 'Then send them through fire.' Patrick said: 'I am prepared to do this.' But the wise man was unwilling and stated: 'This man worships fire and water in alternate years as god: now water is his god, now fire.' The saint replied: 'This is not true. What should happen is this: you should go with one of the boys who accompany me into an enclosed house that is divided into two separate parts.[126] You put on my vestment,[127] while my boy

---

121. Matt. 9:33.
122. Acts 2:37.
123. This miracle appears to be the antitype of that produced by Moses in Egypt (Exod. 10:21).
124. Rom. 1:21.
125. The phrase is modelled on Ex. 20:3.
126. It seems an unequal contest for while the wise man has to enter the house himself, Patrick can use a deputy. However, Muirchú may intend to show by this the great power of Patrick: not only is he mighty in holiness in that he is protected, but his power is such that he can reproduce it in one of his spiritual 'sons'. Just as Christ's power creates an image in the Christian who then shares in his power, so the mighty saint can reproduce himself in his followers, who in turn become extensions of him (I am indebted to Prof. J. Nagy for this suggestion).
127. I translate *uestimentum* with the liturgical term 'vestment' as it is clear from the context, and from the later references to chasubles, that it is not ordinary but ritual clothing that is intended here.

puts on yours. Then let both of you be set on fire "in the sight of the Most High."'[128] The scheme was acceptable and they set about building the house: one half was made from green wood, the other from dry wood. Into the green part stepped the wise man, while in the dry part was placed Benignus, one of Patrick's boys, wearing the magical robe [of the wise man]. Then with the house closed up from outside, it was set ablaze while the whole crowd looked on. 'And it came to pass in that hour,'[129] through Patrick's praying that the flaming fire[130] consumed the wise man and the green wood entirely.[131] St Patrick's chasuble alone surviving intact as the fire did not touch it. Happily, the exact opposite result happened to Benignus. Although he was in the dry part of the house, in his case it was like what was said about the three boys [in the fiery furnace]: 'The fire did not touch them at all and caused them no pain or distress.'[132] Only the wise man's chasuble that the boy was wearing was burnt[133] – and this happened by God's command.

The king 'was greatly infuriated'[134] with Patrick over the death of his wise man and would have killed him except that he was prevented by God. At Patrick's bidding and by his word the anger of God came down upon that blasphemous people,[135] and many of them perished.[136] Then St Patrick spoke thus to the king: 'Unless you now believe, you shall quickly die, for the anger of God has come down upon your head.'[137] And the king feared greatly and

128. Sir. 39:6.

129. Rev. 11:13.

130. The notion of flaming fire seems tautologous, but within Muirchú's physics it is a precise statement of what he saw as the facts: 'fire' is one of the four elements – as such it is the inherent heat that goes to make up material things – and one manifestation of this element is the particular species of 'fire' that we see in a burning fire, i.e. 'flaming fire'.

131. The whole incident appears to be modelled on the clash between Elijah and the prophets of Baal in 1 Kings 18:19–40; this passage is examined in detail in O'Loughlin 2002, pp. 87–108; and O'Loughlin 2002b.

132. Dan. 3:50 (in modern versions this is sometimes numbered 3:27); on the biblical text used by Muirchú – directly related to this passage, see O'Loughlin 2003, pp. 125–6.

133. Cf. Heb. 11:34.

134. Matt. 2:16; again the king is being modelled on Herod.

135. Rom. 1:18.

136. Cf. 1 Macc. 13:49.

137. Cf. Ps. 7:17.

his heart was in turmoil,[138] and with him that of the whole city.[139]

[21] So King Loíguire gathered his elders and whole senate and said to them: 'It is better that I believe, rather than that I die.'[140] So having held the meeting, on the counsel of his fellows he believed on that day and he turned to the eternal Lord God, and in that place many others believed.[141] And Patrick told the king: 'Because you have resisted my teaching and have put obstacles in my way, although the day of your reign shall be prolonged, none of your descendants shall ever be king.'[142]

[22] So then St Patrick, according to the precept of the Lord Jesus, 'went off teaching all the nations and baptising them in the name of the Father and of the Son and of the Holy Spirit.'[143] He 'went out' from Tara 'and proclaimed the good news everywhere, while the Lord worked with him and confirmed the message by the signs that accompanied it.'[144]

Book 2[145]

Headings

1. Of Macc Cuill and his conversion at the word of Patrick.
2. The tale of Dáire, his horse, and his gift of Armagh to Patrick.
3. Of pagans working on the Lord's Day while ignoring Patrick's command.
4. How at Patrick's word fruitful land was turned into a swamp.
5. About the death of Monesan the Saxon.
6. How St Patrick saw the heavens opened and saw the Son of Man and his angels.[146]

138. Cf. 1 Sam. 28:5.
139. The phrase is modelled on Matt. 2:3, but its language follows Matt. 21:10.
140. Cf. Jonah 4:8.
141. Cf. John 7:31; 8:30; 12:42; Acts 17:12.
142. Cf. Jer. 33:26.
143. Matt. 28:19; for the complex use of gospel quotations in this chapter, see O'Loughlin 2002b, p. 129.
144. Mark 16:20.
145. This division is not explicitly indicated in the extant manuscripts.
146. Cf. Acts 7.

7. Of St Patrick's conflict with Coirthech [Coroticus], king of
Ail.

[1] Now, God willing, I want to try to narrate a few of the many
wonders of Patrick, bishop and eminent teacher of the whole of
Ireland.

In Patrick's time, one of the men in the Ulaid region of Ireland
was Macc Cuill Greccae.[147] He was such a wild and wicked tyrant
that he was nicknamed 'the Cyclops'.[148] He was depraved in his
thought, intemperate in his words, evil in his actions, bitter in
spirit, angry in soul, impious in body, unfeeling in mind, a gentile
in lifestyle, and stupid in conscience.[149] This tyrant used to operate from a barren fastness called Druim moccu Echach that was
high in the mountains. Every day he used to cruelly ambush and
kill travellers moving through that region. Indeed, he was so cruel
that he adopted cruelty as his trademark. So deeply had he fallen
into wickedness that one day when he was sitting on his hilltop
and saw St Patrick approaching, his first thought was to kill him.
Patrick walked along the way radiating the clear light of faith and
sparkling with the wondrous halo of heavenly glory, and with the
untroubled trust that comes with Christian teaching. Macc Cuill
then said to his partners in crime: 'Look! Here comes the seducer
and perverter of the people! His game is to make a mighty display
of "power" so that he can deceive and lead astray crowds of people. Let us set out and ensnare him, and then we will know
whether or not this god he keeps talking about has any power.' So
they tempted the holy man thus. They placed a healthy member of
their gang in the middle of the group with a cloak over him. This
man then pretended to be fatally ill. In this manner they wanted
to prove that the saint was a fraud, and then they thought they
could call the saint a seducer, his miracles could then be called
illusions, and his prayers described as spells and witchcraft.

As Patrick and his disciples got closer, the bandits said to him:
'Look over here! One of us has just taken ill. So come closer and

---

147. This story of a murderer who becomes a monk and then a bishop is mod-
    elled on the account of Abba Moses in John Cassian's *Conlationes*, 3,5,2 (cf.
    O'Loughlin 2002b, p. 128).
148. Cf. Isidore of Seville, *Etymologiae*, 14,6,33.
149. This list of the qualities of the evil man, allows us to infer what Muirchú
    considered to be the qualities of sanctity.

sing some of the spells of your sect over him for you might be able to heal him.'[150] Patrick, knowing all[151] their deceits and lies, stoutly and bravely said to them: 'If he had been ill [his death] would be no surprise.' Then the gang uncovered the face of the one who pretended illness and they discovered that he was dead. Stupefied and bewildered by this great miracle the pagans said to one another: 'Truly this is a man of God,[152] and we have done evil in tempting him.'

Then St Patrick turned towards Macc Cuill and asked him: 'Why did you want to tempt me?' The cruel tyrant replied: 'I am repentant of this deed, and whatever you order me to do I will do. Now I deliver myself into the power of this high God of yours whom you preach.' And St Patrick said: 'Then "believe in my Lord" and God "Jesus",[153] and "confess your sins"[154] and be baptised "in the name of the Father and of the Son and of the Holy Spirit."'[155] And, 'at that very hour'[156] he was converted, and he believed in the eternal God, and was baptised. Then Macc Cuill told the saint even more: 'I confess to you, Patrick my holy lord, that I had proposed to kill you. So judge what is the debt that I owe for so great a crime.' Patrick replied: 'I am unable to judge, but God will judge. You must now go down to the sea, unarmed, and leave this part of Ireland. You can take none of your riches except one piece of clothing. Something poor and small that just about covers you. You are not to taste or drink any of the fruits of this island, and you shall bear this as a mark of your sin upon your head.[157] When you arrive at the shore bind your feet with an iron fetter and throw its key into the sea. Then get into a one-hide boat[158] and put to sea without a rudder or an oar. You can then

---

150. This incident is set out as a contrast to the faith of the centurion in Matt. 8:5–13.
151. Cf. John 18:4.
152. Cf. Matt. 27:54.
153. Acts 16:31; the addition of 'and God' is an expansion of the verse by conflation with John 20:28.
154. Sir. 4:31.
155. Matt. 28:19; the instruction itself ('now be baptised') is based on Acts 22:16.
156. Matt. 10:19.
157. Cf. Gen. 4:15.
158. Such a craft was not only small, but also very flimsy as it could be easily holed. I am indebted to Dr Jonathan Wooding for this information.

accept wherever the wind and sea take you. In whichever place divine providence lands you, there you are to dwell and keep God's commandments.' Macc Cuill said: 'I shall do as you have said. But what shall we do about this dead man?' Patrick replied: 'He shall live and rise without pain.' And at that hour Patrick raised him and he returned to life healthy. Meanwhile Macc Cuill departed in silence. He went to the southern shore of Mag Inis having the untroubled trust of faith. He bound himself on the seashore and threw the key into the sea as he had been ordered. He then took to the sea in a small little boat. The north wind blew and propelled him towards the south. Finally, it cast him ashore on the island called Evonia. There he encountered two truly wonderful men, splendid in faith and in teaching. These two had been the first to teach the word of God and [give] baptism on Evonia, and the island's people had been converted to the Catholic faith through their teaching. Their names were Conindrus and Rumilus. When these two saw the man with only one short garment they were amazed and sorry for him. So they lifted him from the sea and received him with joy. He, on the other hand, having discovered spiritual fathers in this place picked for him by God, trained his body and soul in accordance with their rule. He passed the rest of his time on earth in that place with these two holy bishops, and eventually was their successor in the episcopate. This is Macc Cuill, bishop of Mane and prelate of Arde Huimnonn.[159]

[2] 'There was once a rich man'[160] honoured in the eastern region [Airthir] 'who was named'[161] Dáire. St Patrick asked him to give a particular piece of land over to him for the practice of religion. So the rich man said to the saint: 'Which piece are you asking for?' 'I request' said the saint 'that you give me the piece of high ground named Druimm Sailech, and I can build in that place.' But [Dáire] did not want to give that piece of high ground to the saint, so he gave him another piece of low-lying land – what is now the burial mount of the martyrs near Armagh – and St Patrick lived there with his companions.

---

159. This place is identified as the Isle of Man.
160. Luke 16:1, 9; and cf. Matt. 27:57.
161. Cf. Luke 1:27; John 1:6; Acts 13:6.

Some time after that one of the men who looked after Dáire's horses brought one of those horses to pasture in the very grassy place belonging to the Christians. This letting loose of a horse in his place offended Patrick, who said: 'Dáire has done a stupid thing in sending brute animals to upset this little place which he has given to God.' But the handler 'did not hear as if he were deaf, and like one who is dumb he opened not his mouth'[162] and said nothing. However, he left the horse there for the night and went off. On the following morning, however, when he came back to check on the horse he found that it was dead. He then went back to his master's house full of sadness and said to him: 'Behold that Christian killed your horse, because it offended him that his place was disturbed.' Then Dáire said to his men: 'That man also shall be killed. Away now and kill him!' Just then as his men went outside, Dáire was gripped in death. His wife then said: 'This death is caused by the Christian. Someone must go quickly and bring us his blessings and we will be well.[163] Those who have gone off to kill the Christian are to be stopped and called back here.' So two men went off and, not letting on what had occurred, said to [Patrick]: 'Behold Dáire has just been taken ill. We want to carry back something from you which might be able to heal him.' But St Patrick knowing what had happened said: 'You don't say?' So he blessed water and gave it to them saying: 'Go, sprinkle some of this water on your horse and take it with you.' So they did this and the horse came back to life. Then they brought the water with them and when Dáire was sprinkled with this holy water he was restored to health. After this Dáire came and paid homage to St Patrick, and he brought along with him a wondrous bronze bowl from across the seas which could hold three measures.[164] Then Dáire said to the saint: 'Behold this bronze is yours.' And St Patrick responded: 'Grazacham!'[165] On returning home Dáire said: 'This man is a fool. If he can say nothing more than "grazacham" for such as wonderful bronze as can take three measures!' So Dáire told his servants: 'Go off and carry back to us our bronze.' They went away and said to Patrick: 'We shall carry away this bronze.'

162. Ps. 37:14.
163. The text is emended here from 'you will be well'.
164. Cf. Jn 2:6.
165. A colloquial form of *gratias agamus* ('we give you thanks'), something like our simple expression 'thanks'.

Nevertheless, this time Patrick [again] said: 'Grazacham, carry it away!' And the servants carried it off. Later Dáire questioned his fellows: 'What did the Christian say when you carried off the bronze?' They told him: 'He said "grazacham".' Dáire then said in response to this: '"Grazacham" in giving, "grazacham" in taking away.[166] His statement is such a good one that with these uses of "grazacham" his bronze shall be carried back to him again!' This time Dáire himself came to Patrick carrying the bronze. [Dáire] said to him: 'Let this be your bronze. You are a steady and unflappable man. Moreover, that plot of the land which I have, but which you once asked for, that I now give to you so that you can dwell there.' This is the place of the city we call Armagh. And both St Patrick and Dáire went out and surveyed that wonderful offering and most pleasing gift. They then ascended to the high ground there and found a deer with its little fawn lying in the place where now the altar is located in the northern church of Armagh. Patrick's companions wanted to catch and kill the fawn, but the saint did not want this to happen and would not permit it. Instead, the saint himself took hold of the fawn and carried it in his arms and the deer followed him like a loving lamb until he set the fawn free in another valley on the northern side of Armagh.[167] There even today, as those who know about these things relate, some signs of his power still remain.

[3] On another occasion St Patrick was resting on the Lord's Day. He was beside a marsh up above the seashore not far north of Druimm Bó. There he heard the sound of some pagans nearby who were working on the Lord's Day busily digging the ditch that runs around a rath. So Patrick called to them and prohibited them from working on the Lord's Day.[168] But far from listening to the words of the saint, they began to laugh at him and make fun of what he said. Then St Patrick said: 'Mudebroth,[169] though you

---

166. Cf. Job 1:21.

167. The imagery is that of the good shepherd from Isa. 40:11.

168. This reference to the developing notion of refraining from work or travel on Sunday is the earliest indication we have from Irish sources of what would later become a significant element in Christian practice in Ireland as witnessed by the *Cáin Domnaig* ['The Law of Sunday'] (*c.* AD 800); see O'Loughlin 1990; and Maher 1994.

169. This is an Irish corruption of early Welsh, it means 'by the God of judgement'.

labour hard, it will benefit you nothing!' And this happened exactly as the saint had said: on the very next night a great wind came and tossed up the sea, and the tempest wrecked the entire work of those pagans.

[4] It is reported by those who know these things that there was once a tough and very greedy man in Mag Inis. Indeed he was so greedy he had become stupid in his avarice. Thus one day when the two oxen that drew Patrick's cart after the holy work of the day were resting and grazing in one of his meadows this silly man chased them off with force – and he did this in the presence of St Patrick. St Patrick was so angered by this that he uttered this curse: 'Mudebroth!'[170] You have done evil. This field will never again be of any use to you nor to your descendants forever. From this moment forth it will be useless.' 'And it was so.'.[171] On that very same day there was a mighty inundation from the sea which washed over the whole field. It was like what is described in the prophet's words: 'a fruitful land [is turned] into a salty waste, because of the wickedness of its inhabitants'.[172] The result is that it has been sandy and infertile ever since that day when St Patrick cursed it 'down to today.'[173]

[5] At that time when the whole of Britain was held rigid in unbelief, one of its kings had a noble daughter called Monesan. She, 'full of the Holy Spirit,'[174] refused with God's help all the proposals from those who wanted to marry her. Despite frequent drenchings with water, they could not force her to do what she did not want and that which she considered of lesser worth.[175] Now between the beatings and the drenchings her mother and her nurse sought to persuade her to marry, but Monesan kept questioning them if they knew who made the spheres of the heavens by which the universe is given light. When she got the

---

170. This is an Irish corruption of early Welsh, it means 'by the God of judgement'.
171. Cf. Gen. 1:7.
172. Ps. 106:34.
173. See for example Matt. 27:8.
174. Luke 1:41.
175. On this evaluation of virginity in contrast to marriage in Muirchú's ecclesiastical culture, see O'Loughlin 1997c.

answer that the maker of the Sun was he whose seat is in heaven,[176] she, when frequently asked to join in the bond of marriage, said: 'I shall never do this.' And in this she was enlightened with the most luminous counsel of the Holy Spirit. So she searched, like Abraham before her, 'through nature for the maker of all that is created.'[177] Her parents took advice on her behaviour and heard that Patrick was a just man[178] who was visited by the eternal God every seventh day.[179] So they went to Ireland with their daughter and after much labour they encountered Patrick who asked where they had come from. So the travellers began to shout loudly and tell him: 'It is the intensity of the desire of our daughter to see God that has made it necessary for us to travel to you.' So Patrick, 'full of the Holy Spirit,'[180] lifted his voice and asked her: 'Do you believe in God?' She replied: 'I believe!' Then he washed her 'with the washing of water[181] and the Holy Spirit.[182] Just after that, without any delay, she lay on the ground and handed her spirit over into the hands of the angels.[183] Where she died, there she was joined [to Christ]. Then Patrick foretold that after twenty years her body would be taken with honour to a little chapel that was near that place. And later this happened. Indeed, the relics of this woman from across the sea are worshipped there to this day.

[6] We must make brief mention of [another] miraculous deed of

---

176. Cf. Ps. 2:4; 102:19; Isa. 40:22; Heb. 8:1.
177. Book of Jubilees 11:15–7. McNamara 1975, p. 20, said that it could not be stated 'with certainty whether this apocryphon was known in Ireland'; and, at McNamara's suggestion, Bieler in the edition of Muirchú (p. 206) advanced the possibility that this snippet of information was known by way of one of the letters of Jerome. However, this is a direct quotation and therefore offers direct evidence that his book, which was very widely used in Latin in the early Middle Ages in Europe, was available to Muirchú.
178. This title is given to several men in Scripture: Noah (Gen. 6:9), Joseph the husband of Mary (Matt. 1:19) and Lot (2 Pet. 2:7).
179. This passage provides a valuable insight into how Muirchú viewed the Eucharist; there is very little indeed extant from this period in Ireland that can give us such an indication of how the Eucharist was viewed.
180. Luke 1:41.
181. Eph. 5:26.
182. Cf. John 3:5 (and note John 1:33).
183. Echo of Luke 23:46.

Patrick, that apostolic man of the Lord, while he still stood here in the flesh. Indeed it is so wondrous that it is only written about him and Stephen.[184] Once just before he went to his usual nightly place for solitary prayer, Patrick saw the wonders of the heavens.[185] The saint then wishing to test his most beloved and faithful boy, Benignus, said to him: 'O my son, tell me, I beg you, if you see those things which I see?' The little fellow replied with confidence: 'It is known to me already what you sense, for I see heaven opened and the Son of God and his angels.'[186] The Patrick said: 'I now realise that you are worthy to be my successor.'[187] Then without delay and with hastened step they arrived at the usual place of prayer which was a river bed in mid-river. During the prayers the young fellow said: 'I cannot take the cold of this water any longer!' for the water was exceedingly cold for him. Patrick told him to move down from the upper part of the river to a place lower down. But Benignus could not stand there either for he declared that now he felt the water to be exceedingly hot. So not being able to stay there any longer, he got up out of the river and onto the land.

[7] I must not omit mention of another of Patrick's wonderful deeds. He had heard of the most wicked act committed by one of the kings of the British. This was that foul and cruel tyrant Coroticus who was a great persecutor and killer of Christians. Patrick sent him a letter in which he attempted to call him back to the way of truth.[188] But Coroticus only sneered at these saving admonitions. When it was conveyed to Patrick that sneering was

184. The allusion is to Acts 7; but it should be noted that seeing into heaven is a common saintly attribute, and second, that Muirchú takes the notion that miracles fall into specific categories – and therefore the same miracle can be found in saint after saint – for granted; he then makes a point in this case that it is only Patrick and Stephen – thereby indicating their equal stature in holiness.

185. Cf. Job 37:14.

186. Cf. Acts 7:55, but note that in Acts, Stephen sees the Son of Man at the right hand of the Father, whereas here we have the Son of God and the angels. The text here is a silent conflation of Acts with the promise made by Christ of 'the greater things' that will be seen by the disciples in John 1:51.

187. The picture created by Muirchú seems to echo the election of Elisha as the successor to Elijah in 2 Kings 2.

188. The expression is found in several places in Scripture: e.g. Tobit 1:2; Wisd. 5:6; 2 Pet. 2:2.

the only outcome of his letter, he prayed to the Lord and said: 'O Lord, if it be possible,[189] cast out this traitor[190] from the present life and from the life to come.'[191] Only a little time had passed after this when Coroticus heard someone singing in accompaniment to music that he should move off his throne. And then all who were dearest to him burst out in one voice with this song. There and then, in the midst of them all, he miserably took on the form of a fox. At once he left that place and since that very hour and day he has never been seen. It was as if Coroticus was like water: once it has flowed away it is never seen again.

Book 3

Headings

1. Patrick's diligence in prayer.
2. How someone who was dead spoke with him.
3. How a Sunday night was lit up so that they could find horses.
4. About the weekly visit of an angel to Patrick.
5. About the angel preventing him from choosing to die in Armagh.
6. About the burning bush with the angel in it.[192]
7. Concerning Patrick's four requests.
8. About his day of death and his life-span of thirty years.
9. How a barrier was placed against the night and so for twelve nights there was no darkness.
10. How he received the Eucharist[193] from Bishop Tassach.
11. About the angels who kept the vigil beside his body on the first night of his funeral.

---

189. Cf. Rom. 12:18; Matt. 24:24.
190. In the remainder of the text Muirchú gives the impression that Coroticus is a pagan opposed to Christianity. Here by his use of *perfidus* (traitor) he shows his acquaintance with the *Epistola* where Coroticus is treated not as a pagan, but as an 'apostate', this being equivalent to a grievously sinful Christian
191. This linkage of 'the present' and 'future ages' can be found in Mark 10:30 and Eph. 1:21.
192. Cf. Exod. 3:2 with Acts 7:30.
193. The Heading reads 'sacrifice' (*De sacrificio*), and it is clear from the chapter that this was the Eucharist (*uiaticum*), hence the translation here.

12. About the advice given by an angel regarding where Patrick's tomb should be.
13. How fire came out from his tomb.
14. How the sea level rose so that there could not be a war over his body.
15. How the people were happily led astray.

[1] Of his diligence in prayer, we shall try to write down only a few details out of the many things that might be said about Patrick. Daily, whether he was staying in one place or travelling along the road he used to sing all 'the psalms and hymns' and the Apocalypse of John 'and' all 'the spiritual songs'[194] of the scriptures.[195] No less than a hundred times in each hour of the day and each hour of the night he made the sign of the triumphant cross upon himself; and at every cross he saw as he travelled, he used to get down from his chariot and turn towards it in order to pray.

[2] While travelling in his chariot one day Patrick passed by a cross, which had been erected alongside the road, without observing it. But the charioteer, though he said nothing at the time, did see it. After further travelling Patrick and the charioteer arrived at the inn where they were to spend the night. They were inside and about to pray before eating when the charioteer commented to Patrick: 'I saw a cross placed alongside the road we have just travelled.' At once Patrick got up, left the inn, and went back along the road. When he arrived at the cross Patrick began to pray before it, and then noticed that it was located over a tomb. So Patrick questioned the dead man about who he was, about the sort of death he had suffered, and as to whether he was a believer who lived within the faith. The dead man replied to Patrick in this way: 'When I was alive I was a pagan, yet now I am buried here as a Christian. In another province there was a woman whose son died in these parts. The area was quite foreign to her and she did not know where he had been buried. Afterwards while mourning her sad loss she travelled here to find his grave. But she was so upset that she thought my grave was that of her son. So she set up that

194. Eph. 5:19.
195. Clearly the meaning of verse 22 of *Audite omnes* was no clearer to Muirchú than it is to us.

cross beside me by mistake.' Once Patrick heard this and that the cross was located on a pagan tomb he could understand how it had happened that he failed to see the cross when he first passed it.[196] But what is most interesting about this event, and which really shows us the power of the saint, is that he could raise up a dead man in order to converse with him. And moreover, the grave of a man who died in the faith of Christ became known, and the nourishing cross came to be placed in its true location beside him who deserved this sign.

[3] Now Patrick had a custom that he would not move onwards on his journeys from the evening[197] of the night of the Lord's Day[198] until the morning of the Second Day of the Week.[199] Now on the Lord's Day on one occasion, when in honour of the sacred time he was passing the night in a field, a mighty rainstorm began. But while heavy rain fell over the whole peopled area of our fatherland, in that place where the holy bishop was spending the night the ground was bone dry. It was just like what happened to Gideon's bowl and fleece.[200]

[Another time, Patrick's] charioteer realised that the horses had gone astray and was grieving about this as if he had just lost close friends! But as it was dark he could not go and search for them. So Patrick was moved to kindness like a godly father[201] and said to the tearful charioteer: 'God is always ready to help us in our difficulties and he grants us his mercy in all our misfortunes,[202] so you

---

196. This curious incident gives us an insight into Muirchú's eschatology. A Christian tomb was considered a place of power, e.g. the tombs of the saints were places for intercessory prayer, as in such a tomb lay someone who was one of the elect while they awaited the resurrection. As such this presence could radiate itself through the sign; but the sign alone, as here where we have the cross but not the waiting soul it should be marking, did not have this radiance. The obverse of this argument is that the dead pagan is just lying there, his soul stuck in the ground and not possessing any power nor awaiting anything, and as such he is one of the damned (see O'Loughlin 1996b and O'Loughlin 2001a where these beliefs about tombs are examined in detail).

197. Literally: vespers.

198. I.e. Saturday night (the First Vespers of Sunday).

199. I.e. Monday morning.

200. Judg. 6:36–40.

201. Cf. Luke 11:11–2.

202. This statement echoes Ps. 29:11; 24:17; 33:5; Heb. 13:6.

shall find these horses that you are crying over.' Then holding out
his hand, and drawing clear his sleeve, Patrick raised his hand and
his five fingers shone out like spotlights. They lit up all the area
round about them and in that light the man was able to find his
missing horses, and to stop crying. But [we should note] this
miracle was not known about during Patrick's lifetime because
the charioteer told no one about it until after Patrick's death.

[4][203] Now back to the story. Every week on the seventh day an
angel visited Patrick who enjoyed speaking with him as one man
speaks to another.[204] Even when he was sixteen, and spending six
years in slavery,[205] the angel visited him, and Patrick enjoyed the
angel's advice and conversations on thirty occasions before
leaving Ireland for the land of the Latins.[206] Once he lost the pigs
he was herding and the angel came and showed him where they
were. The next day, having talked about several things, the angel
put his foot on the rock of Scirit, beside Slíab Mís, and ascended
in his presence.[207] The imprint can still be seen in that place
where the angel visited him thirty times. It is now a place of prayer
for the faithful for prayers said there obtain the most happy fruit.

[5] Finally, after all the miracles [some recorded here,] others
written about elsewhere, and not to mention those which are
piously passed on by word of mouth, the day of Patrick's death
was drawing near. Indeed, an angel came to speak to him about it.
So Patrick sent word to Armagh since that was the place he loved
above all the lands. He ordered that many men should come to
him and bring him to where he wanted to go. So with his company
about him he began his desired journey to Armagh, to the land of
his great longing.

203. Where this chapter should be located in the text is unclear – Bieler, with
    some of the manuscripts, placed it after book 1,12, but it certainly does not
    belong there; I am placing it here as the last episode dealing with supernat-
    ural creatures and prior to the tales relating to Patrick's death.
204. There is an echo of what is said in Exod. 33:11 about how Moses spoke with
    God.
205. A gloss in the Book of Armagh adds: 'When he said a hundred prayers by
    day and a hundred by night.'
206. Another conceit: the land of the Latins is opposed to the land of the bar-
    barians, but Muirchú is writing in Latin!
207. See the note on book 1, 11 above.

[6] However, as he travelled he saw near the road, just like Moses before him, 'a bush that was burning, but not consumed.'[208] Victor, the angel who used to visit Patrick, was in the bush.[209] Victor [sent] another angel to prevent Patrick travelling to where he wanted to go,[210] and this angel said to him: 'Why are you setting out on this journey without the advice of Victor? Victor is calling you now, so deviate from your route and go to him.' In response to this message Patrick changed direction as ordered, and asked what he ought to do. The angel answering his questions said: 'Return to where you have come from[211] (namely Saul), and the four petitions you have prayed for are granted to you.'

[7] 'The first petition was this: that you [Patrick] shall rule in Armagh.

'The second petition was this: that anyone who on the day of his death sings the hymns you [Patrick] composed shall have the correct penance for his sins judged by you.

'The third petition was this: that the offspring of Dichú, who received you in such a generous fashion, shall deserve mercy and not perish.

'The fourth petition was this: that "on the day of judgement"[212] all the Irish shall be judged by you. Just as once it was said to the apostles: "And you shall sit judging the twelve tribes of Israel,"[213] so may you judge those people whose apostle you have been.'[214]

208. Exod. 3:2.
209. This image of an angel in the burning bush is derived from Acts 7:30 which alludes to Exod. 3:2, but says that Moses met an angel in the bush.
210. Cf. John 21:18–9; this is a complex allusion by which Patrick is equated with Peter: in old age Peter cannot determine where he is to go, so too Patrick in old age cannot choose.
211. Cf. Num. 24:11.
212. Matt. 10:15; 11:22, 24; 12:36; and many other places in Scripture.
213. Matt. 19:28.
214. Several lists of 'the petitions of Patrick' have survived, here a particular list which links loyalty to Armagh with survival in the judgement, is given added authority by being uttered by an angel. While notion of a favoured judgement as a result of specific actions (e.g. singing a hymn) may seem very alien to us, we should remember that variants of this formula (e.g. the 'Nine Promises to St Margaret Mary', where the form of intercession had been theologically sanitised by linking it to the Sacred Heart of Jesus) were still a vibrant part of Roman Catholic preaching in the first half of the twentieth century, and still figure in certain eschatological cults within Catholicism.

[8] 'So turn back now as I have told you, and in death you will enter into the way of your fathers.'[215]

And the death of Patrick took place on the sixteenth day of the Kalends of April [i.e. 17 March] and 'the years of his life numbered one hundred and twenty years in all.'[216] [His feast] is celebrated by all the Irish each year [on that day].

[9] 'And you shall set a barrier against the fall of night.'[217] So on the day Patrick died there was no night, nor was there night in that province for the following twelve nights while they celebrated his passing. With its dark wing night did not embrace the earth; nor was there even dusk; and the Evening Star did not bring in its train the star-bearing shadows. The people of the Ulaid tell that until the end of that entire year the nights were not as dark as they had been. All this happened to declare the merit of so great a man. If anyone should doubt that these things took place at the time of Patrick's funeral, let him listen to the scriptures and carefully attend to what happened to Hezekiah. As a sign of health he was shown the Sun moving backwards over 'ten lines' 'on the sundial of Ahaz' so that the day was almost doubled in length.[218] Or let him note [what Joshua said]: 'Sun, stand still at Gibeon, and Moon, in the valley of Aijalon.'[219]

[10] When the hour of his death was drawing near, Patrick received the sacrifice from Bishop Tassach – as the angel Victor had told him that he would – as food for his journey[220] to the blessed life.[221]

[11] Angels kept vigil over his holy body with prayers and psalms

215. Cf. Gen. 31:3; Baruch 2:33; 1 Kings 19:15.
216. Deut. 34:7; Patrick is equated with Moses in having the same length of life, which is identical with the ideal age for mortals as given in Gen 6:3.
217. Cf. Virgil, *Aeneid* 8, 369.
218. Cf. 2 Kings 20, especially verses 8–11.
219. Josh. 10:12, but replaces *ne moueraris* in this verse with *stetit* from Josh. 10:13.
220. The technical word 'viaticum' is used; cf. Grabka 1953.
221. Some of the problems associated with the text of this *Vita* can be seen here: having described the funeral the text now returns to the period before Patrick's death; however, such textual problems are beyond the scope of this work.

during the first night of his funeral, while all those who came for this vigil slept that night.[222] But on the other nights men watched over the body praying and singing psalms. When the angels departed to heaven they left behind in that place the sweetest of smells: it was like honey and had the sweet smell that comes from wine. Thus it was fulfilled[223] what was said in the blessing of the patriarch Jacob: 'Behold the smell of my son is like the scent of a fruitful field blessed by the Lord.'[224]

[12] When the angel visited him he gave [Patrick] advice on where his tomb was to be located: 'Two unbroken oxen are to be selected. Then let them wander while drawing a cart on which lies your body. Wherever they come to rest, in that place let a church be built in honour of your relics.' And as the angel had directed, two untamed young bullocks, with a cart haltered around their necks, steadily pulled the holy body. The chosen, and now famous, cattle belonged to the herd of Conal from the place called Clocher to the east of Findabair. These cattle, ruled directly by the will of God, went out as far as Dún Lethglaisse, and there Patrick is entombed.

[13] The angel also told [Patrick] this: 'So that your relics will not be taken out of the earth, let your body be covered with one cubit of earth.' That this instruction came directly from the will of God was clearly demonstrated in the very recent past. When some men were digging up the ground near the body in the process of building a church over it, they saw a flaming fire rise up out of his tomb and they immediately pulled back for they feared the flaming fire.[225]

[14] At the time of Patrick's death the struggle for his relics was so great that the Uí Néill allied with the Airthir ('Easterners') came to the brink of war with the Ulaid. Once they had lived close by as

---

222. This scene is modelled on Christ in the garden [of Gethsemane] as found in Luke 22:39–46. As that text is found in many ancient witnesses and versions (the Vulgate included), but not in most modern editions or translations, there is a contrast between Christ ignored by the sleeping apostles, while comforted by an angel.

223. Cf. Matt. 2:23, and similar phrases.

224. Gen. 27:27.

225. See the note above on 'flaming fire'.

neighbours, now they are the most bitter of enemies. However, so that bloodshed might be avoided, through the merit of Patrick and the mercy of God, the inlet of the sea known as Druimm Bó rose up with billowing waves and flooded backwards and forwards as if to quench the hatred of these embittered peoples – for bitter people is the sort they are. Thus the fierce sea's rising stopped the warfare of these peoples.

[15] Later on, when Patrick was buried and the inlet of the sea had subsided, the Uí Néill and the Airthir again wanted to do battle with the Ulaid. Fully kitted out for war they burst into the area where the holy body was located. But they were happily led astray through false thinking. The imagined they had found the two oxen with the cart, and that they were grabbing the holy body [of Patrick]. Then with the body, and all they arms and equipment, they travelled as far as the river Cabcenne. Just then the body vanished from their sight. It would have been impossible to have peace over so blessed a body as Patrick's except they were seduced by this vision at that time. If they had not been so seduced, by the directly expressed will of God, the health of innumerable souls[226] would have been turned to death and ruin. It was similar to the time when the Syrians were blinded lest they would kill the holy prophet Elisha, and by divine providence were led by Elisha as far as Samaria.[227] So here in the case of Patrick through this distracting vision was established the concord of the peoples.

226. Cf. 1 Pet. 1:9.
227. Cf. 2 Kings 6:11–20 (in the Vulgate the enemies of Israel are called 'Syrians,' in modern versions they are called 'Arameans').

BIBLIOGRAPHY

Sources pre-1500

Adomnán, *Vita Columbae* (A. O. Anderson and M. O. Anderson, eds and trs, *Adomnan's Life of Columba*, Edinburgh 1961, 2nd edn. Oxford 1991; and R. Sharpe tr., *Adomnán of Iona: Life of St Columba*, Harmondsworth 1995).

— *De locis sanctis* (D. Meehan with L. Bieler, eds, Dublin 1958) [Latin text with facing ET].

Anon, *The Martyrology of Tallaght* (H. J. Lawlor and R. I. Best, eds, London 1931).

Augustine, *Epistula* 10* [*Ad Alypium*] (J. Divjak, ed., *Corpus Scriptorum Ecclesiasticorum Latinorum* 88, 46–51, Vienna 1981).

Bede, *Historia eclesiastica gentis anglorum* (B. Colgrave and R. A. B. Mynors, eds, Oxford 1969) [Latin text with facing ET]; and see the notes in C. Plummer's edition (Oxford 1896).

Claudius Ptolemaeus, *Geographia* (C. Nobbe, ed., *Claudii Ptolemaei Geographia*, Leipzig 1843; and E. L. Stevenson and J. Fisher, eds and trs, *Claudius Ptolemy: The Geography*, New York 1932, reprint 1991).

Columbanus, *Epistula* 5 (G. S. M. Walker, ed., *Sancti Columbani opera*, Dublin 1957), pp. 36–57) [Latin text with facing ET].

Cummian, *De controversia paschali* (see Walsh and Ó Cróinín 1988).

— *De ratione computandi* (see Walsh and Ó Cróinín 1988).

Jerome, *Liber interpretationis hebraicorum nominum* (P. Lagarde, ed., *Corpus Christianorum Series Latina* 72, pp. 59–161, Turnhout 1959).

Leo the Great, *Sermo* 82 (A. Chavasse, ed., *Corpus Christianorum Series Latina* 138A, Turnhout 1973).

Muirchú moccu Mactheni, *Vita Patricii*, see Bieler 1979, pp. 62–125) [Latin text with facing ET; ET by T. O'Loughlin in this volume].

Patrick, see Bieler 1952; Bieler 1953; Howlett 1994; White 1905.

Prosper of Aquitaine, *De uocatione omnium gentium* (PL 51, 647–722; tr. P. De Letter, *The Call of All Nations* [*Ancient Christian Writers* 14], Westminster MD 1952).

— *Epitoma chronicorum* (T. Mommsen, ed., *Monumenta Germaniae Historica: Auctores Antiquissimi* 9 (Berlin 1892), pp. 486–97) [This is the Latin text of the work usually referred to in writings about Patrick as the *Chronicon*].

'Secundinus,' *'Audite omnes amantes'*, see Bieler 1953 and 1953a [1953a contains the Latin text, ET by T. O'Loughlin in this volume].

Willibrord, *Calendar* (H. A. Wilson, ed., *The Calendar of St. Willibrord from MS. Paris. Lat. 10837* (London 1918; rept. Woodbridge, Suffolk 1998)).

Sources post-1500

Achtemeier, P. J., 1990, '*Omne verbum sonat*: The New Testament and the Oral Environment of Late Western Antiquity', *Journal of Biblical Literature* 109:3–27.

Andrews, J. H., 1997, *Shapes of Ireland: Maps and their Makers 1564–1839*, Dublin.

Bartchy, S. C., 1992, 'Slavery: New Testament' in D. N. Freedman, ed., *Anchor Bible Dictionary* 6:65–73, New York, NY.

Barnard, L. W., 1976, 'Bede and Eusebius as Church Historians' in G. Bonner, ed., *Famulus Christi: Essays in Commemoration of the Thirteenth Centenary of the Birth of the Venerable Bede*, London, pp. 106–24.

Baumgarten, R., 1984, 'The Geographical Orientation of Ireland in Isidore and Orosius', *Peritia* 3:189–203.

Bieler, L, 1952, *Libri Epistolarum Sancti Patricii Episcopi*, Dublin.

— 1953, *The Works of St. Patrick, St. Secundinus, Hymn of St. Patrick* [*Ancient Christian Writers* 17], Westminster, MD.

— 1953a, 'The Hymn of St. Secundinus', *Proceedings of the Royal Irish Academy* 55c, pp.117–27.

— 1962, 'The Celtic Hagiographer', *Studia Patristica* 5: 243–65.

— 1975, 'Ancient Hagiography and the Lives of St. Patrick' in F. Paolo and M. Barrera, eds, *Forma Futuri: Studi in onore del Cardinale Michele Pellegrino*, Turin, pp. 650–5.

— *The Patrician Documents in the Book of Armagh*, Dublin 1979.

Binchy, D. A., 1962, 'Patrick and His Biographers, Ancient and Modern,' *Studia Hibernica* 2:7–173.

Borsje, J., 1994, 'The Monster in the River Ness in *Vita sancti Columbae*: A Study of a Miracle', *Peritia* 8:27–34.

— 1996, *From Chaos to Enemy: Encounters with Monsters in Early Irish Texts. An Investigation Related to the Process of Christianization and the Concept of Evil*, Turnhout.

Bray, D. A., 1983, 'The Making of a Hero: The Legend of St. Patrick and the Claims of Armagh', *Monastic Studies* 14:145–60.

Bull, M., 1999, *The Miracles of Our Lady of Rocamadour: Analysis and Translation*, Woodbridge.

Burkitt, F. C., 1902, 'On two early Irish hymns', *Journal of Theological Studies* 3:95–6.

Bury, J. B., 1905, *The Life of St. Patrick and his Place in History*, London.

Charles-Edwards, T., 1993, 'Palladius, Prosper, and Leo the Great: Mission and Primatial Authority' in D. N. Dumville, *et al.*, eds, *Saint Patrick, A.D. 493–1993*, Woodbridge, pp. 1–12.

Charles-Edwards, T., 2000, *Early Christian Ireland*, Cambridge.

Christensen, D. L., 1992, 'Nations' in D. N. Freedman, ed., *Anchor Bible Dictionary* 4:1037–49, New York, NY.

Conneely, D., 1993, *The Letters of Saint Patrick*, Maynooth.

Contreni, J. J., 2002, '"By lions, bishops are meant; by wolves, priests": History, Exegesis, and the Carolingian Church in Haimo of Auxerre's *Commentary on Ezechiel*', *Francia*, 29/1:29–56.

Corcoran, G., 1985, *Saint Augustine on Slavery*, Rome.

Cosgrove, D., ed., 1999, *Mappings*, London.

Curran, M., 1984, *The Antiphonary of Bangor and the Early Irish Monastic Liturgy*, Blackrock.

Cusack, P., 1993, *An Interpretation of the Second Dialogue of Gregory the Great: Hagiography and St. Benedict*, Lampeter.

Delehaye, H., 1998, *The Legends of the Saints*, Dublin [originally: Brussels 1905; ET: London 1962].

Di Berardino, A., 1992, *Encyclopedia of the Early Church* (Cambridge).

Doherty, C., 1982, 'Some Aspects of Hagiography as a Source for Irish Economic History', *Peritia* 1:300–28.

Dumville, D. N., 1993, *Saint Patrick, A.D. 493–1993*, Woodbridge.

Etchingham, C., 1999, *Church Organisation in Ireland A.D. 650 to 1000*, Maynooth.

Freeman, P., 2001, *Ireland and the Classical World*, Austin, TX.

— 2004, *St. Patrick of Ireland*, New York, NY.

Gole, S., 1993, 'Important is Big!' in P. Barber and C. Board, eds, *Tales from the Map Room*, London, pp. 16–7.

Gould, P., and White, R., 1974, *Mental Maps*, Harmondsworth.

Grabka, G., 1953, 'Christian Viaticum: A Study of its Cultural Background', *Traditio* 9:1–43.

Grisbrooke, W. J., 2002, 'Kyrie' in P. F. Bradshaw, ed., *The New SCM Dictionary of Liturgy and Worship*, London, p. 268.

Gwynn, A., 1975–76, 'The Problem of the *Dicta Patricii*', *Seanchas Ard Mhacha* 8:69–80.

Haselock, J., 2002, 'Gestures' in P. F. Bradshaw, ed., *The New SCM Dictionary of Liturgy and Worship*, London, p. 227–30.

Healy, J., 1905, *The life and writings of St. Patrick*, Dublin.

Herbert, M., and McNamara, M., 1989, *Irish Biblical Apocrypha: Selected Texts in Translation*, Edinburgh.

Higgins, J., 1995, 'Two passages in the *Confessio* of Patrick,' *Milltown Studies* 35:131–3.

Howlett, D. R., 1994, *The Book of Letters of Saint Patrick the Bishop*, Dublin.

Huck, A. and Greeven, H., 1981, *Synopse der drei ersten Evangelien*, 13th edn., Tübingen.

Hughes, K., 1966, *The Church in Early Irish Society*, London.

— 1972, *Early Christian Ireland: Introduction to the Sources*, Cambridge.

Herbert, M., 1988, *Iona, Kells, and Derry: The History and Hagiography of the Monastic* Familia *of Columba*, Oxford.

— 1996, 'Hagiography' in K. McCone and K. Simms, eds, *Progress in Medieval Irish Studies*, Maynooth, pp. 79–90.

— 2001, 'Latin and Vernacular Hagiography of Ireland from the origins to the Sixteenth Century', in G. Philippart, ed., *Hagiographies*, Turnhout, vol. 3, pp. 329–60.

Joncas, J. M., 1999, 'Ordination, Orders', in A. D. Fitzgerald, ed., *Augustine through the Ages*, Grand Rapids, MI.

Jones, B. and Keillar, I., 1996, 'Marinus, Ptolemy and the Turning of Scotland', *Britannia* 27:43–49.

Jones, C. W., 1969, 'Some Introductory Remarks on Bede's Commentary of Genesis', *Sacris Erudiri* 19:115–98.

Jungmann, J. A., 1951, *The Mass of the Roman Rite* (2 vols), New York.

Kearns, C., 1969, 'Ecclesiasticus' in R. C. Fuller *et al.*, eds, *A New Catholic Commentary on Holy Scripture*, London, pp. 546–7.

Kelly, F., 1988, *A Guide to Early Irish Law*, Dublin.

Kenney, J. F., 1929, *The Sources for the Early History of Ireland*, New York.

Knowles, M. D., 1963, *Great Historical Enterprises*, London.

Laeuchli, S., 1972, *Power and Sexuality: The Emergence of Canon Law at the Synod of Elvira*, Philadelphia.

Lapidge, M., and Sharpe, R., 1985, *A Bibliography of Celtic-Latin Literature*, Dublin.

Le Brun, J., 2003, 'Martyrologies', *New Catholic Encyclopedia* (second edition), Washington, 9:232–4.

Lynch, K., 1960, *The Image of the City*, Cambridge, MA.

McCone, K., 1989, 'An Introduction to Early Irish Saints' Lives', *Maynooth Review* 11:26–52.

— 1990, *Pagan Past and Christian Present in Early Irish Literature*, Maynooth.

McCready, W. D., 1994, *Miracles and the Venerable Bede*, Toronto.

MacGregor, A. J., 1992, *Fire and Light in the Western Triduum*,

Collegeville, MN.

McManus, D., 1997, *A Guide to Ogam*, Maynooth.

McNamara, M., 1975, *The Apocrypha in the Irish Church*, Dublin.

Maund, K. L., 'The Second Obit of St Patrick in the "Annals of Boyle"' in D. N. Dumville, *et al.*, eds, *Saint Patrick, A.D. 493–1993*, Woodbridge, pp. 35–7.

Meehan, B., 1996, *The Book of Durrow: A medieval masterpiece at Trinity College Dublin*, Dublin.

Maher, M., 1994, 'Sunday in the Irish Church', *Irish Theological Quarterly* 61:161–84.

Meier, J. P., 1994, *A Marginal Jew II: Mentor, Message, and Miracles*, New York, NY.

Ní Dhonnchadha, M., 1982, 'The Guarantor List of *Cáin Adomnáin*', *Peritia* 1:196.

Ó Cróinín, D., 1984, 'Rath Melsigi, Willibrord and the earliest Echternach manuscripts', *Peritia* 3:17–49.

— 1986, 'New Light on Palladius', *Peritia* 5:276–83.

— 2000, 'Who was Palladius "First Bishop of the Irish"?', *Peritia* 12:205–37.

O'Leary, A., 1996, 'An Irish Apocryphal Apostle: Muirchú's Portrayal of Saint Patrick', *Harvard Theological Review* 89:287–301.

O'Loughlin, T., 1990, 'The Significance of Sunday: Three Ninth-century Catecheses', *Worship* 64:533–44.

— 1996, 'The View from Iona: Adomnán's Mental Maps', *Peritia* 10:98–122.

— 1996b, 'The Gates of Hell: From Metaphor to Fact', *Milltown Studies* 38:98–114.

— 1996c, 'Muirchú's *Vita Patricii*: A Note on an Unidentified Source', *Ériu* 46:89–93.

— 1997, 'Living in the Ocean,' in C. Bourke, ed., *Studies in the Cult of Saint Columba*, Dublin, pp. 11–23.

— 1997b, 'Why Adomnán needs Arculf: The Case of an Expert Witness', *Journal of Medieval Latin* 7:127–46.

— 1997c, 'Marriage and Sexuality in the *Hibernensis*', *Peritia* 11:188–206.

— 1999, 'The Eusebian Apparatus in some Vulgate Gospel Books', *Peritia* 13:1–92.

— 2000, *Celtic Theology: Humanity, World and God in Early Irish Writings*, London.

— 2000a, 'Penitentials and Pastoral Care' in G. R. Evans, ed., *A History of Pastoral Care*, London, pp. 93–111.

— 2000b, 'Hagiography: Christian Perspectives' in W. M. Johnston, ed., *Encyclopedia of Monasticism*, Chicago and London, vol. 1, pp. 564–6.

— 2000c, *Journeys on the Edges*, London and New York, NY.

— 2000d, 'Master and Pupil: Christian Perspectives', in W. M. Johnston, ed., *Encyclopedia of Monasticism*, Chicago and London, vol. 2, pp. 831–2.

— 2001a, 'The Tombs of the Saints: Their Significance for Adomnán' in J. Carey, M. Herbert, and P. Ó Riain, eds, *Studies in Irish Hagiography: Saints and Scholars*, Dublin, pp. 1–14.

— 2001b, 'Patrick on the margins of space and time', in K. McGroarty, ed., *Eklogai: Studies in Honour of Thomas Finan and Gerard Watson*, Maynooth, pp. 44–58.

— 2001c, 'One island, one people, one nation: early Latin evidence for this motif in Ireland', *Institute of Technology Blanchardstown Journal* 4:4–13.

— 2002, '"A Celtic Theology": Some Awkward Questions and Observations' in J. F. Nagy, ed. *Identifying the 'Celtic'* [*Celtic Studies Association of North America Yearbook* 2], Dublin, pp. 49–65.

— 2002b, 'Muirchú's theology of conversion in his *Vita Patricii*', in M. Atherton, ed., *Celts and Christians: New Approaches to the Religious Traditions of Britain and Ireland*, Cardiff, pp. 124–45.

— 2003, 'Reading Muirchú's Tara-event within its background as a biblical "trial of divinities"' in J. Cartwright, ed., *Celtic Hagiography and Saints' Cults*, Cardiff, pp. 123–135.

O'Loughlin, T., and Conrad-O'Briain, H., 1993, 'The "baptism of tears" in early Anglo-Saxon sources', *Anglo-Saxon England* 22:65–83.

Orchard, A., 1993, '"*Audite omnes amantes*": A Hymn in Patrick's Praise' in D. N. Dumville, *et al.*, eds, *Saint Patrick, A.D. 493–1993*, Woodbridge, pp. 153–73.

Orpen, G. H., 1913, 'Rathgall, County Wicklow: Dun Galion and the "Dunum" of Ptolemy', *Proceedings of the Royal Irish Academy* 32c:41–57.

Richter, M., 1999, *Ireland and her neighbours in the Seventh Century*, Dublin.

Ryan, J., 1938, 'A Difficult Phrase in the '*Confession*' of St Patrick', *Irish Ecclesiastical Record* 52:293–99.

Salway, P., 1981, *Roman Britain*, Oxford.

Sharpe, R., 1982, 'St Patrick and the See of Armagh', *Cambridge Medieval Celtic Studies* 4:33–59.

— 1983, 'Palaeographical Considerations in the Study of the Patrician Documents in the Book of Armagh', *Scriptorium* 36:3–28.

Shearman, J. F., 1879 [second edition 1882], *Loca Patriciana: an identification of localities, chiefly in Leinster, visted by St Patrick and his assistant missionaries and of some contemporary kings and chieftains; with an essay on the three Patricks, Palladius, Sen Patrick, and Patrick mac Calphurn, apostles in Ireland in the fifth century*, Dublin and London.

Sims-Williams, P., 1998, 'Celtomania and Celtoscepticism', *Cambrian Medieval Celtic Studies* 36:1–35.

Smith J. Z., 1978, *Map is not Territory*, Leiden.

Stancliffe, C., 1983, *St Martin and his Hagiographer: History and Miracle in Sulpicius Severus*, Oxford.

Strang, A., 1997, 'Explaining Ptolemy's Roman Britain', *Britannia* 28:1–30.

Sundberg, A. C., 1959, 'On testimonies', *Novum Testamentum* 3:268–81.

Swift, C., 1994, 'Tírechán's Motives in Compiling the Collectanea: An Alternative Explanation', *Ériu* 45:53–82.

Talley, T. J., 1991, *The Origins of the Liturgical Year*, 2nd edn, Collegeville, MN.

Thompson, E. A., 1980, 'St. Patrick and Coroticus', *Journal of Theological Studies* 31 (new series):12–27.

Throckmorton, B. H., 1949, *Gospel Parallels: A Synopsis of the First Three Gospels*, New York, NY.

Walsh, M. and Ó Cróinín, D., 1988, *Cummian's Letter* De controversia paschali *and the* de ratione computandi, Toronto.

Ward, B., 1976, 'Miracles and History: A Reconsideration of the Miracle Stories used by Bede' in G. Bonner, ed., *Famulus Christi: Essays in Commemoration of the 13th Centenary of the Birth of the Venerable Bede*, London, pp. 70–6.

White, N. J. D., 1905, 'Libri Sancti Patricii: The Latin Writings of St Patrick', *Proceedings of the Royal Irish Academy* 25C:201–326.

— 1918, *Libri Sancti Patricii: The Latin Writings of St Patrick. A Revised Text with a Selection of Various Readings based on all the Known Manuscripts*, London.

Wooding, J. M., 1996a, *Communication and Commerce along the Western Sealanes AD 400–800*, Oxford.

— 1996b, 'Cargoes and Trade along the Western Seaboard', in K. R. Dark, ed., *External Contacts and the Economy of Late Roman and Post-Roman Britain*, Woodbridge, pp. 67–82.

An earlier version of my translation of Patrick's works, with a much more restricted apparatus, appeared in *St Patrick: The Man and His Works*, published by SPCK, London in 1999.

An even earlier version of Patrick's works, along with an earlier version of my translation of Muirchú's *Vita Patricii*, appeared in O. Davies, ed., *Celtic Spirituality*, Paulist Press, Mahwah, NY, 1999.

INDEX OF SCRIPTURAL CITATIONS

GENERAL INDEX